CULTURAL DEMOCRACY

SUNY Series

Interruptions: Border Testimony(ies) and Critical Discourse/s
Henry A. Giroux, Editor

Cultural Democracy

Politics, Media, New Technology

David Trend

State University of
New York Press

Published by
State University of New York Press

Printed in the United States of America

For information, address the State University of New York Press,
State University Plaza, Albany, NY 12246

Production by Bernadine Dawes • Marketing by Theresa Abad Swierzowski

Library of Congress Cataloging-in-Publication Data

Trend, David.
    Cultural democracy : politics, media, new technology / David
Trend.
        p.   cm. — (SUNY series, Interruptions — Border
testimony(ies) and Critical Discourse/s)
    Includes index.
    ISBN 0-7914-3319-6 (hard : alk. paper). — ISBN 0-7914-3320-X
(pbk. : alk. paper)
        1. United States—Social conditions—1980– 2. Democracy—United
States.   3. Politics and culture—United States.   I. Title.
II. Series.
HN65.T7 1997
306'.0973–dc21
                                                        97-629
                                                        CIP

1 2 3 4 5 6 7 8 9 10

CONTENTS

one

Culture and Democracy

We live in an era of democratic contradiction. As the Cold War recedes into history and the apparent triumph of liberal democracy spreads around the globe, the domestic state of democracy within the United States continues to erode. Rather than a nation where citizens feel empowered in their common governance, the United States has become a land where the vast majority of citizens hate their leaders yet never vote. Massive anti-incumbency sentiments and resentment toward representative government parallel the rise of grass roots militia movements and media demagogues. Clearly, something has gone wrong with democracy in the United States—or more precisely with the way democracy is understood and exercised.

Nowhere are these difficulties more pronounced than in battles over cultural issues. Debates about canonical values, revisionist curricula, artistic censorship, and freedom of expression have moved from the margins of public debate to its center. Increasingly, people across the political spectrum recognize the strategic role of the arts and humanities in shaping human identities and influencing politics. At a historical moment lacking in superpower conflicts, ideological debate has become internalized, as it did in the 1950s. Once again, battles that were waged with guns and bullets are now fought with ideas and symbols. And once again access to the debate is a crucial issue, as attempts are made to exclude voices that would contest the status quo.

This book is premised on the regrettable fact that the United States has nothing even approaching an egalitarian realm of public communication and civic ritual. Although identity politics and the so-called "culture wars" have done much to expand the national conversation about pluralism and values, these issues have also induced heightened levels of divisiveness and antagonism. As television and computers have made more information available to people than ever before, the electorate finds itself increasingly uninformed and confused.

1

And while democracy is a word that politicians and media personalities bandy about with great alacrity, its usefulness has become all but exhausted by divergent interests it has come to serve.

Given this crisis of democratic meaning, the purpose of *Cultural Democracy: Politics/Media/New Technology* is twofold. The first is explanatory and historical, describing how various cultural institutions and communications technologies have evolved in the United States within education, entertainment, art, and the media. I explain how deeply entrenched ideological attitudes often frustrate a meaningful national conversation about cultural issues, as discussions about abortion, multiculturalism, gay rights, or school prayer become reduced to polemical, all-or-nothing debates. Rigid divisions between left- and right-wing positions yield little room for the understandings that can grow from genuine dialogue. In part, this results from a philosophical legacy that splits every issue into a binary opposition. In part, this is caused by patterns in public communication that reduce discussion to superficial soundbites and overheated rhetoric. A cultural democracy requires more than this.

The second purpose of this book is prescriptive. People stick with old-style party politics in the United States because other models don't seem viable. This is largely due to the self-marginalizing character of most alternatives. Yet as recent events have demonstrated, public dissatisfaction with "mainstream" institutions stands at an all-time high. Diverse communities seem willing as never before to reach for new answers to old problems. *Cultural Democracy: Politics/ Media/New Technology* suggests that these new answers are not as far away as one might think. The roots of these solutions lie in the very democratic principles upon which the United States was founded, although many of those principles need to be brought up to date and radicalized.

Following the work of a range of public intellectuals like Stanley Aronowitz, Henry Giroux, bell hooks, Chantal Mouffe, and Cornel West, I want to argue for a "radical democracy" capable of subverting traditional divisions of left and right.[1] This is not to be confused with a call for a centrist compromise or with a romantic appeal to pre-industrial communitarianism.[2] Rather than asking people to surrender their identities in the interest of a national consensus, radical democracy stresses the primacy of cultural difference. Its theoretical program recognizes that people are not simple creatures of Republican or Democratic ideology, but comprised of complex histories, needs, cultures, and values. To these ends, radical democracy would reconcile current tensions between national and local governance by reorganizing political constituencies in ways typically considered off-limits to politics. By necessity this will entail the creation of what

Chantal Mouffe has termed "new political spaces" that fall outside traditional definitions of government, civil society, and the family. It will take a good deal of work to put these ideas into practice. Yet the time seems right to spell out some of the ways radical democracy might be applied.

Beyond Liberalism and Conservatism

It is becoming increasingly apparent that old oppositional categories of political analysis are no longer adequate for addressing the complexity of the contemporary world. The 1980s were largely defined in "us versus them" terms. Presidents Reagan and Bush sought to construct a world of good and evil, in which the noble forces of free enterprise struggled against the red menace of communism. Of course, this simple opposition was more than a tool for foreign policy analysis. The model was applied to all manner of issues involving education, work, religion, the family, and culture to produce convenient all-or-nothing answers for difficult social questions.

To a great extent this polarizing impulse derived from the split between *orthodox* and *progressive* philosophies that emerged during the early Enlightenment. René Descartes's seventeenth-century formulation of a separation of mind and body gave form to a broader opposition between idealized abstraction and everyday actuality. For this reason, groups in the orthodox tradition—while varying considerably in style and motivation—generally support a faith in timeless truths to be learned and obeyed. They see a fundamental correctness in existing arrangements, but fear that society's enabling values are eroding. Progressives, a similarly diverse and contradictory category, embrace an evolving concept of truth. The rules of social organization are hardly static or universal, and thus merit continual revision. Orthodox and progressive positions yield radically different views of moral authority, resulting in conflicting attitudes toward the way people should act. Most typically, these philosophies find contemporary form in mutually exclusive views of the political right and left.[3]

Groups on the right tend to put their emphasis on *behavior*, attributing human success or failure to attitudes people bring to their exercise of free agency. Great importance is afforded to cultural issues, as manifest in recent controversies over literary canons, artistic censorship, and the labelling of records and video games. Minimizing the significance of economic inequity, conservatives make assertions that job discrimination, sexual harassment, and unfair housing practices really aren't that much of a problem and the government programs to rectify them provide inegalitarian preferences upon which "minority" groups become dependent. Rarely is any consideration given to the corrupting influence of a market that emphasizes competition, greed, and wealth as measures of human worth.

Most often, the left focuses on issues of economic *structure* and argues that government should intervene in correcting the inevitable inequities produced by the market. In contrast to the right, leftist ideology is often critical of a society it claims emphasizes greed and competition instead of social justice. Rather than emphasizing cultural programs that might influence human behaviors, the left more strongly favors a fundamental redistribution of wealth through such measures as welfare programs, government subsidies, and progressive tax legislation. Arguments that some people might lack motivation or require forms of moral education are rejected as biased. This fundamentally redistributive program has made leftists vulnerable to the charge that they simply want to throw resources at problems. As Molly Ivins jokingly has stated, "this may sound simple, but the *real* problem with poor people is that they don't have enough money."[4]

In their postures of mutual exclusion both right and left camps hold part, but not all, of the means to address social problems. The inadequacy of such polarized thinking became particularly apparent in the early 1990s, with the collapse of the Eastern bloc and the election of moderate Democrat Bill Clinton. The extremist black-and-white logic of the 1980s needs to be replaced with a political imaginary to account for what some have termed the new "gray times."[5] Approaches to politics that would issues economic structure from cultural behavior no longer seem viable. As Cornel West has commented:

> We must acknowledge that structure and behavior are inseparable, that institutions and values go hand in hand. How people act and live are shaped— though in no way dictated or determined—by larger circumstances in which they find themselves. These circumstances can be changed, their limits attenuated, by positive actions to elevate living conditions. . . . We should reject the idea that structures are primarily economic and political creatures—an idea that sees culture as an ephemeral set of behavioral attitudes and values. Culture is as much a structure as the economy or politics; it is rooted in institutions such as families, schools, churches, synagogues, mosques, and communication industries (television, radio, video, music).[6]

As the 1996 presidential elections demonstrated, these cultural answers to material questions hold enormous public appeal. Exit polls indicated that the majority of voters had been motivated more by "values" than any other interest. In response, the rhetoric of both Democrats and Republicans is increasingly driven by a vocabulary of cultural concern. Yet despite these changes in the political climate, the polarized character of the debate remains intact.

Models of Democracy in Context

To clarify the principles of radical democracy, it is helpful to examine the doctrines of liberal, socialist, and pluralist practice from which it emerged. First of all, one should understand that in the context of democracy the word "liberal" is applied in the classical sense to designate an emphasis on individual freedom, rather than the term's more contemporary association with progressive reform. Liberal (or "representative") democracy evolved in direct response to the perceived encroachment of the state on personal liberty. At the center of the liberal democratic ethos lies the Western notion of the autonomous subject, capable of free choice and motivated by capitalistic self-interest. Most important is the separability of existence into public and private domains. The public comprises the arena of laws, legislatures, and other civic structures, whose ultimate logic is reducible to an apolitical ideal of the common good.[7] As with orthodox and progressive impulses, the formation of a disinterested and distinct public sphere can be traced to the uniquely Western belief in Cartesian epistemology—a belief in the possibility of a knowable independent ground apart from humanity's base instincts. The transcendental universalism of the public sphere is the antithesis of the self-interested specificity of the private realm of personal interests and market competition.

The unifying element for many liberal democratic theorists is belief that individual interest can be enhanced by mutual cooperation. As John Locke put it, "the great and chief end therefore of men uniting into commonwealths and putting themselves under government . . . is the mutual preservation of their lives, liberties, and estates, which shall call by the general name property."[8] This impulse for accumulation is both enabled and limited by the state. Hence, liberal democracy assumes a two-stroke function as a justification and limit for the exercise of state authority. Regular elections serve the philosophical goal of obliging the public to clarify public issues while assuring that no government or set of public officials may remain in office forever.

Opinions differ among liberal democrats over how much the general consensus should apply to all citizens. This is both the rationale for local government and the reasoning behind various pluralist versions of liberal democracy.

Pluralists agree that different groups deserve different degrees of influence over various matters according to the proportion of their interest in them. Within the liberal logic of self-interest, people are more likely to exercise their agency as citizens over matters that affect them most directly.

This principle has led some liberals to advocate a strengthening of the civil society as a means of decentralizing democracy and lessening the role of the state. The civil society argument, occasionally termed the "associationalist" view, asserts that the goals of social justice and human welfare are best served by voluntary and self-governing private bodies, such as unions, political parties, religious organizations, schools, neighborhood groups, clubs, and societies.[9] This position gained popularity in the Western world during the nineteenth century, but was squeezed out of existence with the growing dominance of collectivist and individualist politics. Although similar to liberal democracy, this view differs in according voluntary bodies a primary role in organizing social life, rather that an ancillary function to government. These smaller private entities, which may or may not be governed by democratic principles, are viewed as more flexible and responsive to community needs. Representative government assumes a regulatory function as guarantor of services, rather than acting as their provider. Limited to this oversight role, government bureaucracy is lessened and its efficiency enhanced as a consequence.

If democracy is conceptualized as a series of compromises between individual and collective interest, socialist democracy clearly leans in the latter direction. Critical of the liberal emphasis on competition, Karl Marx and Friedrich Engels viewed material inequities not merely as byproducts of such a model, but as necessary components of it. To create winners in the game of acquisition, a system must also generate losers. The much-ballyhooed "opportunities" for liberty offered by liberal capitalism mean little if they are not universally accessible. The inequities produced by capital in turn spoil the very functioning of democracy, as the state becomes little more than the tool of the privileged. In this scheme, the very idea of a separation between private and public is thrown into question. Rather than serving as an idealized and apolitical mediator of the common good, government is perverted by the ability of some citizens to exert more control over it than others.

Like liberal democracy, the principles of socialist democracies have suffered somewhat in practical application. As demonstrated by the Soviet Union and other nations of the Eastern European bloc, difficulties emerged in the capacities of single-party bureaucracies to remain responsive to local constituencies. This anti-democratic drive to single-party agreement and conformity was worsened by the development over time of a managerial class of party bureaucrats and government officials. Moreover, the structure of state ownership of property has the effect of denying resources to oppositional groups. The ability to mount political alternatives to the state, while not completely foreclosed by a socialist system, is significantly hampered.

The post-World War II atmosphere of growing Cold War tension eventually produced a range of efforts to ameliorate antagonisms between liberal and socialist democrats.[10] Not surprisingly, these hybrid democracies differ considerably. One of the most significant distinctions lies in the degree to which these hybrids emphasize material or cultural matters. The materialist camp is exemplified by the work of John Dunn, Samuel Bowles, and Herbert Gintis, who focus on the system inequities of capitalism in their calls for economic democracy (what Bowles and Gintis term "postliberal" democracy).[11] These authors argue that democracy emerges from the participatory management of property and production. Unlike traditional socialists who advocate the centralized organization of this authority, economic democrats typically favor more heterogeneous sites of power, where decisions can be made by constituencies identified by rights claims.

The culturalist solution to the liberalism/socialism divide can be seen as an important precursor to the radical democracy movement. In contrast to economic democracy, the culturalist hybrid line argues that capitalism will be undone by enhanced civic participation itself. Once people understand the potentials of equality in one sphere, they will attempt to extend it into every other area of life. This approach to politics was codified by Norberto Bobbio, who was strongly influenced by the populist sentiments of Antonio Gramsci. Although critical of the inequities inherent in liberal capitalism, Bobbio saw the modernist assertion of individual agency as a social force that was too powerful to be undone. To accommodate the values of freedom and equality Bobbio proposed a strongly constitutional democracy, in which competitive parties would represent constituent interests. The importance of the party stemmed from a perception of a society too diverse to achieve a single "common sense. " Setting this form of politics apart from typical representative democracies would be a series of compacts designed to block what Bobbio termed the "invisible powers" of industry and finance from exerting undue influence. To achieve this, citizens would be given not simply equal "political rights," but also equal "social rights" to assure that their political rights would not suffer interference.

Central to Bobbio's thinking was a reorientation of the conventional distinction between "public" and "private" realms. Loosely speaking, these terms separate human activity into categories of general and particular concern—with the latter typically considered "off limits" to political discussion. As Bobbio and others subsequently came to believe, this separation has created a dangerous trade-off, as so-called public decision making increasingly takes on a life of its own and becomes distanced from the daily lives of the citizenry. To remedy the situation, the means of political representation need to be spread further into the basic fabric of daily life: work, education, leisure, and the home. As Bobbio explained in a famous quotation, the problem of democracy is no longer "who votes," but "where one votes."[12] As is probably evident, the discussions in this book derive in large part from Bobbio's thinking in this area.

In the contemporary United States, this distancing of the general from the particular has become manifest in a broad-based suspicion among voters of public officials and the anti-incumbency sentiments that led to massive congressional overhaul in the 1994 elections. In that circumstance, opportunistic conservatives successfully exacerbated public anxieties about a federal government grown too large and intrusive. As in other instances the conventional solution to the public/private dilemma has been to place increased emphasis on local ballots, in which communities need not acquiesce to general social mandates. Regrettably, this solution has proven ineffective in serving the needs of diverse groups—such as those defined by age, gender, occupation, race, ethnicity, or sexual orientation—within and across geographical communities. This dilemma has led certain theorists to advocate an enhanced emphasis on pluralism, with approaches ranging from a reassertion of the civil society to more radical prescriptions.

Twentieth-century pluralist arguments in the West can be traced to the liberal discontent with state centrism, exacerbated by the increasing social diversification and class stratification brought on by industrialization. Groups in Europe and the United States began to argue that the liberal dyad of individual and state insufficiently represented the complexity of civil subjectivity. Needed was a way of accounting for the more complex differentiation of individuals into groups and identities. The emphasis on locating a "middle ground" between state authority and individual autonomy was further tempered by an antagonism toward what C. Wright Mills termed "the power elite"—a hegemonic class of business interests perceived to dominate capitalist society. Despite this apparent awareness of the tendency of private interests to impinge upon and influence the public functions of government, most U.S. pluralist thinking of this period did little to question conventional demarcations between the two. In other words, although postwar pluralism failed to recognize the permeability of the categories pubic and private, it failed to see this as more than a structural problem. Instead, it sought to promote the interests of diverse groups by pushing private interests back in their place as equal competitors, hence rebuttressing the public/private divide.

To subsequent poststructuralist theorists this move did little more than resinscribe the notion of the modernist subject. Not only did the postwar U.S. pluralists reinforce conventional public/private categories, but they also were incapable of recognizing the subjects of politics as anything other then members of discrete groups. Postwar pluralism marked a significant advance over unreconstructed liberalism in carving out a larger role and a more complex arena for citizens to act politically, but it did so only within existing understandings of citizens roles. Theorists such Ernesto Laclau and Chantal Mouffe proposed what they termed a "radical democratic" reconceptualization of the citizen unencumbered by essentialist categories of modernist subjectivity. Far from a unified and autonomous member of a particular constituency, within this formulation each person belongs to numerous overlapping groups and multiple intersecting identities. As Mouffe explains, "it is not a matter of establishing a mere alliance between given interests but of actually modifying their identity to bring about a new political identity."[13] As this group-identification model ties its subjects irrevocably to the social, individuality is also maintained because of the relatively unique mix of association within each person.

This radical democratic model of the subject has profound implications for political organization, for it shatters convenient distinctions between public and private. As speculated by Kirstie McClure, this formulation could imply a reinscription of the "subject of rights," which implies not so much an escape from the state, nor an "abdication from political participation more conventionally understood, but rather a potential refusal of a unitary construct of citizenship as exhaustive of the political tasks of the present."[14] This reformulation of the subject need not be understood as a simple collapse of formerly private concerns into the public arena, or vice versa. According to Laclau and Mouffe, this should be seen instead as an opportunity for the creation of "new political spaces."[15] In the expanded view of the multiple subject, the very definition of the political becomes broadened to a new range of sites beyond the conventional jurisdiction of state institutions into the far more dynamic domain of cultural representations and social practices.

In such a context, this poststructuralist approach to pluralism does not negate subjective agency, as it is often accused of doing. Instead, by opening new territory for scrutiny the model gives new vitality to the impetus for democratic principles. The politicization of formerly social spaces formerly considered neutral makes apparent the often unacknowledged power relations in everyday activities. In this way such "off-limits" territories as culture, education, and the family become sites of critical investigation and emancipatory contestation. Rather than diminishing a sense of political agency by negating essential notions of the subject, the principles of radical democracy have the potential of reinvigorating the subject within new domains of influence. Just as importantly, in arguing against the notion of a fixed or universal subject, the project of a radical democracy is by definition never complete.[16]

Populism and Elitism

Within the contemporary United States the task ahead obviously is far from easy. In recent years, left and right have replicated their oppositional logic in a battle to claim the political center as their own (see chapter 2, "What's in a Name? Beyond the Politics of Left and Right"). This is encouraged by an electoral process that produces a totalizing rhetoric of "mandates" and landslides" from narrow margins of the vote. Our current winner-take-all process yields little understanding of the important relationship between minority and majority stockholders in the participatory government.[17] This encourages a strange denial of oppositional possibility.

Essential to the majoritarian visions of both Democrats and Republicans is a devaluation of human diversity. Within this seemingly contradictory reasoning, differences are viewed as obstacles to be suppressed in favor of a broader consensus.[18] Put another way, groups identified as "special interests" are constructed as antithetical the standard of the social "mainstream." But what are the epistemological grounds on which such notions are based? Although this imaginary mainstream purportedly includes a majority of people, in fact it excludes everyone. Instead of functioning as a marker of the civil middle ground, it works as a mechanism to naturalize social hierarchies. When stripped of its mystifying pretensions, the mainstream can be seen as an abstract representation that at best describes a rather small minority of people.

This is how vague appeals to populism can really represent an elitism of their own—not far from the primary referents of male, European heterosexuality around which Western law and culture have always been organized. This structural hegemony converts efforts to contest, infiltrate, or subvert it into acknowledgments of its dominance. In this manner the relation of margin to center has been maintained. To achieve these monolithic visions of national identity both left and right have assaulted—in admittedly different ways—as divisive the proponents of multiculturalism or identity politics. Ignoring historically entrenched power asymmetries among social groups, they have argued that such "separatist" and "ethnocentric" views subvert the potential of a national accord.[19] Promoted instead is a monolithic definition of citizenship, which dismisses the specificity of human variety as either irrelevant or selfish.

The promotion of this pseudo-populism has paralleled a widening of the gap between rich and poor in the United States. This covert reconsolidation of race and class divisions has been chronicled in recent years by a diverse spectrum of writers. Christopher Lasch describes what he terms the "revolt of the elites" within both political parties against the very middle class they purport to represent. Jerry Adler identifies the "rise of the overclass" as the consolidation of yuppie smugness and power. As Adler puts it, "if the overclass is hard to define, it's because it is a state of mind and a slice of the income curve." Lani Guinier resurrects Alexis de Tocqueville's expression the "tyranny of the majority" in her analysis of a permanent bipartisan ruling order, that uses its political leverage to exclude the interests of the disenfranchised.[20]

The anti-democratic implications of this pseudo-populism become apparent in the way extreme political attitudes become naturalized in partisan discourses. Take education for example. Republicans and Democrats seem incapable of reconciling their political appeal to a mainstream identity and a cultural appeal to idealized notions of "the best" of Western culture. Implicit in recent school reform plans from both Bush and Clinton—with their programs of universal testing, their implication of a national curriculum, and their invitation to business interests to manage public education—is the belief that the nation has spent too much time pursuing educational equity and too little time advancing rarefied standards of "world class" excellence.[21] These attitudes have helped produce an atmosphere in which many of today's young people feel powerless, alienated, and angry.

In the art and entertainment worlds these debates have taken a similarly vicious turn, as the rhetoric of political extremists once again heats up in Congress. Again, both right and left seem bent on eliminating dissenting opinion with a more directed assault on democracy that fails to consider any aspect of an opposing position. The parameters of the debate as seen by the conservative camp are well framed by the late National Endowment for the Arts council member Samuel Lippman, who wrote that "culture and democracy cannot co-exist, for democracy by its very nature represents the many, and culture, by its nature, is created for the few."[22] With these words, Lippman articulated what many people perceive to be a primary contradiction in public life: the inherent distance between objects of aesthetic worth and the popular universe in which they exist. Rather than grappling with the complex political implications of this apparent paradox, for most legislators the solution is to get government out of the picture.

Contrary to common assumptions, this problematic stratification of high and low culture implicit in Lippmann's remarks is not promoted by only the right. This high-minded idealism has long characterized leftist cultural practice as well. Certainly recent attacks on public broadcasting and the NEA hardly would have been so successful if those entities had ever cultivated a genuine constituency. The NEA and the Corporation for Public Broadcasting have continued to make a strategic error in basing their existence on the need for "balance" in programming (that is, compensation for what the marketplace provides). In this way public media and culture themselves have remained exclusionary and to a certain extent unrepresentative.

Who Will Tell the People?

Discussions of media and entertainment have become similarly polarized and exclusionary. Tune in nearly any talk radio program and you'll hear complaints about a leftist "cultural elite" promoting bias in the news and ideological imbalance in other programming. Conservatives argue that Hollywood liberals are brainwashing the public with increasingly politicized media content (chapter 3, "Movies, Histories, and the Politics of Utopia"). Meanwhile, from the left one hears similar claims. The corporate media, so that argument goes, systematically exclude dissenting opinion from cultural institutions and the airwaves, thus creating a nation of clueless converts. Browse through the shelves of any college library and you'll find title after title decrying the ownership of the media by a right-wing monopoly. Certainly within academic circles, decades of residual Frankfurt School social theory have supported contentions that commercial media irrevocably serve the interests of the conservative "consciousness industry."[23] A figure like Rush Limbaugh purportedly achieves popularity because oppositional voices never get to speak.

The flaw in both arguments is that the United States is just too big to be sold a line of propaganda so easily (chapter 4, "Video Culture and National Identity"). Production entities and reception contexts are too diverse for the situation to be so simply explained. For one thing, most commercial media outlets are far more concerned with profits than with ideology. Partisan programming exists because someone is willing to pay for it. Similarly, there must be a demand for what the self-proclaimed radio "doctor of democracy " is offering. Conservative demagogues like Limbaugh are popular because they sanction their audience's anger over its economic frustrations and social fears. They tell citizens that it is okay to demand what they have worked hard to achieve.

What are the consequences of this elite versus populist war of positions? For one thing, it encourages the ambivalence and confusion people feel toward government. While varying considerably in philosophy and style, both left and right have painted a picture of a federal bureaucracy out of control in its spending and inefficiency. Taken to an extreme, these sentiments foster the type of anti-government paranoia behind the militia movement and such atrocities and the 1995 bombing of the federal building in Oklahoma City. Ironically, if you ask people about the things government does—like building highways, helping the poor, and cleaning up the environment—they express resounding support. In this light, the alienation citizens feel from their common institutions is partly one of perception.

The Phantom Public Sphere

How did this public disaffection come about? The gradual collapse of civic accords, and the growth of political alienation, has a long history. To many analysts these problems are attributable to a contemporary decline in the quality of common discourse—to a deterioration of political debate itself. Before the existence of modern telecommunications, the print era afforded citizens unrelated by physical geography, native ethnicity, or religious tradition an enhanced experience of a mutual culture and shared a perception of nationality. The resulting respect for published forums prompted the framers of the U.S. Constitution and the French Declaration of Rights to legislate journalistic freedom. As James Madison wrote, "the People shall not be deprived or abridged of their Right to speak, to write, or to publish their sentiments; and the Freedom of the Press, as one of the great Bulwarks of Liberty, shall be inviolable."[24]

This desire for a free press developed from a number of quite specific historical conditions. Politically, these convictions emerged from fears that an all-powerful state might exert influence over the precious medium of print. Philosophically, early free speech arguments grew from the Enlightenment belief (shared by many contemporary anti-censorship advocates) that individuals could resist external influence in making autonomous personal judgments.

Socially, free speech was premised on the faith that existing communications media could adequately convey the views of all citizens.

The idealized space in which this "free and open" communication would occur has been labeled by Jürgen Habermas the "bourgeois public sphere."[25] According to Habermas,

> By "public sphere" we mean first of all a domain of our social life in which such a thing as public opinion can be formed. Access to the public sphere is open in principle to all citizens. A portion of the public sphere is constituted in every conversation in which private persons come together to form a public. They are then acting neither as business or professional people conducting their private affairs, nor as legal associates subject to the legal regulations of state bureaucracy and obligated to obedience. Citizens act as a public when they deal with matters of general interest without being subject to coercion; thus with the guarantee that they may assemble and unite freely; and express and publicize there opinions freely.[26]

It's important to stress that the pubic sphere was never an achievable fact but an idealized horizon. To Habermas, a key analytical question of contemporary social analysis has become one of accounting for the growing discrepancy between the conceptual frame of the public sphere and actual social relations.

In historical actuality, while certain venues occasionally offered relatively open spaces for the common exchange of views and the testing of civic arguments, they couldn't provide a perfect incubator for democracy. No public medium has ever provided a completely unmediated conduit of civic discourse. Nor has any public sphere been capable of compensating for the differing backgrounds, perceptions, and social locations of those entering it. Moreover, despite assertions of "universal rights" by its early proponents, the public sphere never did much for those kept out—which in the Enlightenment era meant women, slaves, and immigrant communities.

Democracy and Modern Communications

The horizon of a public sphere receded further into the distance near the end of the nineteenth century, as the democratic aspirations of liberal philosophy became subverted by advanced capitalism. Technology played an important role. Emergent forms of audio and visual communication helped create a myriad of new delivery contexts, each with its own reception characteristics. Such developments were accompanied by shifting approaches to commerce based on advertising and public relations, which further complicated the style and function of mass communication. Some analysts attribute to these changes a corresponding loss of agency within the population at large, as citizens began to see themselves less as participants in the ongoing drama of democracy than as observers of its effects.[27] Others see media technologies as enhancements to democracy that provide more opportunities for viewers to exchange messages and engage in common decision making.[28]

Either way, within this technological transition the growth of electronic media produced the most profound consequences. With the declining readership of the newspaper—what Walter Lippman called the "bible of democracy"—radio and television stations became the principle means through which political discourse flowed to the general public.[29] Although primarily owned by commercial interests, during the 1930s and 1940s the airwaves carried a relatively broad range of opinion because so much of network time remained unsponsored.

With the gradual rise of commercial advertising in the 1950s and 1960s, the potential to influence programming increased. Yet regulatory protections helped insulate this electronic discourse from direct manipulation until decades later. This was largely due to governmental efforts—notably through the Federal Communication Commission—to maintain this public sphere as a civic "trust." When the Reagan administration assumed power, it effected historic shifts in the democratic function of media through a series of deregulatory measures that aided network consolidation of ownership, increased the role of advertisers and corporate sponsors, and loosened rules of public accountability. With the economic downturns of the late 1980s and early 1990s, the role of market forces grew with budget cutbacks in broadcast journalism, as well as the concomitant rise of government spokespeople and corporate publicists. More recently, the Republican majority in Congress has extended deregulation into the cable and telephone industries, a move that will have a devastating effect on the democratic potential of the information superhighway.[30]

Radical Potentials

Not that this marks the end of the story. Numerous studies have demonstrated the inability of media outlets to exert anything like a uniform regime of control over audiences, for the simple reason that different people consume the same messages in different ways.[31] To proponents of the new media literacy movement, this suggests that viewers possess capacities to make critical assessments of what they see—capacities that can be improved with education. It also bears acknowledging that the entertainment industries are not monolithic structures. If anything, Hollywood has become more heterogeneous in recent decades as the hegemony of the studio system has diminished and "independent" production has increased. Indeed, even many market advocates are quick to point out that the same mechanisms that limit production access for some also remove barriers for others. As John Keane contends,

> Critical theories of media which obscure the *self-paralyzing tendencies* or *internal limits* of commodified systems of communication are inadequate. They fail to see that the production and distribution of opinion according to market criteria is possible only within narrow limits. Market-based-media are not seamless and trouble-free.[32]

This permeability of corporate culture is further advanced by the restructuring of segments of the capitalist enterprise along "post-Fordist" lines. Unlike the days of early industrialism—with giant factories pouring out goods for masses of consumers—new financial structures and communications technologies permit highly decentralized means of production aimed at tiny segments of consumer markets. Although still subject to familiar hierarchies of management and control, the resultant micro-economies offer enhanced opportunities for localized subversion.

In a similar fashion, the dynamic character of technological change continues to offer possibilities for diversity and democratic intervention in small-format video production, digital broadcasting, and telecommunications via the internet (chapter 5, "Fantasies of Power on the Information Superhighway").[33] This is not to suggest technology alone will yield the sort of utopian "global village" envisioned by Marshall McLuhan.[34] In fact, there is increasing evidence of potential problems raised by an unrepresentative and reactionary "cyberdemocracy."[35] But I do want to make the more modest suggestion that a communications environment has begun to develop in which it becomes difficult for a single message to be manipulated for the entire nation.

These economic and technological changes are paralleled by cultural and political shifts. Postmodern and postcolonial critiques of centralized power have lent support to an expanding range of social movements around such issues as gender, sexual orientation, race, nationality, age, and disability. Not so coincidentally, these identity-based movements are emerging at a time when the authority of the bureaucratic state is increasingly under siege.[36] Nancy Fraser has pointed out that rather than one gigantic public arena, one should envision the nation in terms of numerous conversations among different groups and around different issues.[37] This critique of a single public holds significance as well because it undermines any rigid notions of what the "public" means.

Needed are new kinds of organizations and new kinds of practices to take advantage of this new technology. In theoretical terms, such issues of structure can be addressed through what writers from Louis Althusser to Michel Foucault have identified as the capillary conduits of ideology and power. By addressing the way power emanates through the "social technologies" of the school, the workplace, and the courthouse, one can begin to analyze the way the dominant social order reproduces itself in personal identities, cultural practices, disciplinary structures, and attitudes toward authority (chapter 6, "Problem Youth: Pedagogies of Representation"). Hence, any effort to reform the workings of social technology needs to be supported in the contextual frames that utilize media. This also means creating (or rebuilding) the type of "free" spaces where democratic dialogue can again begin to grow outside such institutions.[38] Finally, it entails attention to the economic, political, and cultural factors that limit the potential of any such endeavor.

Establishing these conditions will take more than utopian vision and good will. It will require concerted political organization to carve out the economic and social theaters for such activity (chapter 7, "From Victim Aesthetics to Postmodern Citizenship"). Unfortunately, great flaws exist in the current communication policy promoted by both the right and the left. At issue are the fundamentally anti-democratic principles that lie at the heart of either approach.

Conservatives advocate the purportedly unparalleled capacity of the marketplace to produce egalitarian opportunity and to stimulate quality through competition. But the commercial sector's tendency toward consolidated ownership and the elimination of unprofitable voices contradicts these utopian claims. In contrast, the left favored governmentally sponsored media and cultural programs as an antidote to the market, arguing that equality can only result from a compensating system. Supposedly this non-commercial sector encourages the development of quality programs that the commercial sector won't support. Yet as recent funding controversies have demonstrated, the totality of projects supported by tax dollars do indeed ignore the interests of many citizens.

These absences call for novel approaches to cultural democracy that do not succumb to either exclusionary impulse (chapter 8, "Toward a Radical Cultural Democracy"). Unlike today's subsidized or commercial media, this new cultural infrastructure would be developed according to radical democratic principles to represent the diverse interests of many citizen groups. Legislative measures and public funding might be required to insulate this new media sector from undue state or corporate pressure. Finally, this cultural radical democracy would be organized in transnational terms to reflect the global character of media, capital, and society.

The chapters that follow will provide a more detailed account of this scenario. My fundamental premise is that great flaws exist in left, liberal, and conservative approaches to cultural democracy—flaws that can be traced to specific historical sources. But rather than dwelling on the problems radical democrats have inherited—or lamenting recent skirmishes between left and right—the time has come to begin formulating a new agenda rooted in egalitarian principles. A partial framework for the infrastructure of a renewed "public conversation"—to use Guinier's term— exists in models from the past.[39] These original sites are finding novel extensions in the emerging technological environment. They also make possible new forms of cultural pedagogy to extend the critical capabilities of citizens and activists in ways that foreground alternative definitions of citizenship. The old town square has reappeared in the e-mail networks and electronic conferences of the information superhighway. These new political spaces call out to be claimed.

two

What's in a Name?
Beyond the Ideology of Left and Right

At the height of the recent arts censorship controversies, conservative columnist Patrick Buchanan wrote a column entitled, "In the War for America's Culture the 'Right' Side is Losing."[1] In this frequently quoted story Buchanan claimed that while conservatives had been busy defending democracy around the globe, leftists had been infiltrating schools, the media, and the art world at home. It's no secret what happened next, as numerous legislators, religious figures, and journalists cashed in on the publicity of the ensuing "culture war."[2] It also should go without saying that the left has never held "all the commanding heights of art and culture," as Buchanan asserted.[3]

Nevertheless, the myth of a radical juggernaut took hold, as manifest in countless outcries over arts funding, multiculturalism, political correctness, and school curricula. But close examination of recent controversies demonstrates that they hardly represent progressive victories in a broad-based war. Instead they constitute a few a highly publicized skirmishes (that the left has actually lost) generated by headline-hungry politicians with little interest in movies or schools, but with great interest in diverting public attention from failing social policies.

Unfortunately, the scheme seems to be working. If the left is winning the so-called culture war, why are musicians and record store owners now routinely arrested for playing concerts or selling CDs? If the left is winning the culture war, why are museums and art galleries closed for showing "unpatriotic" art?[4] If the left is winning the culture war, how can a reactionary figure like Rush Limbaugh top the best seller list? The nation's cultural sphere (both its "low" and "high" ends) has always been dominated by the wealthy business people. This isn't to say that *liberalism* hasn't made its mark in many areas, only to point out that the majority of American cultural institutions are strongly influenced by the moneyed interests that support them.[5]

19

This chapter will discuss the failure of democratic principles in three areas of public life: education, media, and the arts. To some extent this will be a familiar narrative, as it chronicles some of the more extreme challenges made by conservative bureaucrats and religious figures in recent years. Perhaps not so familiar will be a similar set of critiques made from liberal and left quarters. These culture wars have caused the erosion of a number of key democratic principles—foremost of which is the ability of diverse groups to participate in public discourse. Rather than attributing this circumstance to a partisan conspiracy, I will focus on the way both mainstream conservatives and liberals cooperate in foreclosing opportunities for anyone to challenge their authority. This atmosphere discourages any criticism of the emerging political centrism. In many ways, what remains is far more insidious than the brute political dichotomies of the cold war era. It obscures otherwise overt ideology with a seemingly neutral language of technological efficiency and corporate productivity. Worker grievances are addressed by "focus groups" rather than collective bargaining; employment discrimination is treated by "sensitivity training" rather than equitable hiring practices. In short, dissent is managed and depoliticized in the interest of maintaining the liberal/conservative order.

Within this regime, the language of politics and political possibility becomes reduced to the options offered by the Republican or Democratic parties—as choice is rendered a shallow dichotomy. Disagreements over complex social issues becomes a simple matter of "yes" or "no" in a winner-take-all electoral game that eliminates the possibility of alternative answers. Complicated questions of ethics, culture, and philosophy are removed from public discusion, as confrontations between opposing factions are rendered as struggles of raw political power.[6]

As a consequence, civic debate—the very stuff of a vital democracy—becomes distorted into polemical discourse and extremist rhetoric.[7] These circumstances are only exacerbated by a sensation-driven media driven by commercial pressures to turn every story into a headline. The result is an overheated left/right exchange in which neither side is capable of understanding the other. Needed to restore the atmosphere of civic dialogue is a regeneration of the common institutions of society in which meaningful discussion can occur. I'm speaking of those spaces between individuals and government like social clubs, the press, public schools, arts organizations, neighborhood centers, religious and ethnic associations, professional and philanthropic institutions, commonly known as the "civil society"—as well as newly emergent discursive spaces made possible by new computer, media, and telecommunication technologies. These intermediate grounds give articulation to people's identities and interests without asking for the surrender of the differences among them. In this sense they represent the sites of a cultural democracy.

Tenured Radicals and Other Fictions

To begin this democratic restoration, it is important to recognize the profoundly fictional terms in which such designations as "left" and "right" are characterized. Despite the recent brouhaha on college campuses about political correctness, speech codes, literary canons, multiculturalism, and intellectual freedom of expression, many conservatives now admit that the left presents little real threat in the academy. After nearly a decade of media hysteria over the presumed subversion of "tenured radicals" and a leftist "thought police," the credibility of such assertions is wearing thin. As free-market apologist David Rieff wrote in *Harpers Magazine*, "radicals on campus are no more dangerous than a display of Mao caps and jackets would be in Bloomingdales."[8] Moreover, the ranks of the enemy turn out to be much smaller than advertised. In a recent survey of college professors conducted by the Carnegie Foundation for the Advancement of Teaching, when given a choice from among five labels to describe themselves (left, liberal, middle-of-the-road, moderately conservative, and strongly conservative) a mere 5.8 percent described themselves as "left" and only 33.8 percent as "liberal."[9] These statistics suggest that the danger of radicals on campus may more of an illusion than an imminent catastrophe. Another more subtle indication of the ideological climate in academic circles can be determined from what scholars are reading. A recent study conducted by Steven Brint indicated that the following comprise the ten "most influential periodicals among American intellectuals": *The New York Review of Books, The New Republic, The New York Times Book Review, Foreign Affairs, Commentary, The Atlantic Monthly, The New Yorker, The Public Interest, National Review,* and *The New Criterion.*[10]

When it comes to publishing political journals, conservative money talks. As reported in *Extra!*, the monthly publication of Fairness and Accuracy in Media, the right has far outspent the left in supporting periodicals. Between 1990 and 1993, right-wing foundations invested $2.7 million in four conservative publications: *The New Criterion, National Interest, Public Interest,* and *American Spectator.* In contrast, during the same period, left foundations invested just ten percent that amount, $269,000, in *The Nation, The Progressive, Mother Jones,* and *In These Times.*[11]

Actually, the fear of a leftist menace in the academy has a contemporary history dating to the communist witch hunts of the McCarthy era. These anxieties surfaced again in a more subtle form in the 1980s, when the right started to mobilize against a perceived crisis in the humanities. With the ascendance of Ronald Reagan to the White House, conservatives launched a governmentally sanctioned reform program. Resentful of the social changes of the 1960s and 1970s, calls were issued by administration appointees like William J. Bennett (chair of the National Endowment for the Humanities) to "reclaim a legacy" and T. E. Bell (Secretary of Education) to attend to a "nation at risk."[12] These efforts fuelled concerns within higher education over the challenges posed to traditional regimes of knowledge from new interdisciplinary areas like ethnic studies, media studies, and women's studies.

A trickle-down effect to public schools soon followed. In K-12 education, conservative reformers called for an end to what were termed "cafeteria style" course offerings like social studies and current events—and a return to a basic curriculum of core courses.[13] Such curricular critiques were part of a broader program to discredit the very concept of a public system of education, which conservatives claimed had lost touch with mainstream values and had inappropriately "overeducated" certain segments of the workforce.[14] Thus began a twelve-year initiative to privatize the nation's schools—an effort that culminated in "education president" George Bush's infamous "America 2000" reform plan.[15] Perhaps not so surprisingly, Bill Clinton has appropriated large portions of the Bush agenda into his own "Goals 2000" education initiative of standardized core curricula and national achievement tests. Although it lacks the free-market zeal of Bush's scheme of government vouchers to encourage the abandonment of public schools, it shares a pro-business emphasis on competition, hierarchical reward structures, and "world class standards."[16]

Central to this corporatist agenda has been a systematic depoliticization of formerly public areas of civic life. Evoking the crude logic that government erodes individual liberty and choice, arguments are made for the privatization of education, communication, and culture—in effect, placing such policy issues beyond the reach of the electorate. To rationalize these efforts, conservatives accused leftists of using such public institutions as education to indoctrinate unsuspecting young people. Efforts by women, people of color, lesbians, gay men, students, the disabled, and other groups to gain admission to campuses or effect curricular changes were labeled partisan incursions into a realm of otherwise detached scholarship.

Aggravating these tensions were the questions posed by postmodernism to the foundational truths on which so many scholarly institutions were founded. Proponents of these views were characterized as placing "the academy under siege by leftists, muticulturalists, deconstructionists, and other radicals who are politicizing the university and threatening to undermine the very foundations of Western intellectual traditions."[17] Political correctness similarly was branded a national blight, or, more ominously, as the first indication of a creeping socialism. Writing in *Newsweek,* Jerry Adler admonished that there are many " who recognize the tyranny of PC, but see it only as a transitional phase, which will no longer be necessary once the virtues of tolerance are internalized. Does that sound familiar? It's the dictatorship of the proletariat."[18]

This nervousness over the purported ideological "pollution" of the academy became manifest in titles of books like Roger Kimball's *Tenured Radicals; How Politics Has Corrupted Higher Education* and Dinesh D'Sousa's *Illiberal Education: The Politics of Race and Sex on Campus.*[19] Rather than treating changes on university campuses as the healthy outgrowth of collegial debate, writers like Kimball and D'Sousa blamed them for ills ranging from the decline in national productivity to the rise in urban violence. To Kimball in particular, the incursion of campus leftists constituted nothing less than an absolute takeover of higher education:

> Far from being the work of a besieged minority, these voices represent the new academic establishment of tenured radicals. Often they are among the most highly paid professors—those for whose services our leading universities bid against each other in little-publicized auctions. Nor is the influence of these professors confined to the present moment. At many prestigious institutions they are precisely the people helping to shape the future by making faculty appointments, overseeing promotions, and devising the educational program in the humanities—efforts at self-propagation that virtually ensure their continued domination for another generation.[20]

This suspicion over the politicization of learning has very old roots in the Cartesian distancing of intellect from material existence. Within this logic the subjective pursuits of the mind are strictly separated from the dispassionate rules by which society is governed. This disinterestedness is said to emerge from a common respect for universal principles that lie beyond human challenge or revision. Education functions to preserve these traditions by transmitting them to future generations. As D'Sousa puts it,

> The liberal university is a distinctive and fragile institution. It is not an all-pur-
> pose instrument of social change. Its function is indeed to serve the larger society
> which supports and sustains it, yet it does not best do this when it makes itself
> indistinguishable from the helter-skelter of pressure politics.[21]

By the early 1990s, these arguments began to surface outside the academy, as politicians and religious personalities like Alfonse D'Amato, Buchanan, Rev. Jerry Falwell, Jesse Helms, Dan Quayle, and Rev. Pat Robertson sought to cash in on the political capital to be gained by scapegoating radical academics. Evoking a reactionary populism to capitalize on the distance of intellectuals from the average citizen, conservatives successfully constructed the specter of a left-wing "thought police."[22] Meanwhile, within colleges and universities the right began mobilizing its own backlash with the organization of "young conservative" student groups and faculty associations like the National Association of Scholars.

What limited gains the left had made in the ensuing culture wars quickly began to erode. In all fairness, many proponents of political correctness *were* former socialists, but very few of them were making the sort of broad-based assaults on higher education they were accused of committing. Nevertheless, from presidential addresses to cover stories in publications like *Time* and *Newsweek* the public was inundated with accounts of a "new McCarthyism" on campuses inflicted by the left wing. At the center of the hoopla was the ironic assertion that political correctness had itself become a tyrannizing practice, threatening to silence all who would dare to dissent. Rosa Ehrenreich counters such charges of academic piracy with the comment:

> A national survey of college administrators released last summer found that
> "political correctness" is not the campus issue it has been portrayed to be by
> pundits and politicians of the political right. . . . According to the survey's find-
> ings, faculty members complained of pressure from students and fellow profes-
> sors to alter the political and cultural content of their courses at only 5 percent
> of all colleges. So much for the influence of radicals, tenured or otherwise.[23]

Within a short time, proponents of diversity and deconstruction were alternating between damage control and self-reassurance. Speaking of what small progressive advances had been made, Gregory Jay observed that "judged by an absolute standard, these successes may seem pathetic, but in the practical world of everyday struggle they deserve our support," adding that "today's institutions of higher learning remain dominated by traditional groups and ideologies that perpetuate misrepresentation. It's true."[24] The overall impact of what has been termed "the mugging of the academic left" has been a further marginalization of radical educators and a generalized chilling of free speech on campuses. What began as a series of progressive movements to open the university to formerly excluded voices ended as an excuse for extremists and demagogues to further reduce such possibilities.

How did this misunderstanding come about? In some accounts, the scapegoating of the academic left is a result of its ghettoization within the university. Following World War II a pair of significant changes in the job market left radical intellectual with little choice but to become college professors.[25] The first was the much-lamented decline in "little magazines" that provided publishing outlets—and a modest source of income—for a range of "public intellectuals" on both sides of the political spectrum. This impingement on the livelihood and the sense of community among scholars coincided neatly with educational demands of the GI Bill and postwar baby boom. Aided by a massive influx of federal money through such subsequent measures as the 1958 National Defense Education Act (which for the first time give direct aid to non-veterans), colleges and their professoriates grew at a staggering pace. At the close of the 1960s, the number of graduate students had become greater than that of undergraduates in 1940. By the late 1980s, the number of colleges and universities would double and the overall number of students would grow by 800 percent.[26] As a result, the university became a vocational centrifuge for intellectuals of all political stripes—that is, until the rise of privately funded, non-university conservative think tanks in the Reagan years.

Once committed to the gulag of the ivory tower, the academic left's ability for popular communication soon atrophied. In part this estrangement from "the people" grew from a simple deskilling. Experts at such discursive forms as the graduate seminar, the grant application, or the arcane footnote found themselves at a loss in the strange context of the network sound bite or the newspaper op-ed page.[27] Such is the natural consequence of working in an atmosphere in which obscure specialization is the norm and esoteric language the rule. Finally, the estrangement of the academic left from mainstream culture resulted from a genuine contempt for it. The development of these attitudes during 1960s and 1970s will be discussed at length in the next chapter. Of importance here is the extent to which groups on the left have abandoned popular culture—especially the mass media—in their political theorizing. No wonder radicals have found themselves with a public relations problem.

Those small contingents of leftists that have made forays into the popular realm are villainized—often in racial terms. Serious thinkers from communities of color have made consistent efforts to bridge the popular/elite divide. Partly motivated by the historic exclusions of the academy, writers like Michael Dyson, Richard Rodriguez, Lani Guinier, Gayatri Spivak, Edward Said, Toni Morrison, and Vine Deloria have successfully established themselves as "public intellectuals." Early in 1995, a rash of reactionary press accounts—focusing primarily on writings by African-American scholars—began to discuss this phenomenon in the pages of periodicals like the *New Republic, Atlantic, The New Yorker* and *The Village Voice.* In the most benign instances, these articles have treated the successes of certain figures as historical anomalies created by an insurgent politics of identity. In their more pernicious forms, these stories have conveyed a thinly veiled contempt. The latter view is exemplified by Leon Wieseltier's scorching condemnation of Cornel West in the *New Republic,* an essay long on rhetoric and short on substance. Wieseltier contends that "since there is no crisis in America more insurgent than the crisis of race, and since there is no intellectual in America more celebrated for his consideration of race, I turned to West, and read his books. They are almost completely useless."[28] This is not to suggest that West is beyond criticism, or even that he is in need of criticism due to the timidness of a liberal press. However, as Salim Mukakkil has suggested, this quick condemnation of the new public intellectuals has coincidentally arrived at exactly the point when their ranks are no longer a white preserve. To Mukakkil

> The addition of the word "public" to any institution instantly values it in our current cultural iconography: public schools, public pools, public transportation, public hospitals. These institutions are devalued in part because they are associated with minorities. In that sense, the rise of the black public intellectuals may represent less than it seems.[29]

The Medium is the Message?

Although frequently painted as a leftist preserve, public communications in the United States has always been the home of good old fashioned free enterprise. In this regard, the United States stands in stark contrast to many other nations, where television, radio, and (to a lesser extent) publishing have been perceived as public resources too valuable to be left to the whims of the market. The resulting consolidation of American communications resources in the hands of a few large corporations has foreclosed their accountability to the public at large. At the same time, what small space remains for non-commercial media is increasingly reduced by pressures from corporate sponsors.

In this sense, the critique of the left's estrangement from mainstream culture should not be permitted to overshadow the considerably more pervasive elitism of the Hollywood entertainment industry. As Victor Burgin has pointed out, the word "elite" applies to any minority designated to exert control over a majority. In this sense, the members of a government constitute an elite, as does the faculty of a university, or the management of a corporation. Taken a step further, "elitism" can be said to identify any practice that supports the interests of such a dominant group over those it supposedly represents. Burgin explains that

> Much of the production of the so-called "popular" or "mass" media must therefore be considered "elitist," to the extent that it perpetuates and disseminates hegemonic corporate values and beliefs. The charge of "elitism," therefore, is applicable to much of the "popular culture" that cultural populists find most "accessible."[30]

Certainly, in this environment progressives have never held a firm footing. As debates wage over canons and curricula, those on the left need to be aware of the formidable forces confronting them. The sustenance of academic and political conservativism lies in the consolidated economic strength supporting it. No amount of theorizing by itself will place an alternative textbook on a store shelf or an independent video on television. Those institutions are firmly under the thumb of a corporate power structure that functions strictly in its own interest. Utopian speculations of the 1960s promised to replace alienating written texts with a humanizing electronic network. But such aspirations of technological determinism could not forecast that the mere exchange of medium would not disentangle the message from the capitalist order.[31]

The capacity of corporate America to consolidate its influence across a range of industries was documented dramatically by Ben J. Bagdikian in his often quoted study of the 1980s, *The Media Monopoly*. Bagdikian described the near-complete control of U.S. publishing by a handful of multinational conglomerates.[32] The book opens with the following ominous prediction:

> No single corporation controls all the mass media in the United States. But the daily newspapers, magazines, broadcasting systems, books, motion pictures, and most other mass media are rapidly moving in the direction of tight control by a handful of huge multinational corporations. If mergers, acquisitions, and takeovers continue at the present rate, one massive firm will be in virtual control of all major media by the 1990s.[33]

Although Badikian's dystopian vision has not yet been realized, there is striking evidence to support his claim. In print media alone, the statistics are staggering. While twenty major companies controlled more than half of the daily newspaper business seven years ago, now the number of companies is fourteen. Although eleven companies controlled half of book publishing seven years ago, now the number is six. While twenty companies controlled magazine publishing, now the number is three.[34] Due to overlapping interests among corporations involved in multiple areas, the same twenty-three companies control virtually all print media. They include Disney/Capital Cities/ABC, Gannett, Harcourt Brace Jovanovich, Newhouse, The New York Times, Scripps-Howard, and Time Warner, among others. More to the point, the corporate directors of these media outlets also often sit on the boards of the very companies their magazines and newspapers cover. As Bagdikian explains,

> This is more than an industrial statistic. It goes to the heart of American democracy. As the world becomes more volatile, as changes accelerate and create new problems that demand new solutions, there is an urgent need for broader and more diverse sources of public information. But the reverse is happening.
>
> Today there is hardly an American industry that does not own a major media outlet, or a major media outlet grown so large that it does not own a firm in a major industry. These media report the news of industries in which they either are owners or share directors and policies.[35]

One rarely examined but enormously influential subsidiary of this system is the school textbook industry. With ninety percent of titles produced by the top twenty educational publishers, the top four publishers—Prentice-Hall, McGraw-Hill, CBS Publishing, and Scott Foresman—control forty percent of all sales. One might think that with such large market shares, the producing companies might command a modicum of autonomy. But the costs of large-scale production for massive educational markets creates a tendency instead to appeal to the lowest common denominator. Because costs for introductory college texts can run as high as $250,000, publishers are extremely cautious about what they choose to print.[36] The editorial process is akin to that of a Hollywood film, with an endless cast of professional editors, executive consultants, and marketing analysts joining to orchestrate the "managed" text.

Given that the commercial success of these books often hinges on bulk purchasing, their contents are often geared to the largest customers—the handful of states in the Southern tier and the Western sun belt that approves books on a statewide basis. As Michael Apple explains:

> The simple fact of getting one's volume on such a list can make all the difference for a text's profitability. Thus, for instance, sales to California or Texas can account for over twenty percent of the total sales of any particular book—a considerable percentage in the highly competitive world of elementary and secondary school book production. Because of this, the writing, editing, promotion, and general orientation and strategy of such production is quite often aimed toward guaranteeing a place on the list of state approved material.[37]

Because of this, the political and ideological climate of such states often tempers the content of curricular materials offered to the rest of the nation.

The political implications of this relationship have grown as educational reform movements have intensified demands for a quantifiable "basic" curriculum. More than ever, teachers have come to rely more on pre-packaged materials that help them "teach to the test." As a tightening economy has given teachers larger classes, less time, and fewer resources, the practical appeal of text-driven teaching is likewise enhanced. Within the United States, resistance to mandated texts continues to be primarily a local matter. Yet even these decisions are frustrated in the twenty-two states that select books for local use. Obviously, in such an atmosphere many districts have little latitude in supplementing book purchases.

Aside from publishing, a more obvious narrowing of corporate influence exists in the film and television industries, where fewer than a dozen corporations control seventy-five percent of the leading movie studios (including Buena Vista Films, Paramount Communications, Twentieth-Century Fox, and Time Warner), and seventy percent of the major radio networks (such as ABC, Capital Cities, CBS, Westinghouse, and Metromedia) and virtually all television production (like Capital Cities/ABC, CBS/QVC, NBC, and Fox). With recent mergers, the number of corporations continues to fall. Furthermore, although the United States is now wired by more than 11,000 cable television systems, the majority of the nation's sixty million cable subscribers are served by seven companies (such as Viacom, Time Warner, MCA), many of which hold monopolies in the localities in which they operate.[38] Not surprisingly, these very same public media are currently hyping the threat purportedly posed by the Clinton-friendly "Hollywood Left." Yet as Elayne Rapping commented in a recent issue of *The Progressive,* this is another false alarm sounded by conservatives: "The myth that these people have, in fact, any power at all over the content of Hollywood films is ludicrous and serves to obfuscate, for an already confused public, the actual economic and political workings of the movie industry. . . . Racism, sexism, and the glorification of violence in the service of illegitimate power are thriving in Hollywood as never before. And the Hollywood Left has absolutely no inclination or power to do anything about it."[39]

Frustration over this increasingly anti-democratic consolidation of media and publishing has led many to look for futuristic solutions. Historically, technology has sparked the imagination of liberals and conservatives alike, as evidenced in the utopian speculation over the potentials of cable television. Regrettably, cable's promise of programming variety and viewer choice was undermined when its delivery system was gobbled up by commercial interests. Rather than a genuine diversity of programming options, audiences found more of the same, duplicated on endless channels. Whatever added venues were developed were either adapted to the commercial potentials of the new medium (MTV, CNN, TBS) or, in the case of community access cable programming, were relegated to a small and marginalized spectrum of the dial.[40]

Like cable, the information superhighway is currently being touted as the medium that will finally realize Marshall McLuhan's dream of a "global village." During the late 1960s, McLuhan attracted a devoted following based on his vision of a global telecommunications network designed on biological (and therefore "natural") principles, which would undermine all hierarchical structures. At the core of McLuhan's program lay a concept of media as "information without content" that defined international turmoil as the result of failed communication rather than ideological confrontation.[41] The flaw in McLuhan's reasoning lay in its formalism—its complete willingness to overlook the profit motives or political motivations of those controlling the media.

Such less-than-utopian interests are quickly becoming apparent in the scramble to develop the information superhighway, as megacorporations battle each other to stake claims on whatever they can get. On the more innocuous levels, this move is manifest in the rapid proliferation of electronic mail networks (e-mail), bulletin board systems (BBSs), or sites on the World Wide Web (WWW), all of which function like post offices for sending and receiving written (and increasingly pictorial) messages. Often touted as a "free" medium of communication, the most readily accessible ways of using the Internet, like America-on-Line and Prodigy, are metered to exact a fee for every minute of use. Telephone access via computer to libraries, public archives, and databases is similarly limited to those willing to pay for service.

Even more ominous are the planned mergers of telephone and cable television companies to combine these services in a medium. Corporate giants like

Bell Atlantic, Telecommunications Inc. (TCI), Time Warner, and Viacom are currently vying for the rights to offer a video phone service that would provide not merely the capacity to "see" the person one is calling, but also a broad range of entertainment, information, business, and—most importantly— shopping services into the home. At issue is the fundamental difference between the telephone (which is a two-directional medium) and the cable box (which simply permits choice from among one-directional messages). Will individuals, community groups, and non-profit organizations be able to "broadcast" their messages over the over the new telephone/cable information superhighway? Such decentralized capacities could have a genuinely positive effect on the quality of U.S. democracy. But without legislation to ensure such access these new services will probably end up much like cable television.[42]

The Cultural Club

Nowhere has cultural democracy taken more of a beating in recent years that in the art community. It's worth reiterating that the censorship controversies of the early 1990s over David Avalos, Mel Chin, Holly Hughes, Karen Finly, Tim Miller, Andres Serrano, and David Wojnarovitch, among others, were driven more by a hunger for publicity on the parts of their partisan instigators than by any genuine concern for the nation's cultural well-being. Moreover, as revealed in efforts by the new Republican majority in Congress, their secondary motivation was less to penalize a few unruly artists than it was to dismantle an entire system of government programs from public broadcasting to food stamps. Hence, in both subtle and not-so-subtle ways the privatization of public patronage stands at the center of these events.

The right is quick to decry the evils of big government and its associations with bureaucratic inefficiency and lack of competitive drive. It argues that government arts and humanities programs typically use the money of the common taxpayer to finance projects of specialized constituencies—when instead this should be left to "private" patronage. What this argument fails to acknowledge is the extent to which private donations are subsidized by the government in the form of forgone taxes.[43] The development of the private foundation as an institutional form can be dated to the 1916 reinstitution of corporate income tax and the subsequent introduction of philanthropic tax incentives.

The major difference between public and private charities is that the former operate under public scrutiny and that the latter do not. It is now a commonly known statistic, for example, that the obscenity controversies surrounding the National Endowment for the Arts were the result of problems associated with fewer than twenty of the 95,000 grants scrutinized by congressional staff. In contrast, the idiosyncratic giving of an entity like the John D. and Catherine T. MacArthur Foundation through its "genius" grant program continues to be both a public mystery—and, in some instances, a capricious joke. Yet the uncollected taxes on the MacArthur Foundation's $2-billion nest egg approximate the total yearly budget of the NEA.

The now all-too-common practice of censoring government-sponsored artists can be traced to the Reagan administration's 1981 Mandate for Leadership transition document prepared by the Heritage Foundation. Fore-shadowing campus pc/multiculturalism debates, it argued that the National Endowment for the Arts had grown "more concerned with the politically calculated goals of social policy than with the arts it was created to support. To accomplish goals of social intervention and change . . . the Endowment . . . serve(s) audiences rather than art, vocal constituencies rather than individually motivated artistic impulses."[44] In a similar fashion, the report suggested that the NEH should stick to the ideologically "neutral" business of supporting "humanities, rather than social crusades, political action, or political education as demanded by narrowly partisan interests."[45] In the name of "de-politicizing" the non-profit sector, the government restructured funding with a conservative vengeance—purportedly to increase the proportion of private philanthropy.

Yet the changes had very specific political and economic consequences. As Martha Rosler pointed out in a 1982 essay, rather than prompting compensatory funding from the private sector, the move to reduce government cultural support had the opposite effect, as corporations perceived a signal to either reduce their contributions or focus on more traditional cultural forms.[46] The result was a disproportionate reduction of support to community-based arts organizations, many of which served constituencies comprising people of color, sexual minorities, the elderly, or the infirm. (It is important to note that even in the best of times such groups have been a low priority at the NEA due to its mandate for serving "professional" artists.) Rosler correctly predicted an increasing bifurcation of the art system, mirroring the labor-market segmentation in the economy as a whole: "The lower end of the art system will continue to strangle, and the upper will swell and stretch as more of the money available from all sources will be concentrated in it. . . . Many small organizations, especially those serving ethnic communities, will close."[47] In the years since Rosler's article, her predictions have proven prophetic. Dozens of left-leaning organizations have indeed gone out of business, while entities like museums and symphonies with conservative appeal have continued to prosper. With an emphasis on more traditional or historic programs, these mainstream institutions are less likely to present programs that might offend audiences. They are therefore more attractive to both governmental and corporate funders.

In analyzing less powerful "mass constituency" programs like Architecture, Expansion Arts, Education, Jazz, and Folk Arts (as opposed to "elite constituency" programs like opera and dance), Robert Arian recorded radical cut-backs enacted by the Reagan/Bush government. From 1978 to 1981, funding for mass constituency programs was reduced from twenty-seven percent to fourteen percent of total grants.[48] In later years, those numbers dropped even further. By 1987, the Expansion Arts program for "minority" constituencies received but 2.3 percent of NEA funding, with Arts-in-Education just slightly ahead at 3.9 percent.[49]

These dynamics were exacerbated by periodic assaults from conservative extremists angered by the progressive character of some NEA-sponsored projects. Those attacks hit home in the censorship controversies of the early 1990s. Led by politicians such as William Dannemeyer, Jesse Helms, Dana Rohrabacher and religious fundamentalist groups like the American Family Association and the Christian Coalition, a movement emerged in 1989 to expose allegedly immoral and anti-American projects supported by tax dollars. Despite the Right's ultimate failure in enacting such sanctions, the battle that ensued on the floor of congress and in the national news media exacted a heavy toll on the cultural funding apparatus. In addition to further alienating artists from the general public, endowment critics obtained a reallocation of twenty-five percent of NEA money for state and local distribution, thus damaging the prospects of many progressive groups in conservative regions. The preeminence of the presidentially-appointed chair of the endowment over artists juries was also reaffirmed, thus casting an additional cloud over grantmaking.

Campaign promises to the contrary, Bill Clinton has demonstrated his propensity for supporting only uncontroversial arts projects. In 1992 then-candidate Clinton promised an arts policy "free from political manipulation and firmly rooted in the First Amendments freedom of expression guarantee."[50] Following the election Clinton quickly grasped the need to conserve his political capital for other issues. In what Clinton officials now assert was an unintentional blunder, the administration even reinstated a Justice Department law suit to overturn free speech advances won by artists in court during the Bush years. Meanwhile, Clinton's NEA chair—actress Jane Alexander—has performed more as public relations figure than as an advocate of free speech.

Left failures

The right's advances in education, media, and the arts have not gone unchallenged. Historically, there have been as many approaches to cracking this conservative hegemony as there have been "lefts"— almost all of them failing for one
reason or another. A detailed analysis of such efforts will appear in the next
chapter, with specific emphasis on the role of "alternative" or "independent"
media and computer technologies. From their inception, photographic and electronic media promised to play an important role in progressive politics, as a
means of both recording the putative "truth" of social circumstance and circulat-
ing this message to a mass audience. Due to the accessibility of photographic
equipment and the reproducibility of prints and films, photography was touted
as the most "democratic" of media in the early decades of the twentieth century.[51]
Similarly democratic aspirations subsequently were advanced with the development of portable video and home computer equipment. Regrettably, much of the
left has failed to capitalize on these utopian promises. Besides a troubling tendency
to ignore media altogether, left activists often have unintentionally replicated relations of class privilege and ethnocentrism in those projects they have produced.

The difficulties of many radical groups in the culture war have emerged as
much from their own attitudes as from the material domination of the right.
These attitudinal problems fall into three general categories. The first and most
familiar is the seemingly unresolvable antagonism between "textualist" and
"materialist" camps, which perpetuates a debilitating separatism between such
areas as cultural studies and political economy. Despite years of discussions
about multiple subject positions and the need to build coalitions, this rigid
divide persists. The second problem centers on debates over identity, and similarly results in a tendency of progressive groups to discount the efforts of "others." This critique of identity politics stems from the absence of a political imaginary capable of containing the very diversity that has been the left's strength.
Socialists in particular often still cling to a crude materialism that dismisses
issues like race or sexuality. The third difficulty involves viewing issues of media
and culture as apolitical and somehow harmless. As a consequence, many groups
on the left simply ignore the politics of representation.

Is There a Class in This Text?

In part, the left's perpetuation of the archaic textualist/materialist divide results
from a theoretical impasse: a recurrent misinterpretation of the late works of

Marx himself. Often forgotten is the historical significance Marx placed in grounding social thought in the lived relations people have with actual things. Marx's famous formulations of the commodity form evolved from Hegel's theory of subject/object relations. Marx extended this metaphor by insisting that philosophical ideas had to have applications in physical reality. For this reason, Marx literalized the idea of the externalized Other to represent actual commodities.[52] Thus he attributed the processes of acquisition, growth, and change through sublation to the relations between people and actual goods. In a utopian communist environment, workers would have unstymied access to the products they produce, and the process of social development would advance unproblematically. Under capitalism, this process is distorted as workers become estranged from their creative products by the operations of the market. To produce profits the market must interfere with the sublation process. This produces a frustrated mode of consumption in which the commodity is fetishized and the consumer willingly pays more than a product is worth.

In the context of this chapter, Marx's ideas hold a special significance in their insistence on the simultaneous existence of commodities in both material and cognitive realms. Yet as Marx's ideas were reinterpreted and adapted to changing historical circumstances of the twentieth century, the dual character of commodities was often forgotten. The phenomenological side of the equation that privileged the direct experience of the subject was split from the side of cognitive objectivism. Unexamined experience of the subject was critiqued by the emergent discipline of structuralism as being unscientific, ahistorical, essentializing, and "subjective." A need was perceived for systems to "objectively" organize and rationally explain experience. As important as these developments were in correcting the solipsistic tendencies of phenomenology, they were often taken to extremes that afforded the subject no role whatsoever.

The result was a rigid materialism that would deny of the role of human agency or culture. Given this extreme circumstance, it is not surprising that generations of Marxists would struggle with the problem of returning culture to the realm of political significance. In separate trajectories, both Gramscian and Frankfurt School scholars worked to integrate economic concerns with areas of popular culture and everyday creativity. In this light it is worth emphasizing that subsequent inquiries into critical pedagogy, commodity aesthetics, media studies, and material culture were exercised, not by intellectuals operating from outside the Marxist tradition, but by those seeking to extend its relevance in a postindustrial society. The resultant antagonisms to this work came largely from orthodox Marxists who felt their cause had been betrayed in these shifts.

Related to the textualist/materialist divide, another source of antagonism within the left stems from the perception of a boom in cultural studies.[53] A short-lived flurry of cultural studies publishing in the early 1990s, capped by the mammoth 788-page Routledge *Cultural Studies* anthology, produced the impression of an approaching revolution in the American academy.[54] Yet a quick scan of the list of forty contributors to that volume reveals that not one of them was employed in an actual university "cultural studies" program or department, but instead had found jobs in fields like sociology, anthropology, English, and art. Despite its momentary fashion, real institutional support for cultural studies never materialized. This can be attributed in part to the anti-disciplinary character of the field, emerging as it did in response to the failure of traditional disciplines in British higher education to respond to the interests of working-class students and communities of color.[55] As Stuart Hall explained, cultural studies saw its task as "unmasking what it considered to be the unstated presuppositions of the humanist tradition itself. It had to . . . conduct an ideological critique of the way the humanities and the arts presented themselves as parts of disinterested knowledge."[56]

Not surprisingly, cultural studies was rejected as a bastardized discourse by most recognized scholars within established fields, a circumstance exacerbated by the focus on popular culture. Particularly of interest were the habits and artifacts of groups typically excluded from academic analysis. In Britain, cultural studies initially focused on teenagers (primarily boys), whose rebellious attitudes toward clothing, music, sexuality, and schooling generated affinities among comparably rebellious academics. Transplanted to the United States in the mid-1980s, cultural studies became a catch-all for the study of groups ranging from urban gangs to Star Trek fans.

In this sense, the very mutability of cultural studies came to undermine its success. For one thing, conservatives haven't been the only ones to harbor ambivalence about the embrace of mass culture. Many on the left simply haven't taken cultural studies seriously on purely intellectual terms. Despite its professed embrace of the popular, the left often has supported what is typically seen as a conservative valorization of elite expression. One need look no further than the pages of publications like *The Nation* or *In These Times* to find an objectified view of culture as a substance set apart from political reality. As explained by former *In These Times* cultural editor Pat Aufderheide, "although there is widespread consensus on the Left that cultural expression is empowering, the notion that art offers a way to envision other ways of being is less common than the notion that art is something pleasant and extra at the end of a hard day."[57] Indeed, this narrow view of culture among educated leftists has itself been a major stumbling block in the formation of a broader progressive coalition.

Beyond this elitism have been grievances over the strategic viability of the kind of interdisciplinary approach cultural studies represents. Stanley Fish, among others, has argued that such approaches suffer from an inadequate concept of what constitutes a discipline.[58] Fish argues that assaulting the "local knowledge" of traditional disciplines doesn't eradicate the boundaries between areas of inquiry; it simply redraws them. More significantly, in redrawing boundaries one abandons both language and the community it contains. One's effectiveness is compromised as a consequence. This is not the only difficulty associated with the aspiration of cultural studies to reach beyond traditional disciplines. In extending into "non-academic" domains, cultural studies was accused of lacking genuine contact with the constituencies under analysis. Attention has focused on the movies, music, or fashion accouterments of various groups as objects for scholarly discourse—but often at the expense of the people themselves. This is especially true of the brands of cultural studies emerging outside Britain in such countries as the United States. Despite its high-minded intentions, cultural studies has been criticized for contributing to the very academization it seeks to combat. As Judith Williamson observes, "to study a culture presumes to some extent that one is outside it, though it is fashionable to 'slum it' culturally . . . there is a perverse contradiction whereby the higher up the educational scale you are, the more fun is to be had from consuming (while criticizing) the artifacts of mass culture."[59]

This intellectual distance also has been accused of indirectly harming those studied. Besides exploiting disadvantaged communities, academics have at times exaggerated the ability of "the people" to outsmart capitalist manipulation. By romanticizing this ability to escape material reality, cultural studies has underplayed the significance of "real" racism, sexism, homophobia, or economic injustice.[60] At the same time the academic objectification of the popular has ironically romanticized the ability of groups to escape the economic realities they inhabit.

Recently, these assaults have taken a more strident tone as leftist intellectuals have argued that engagement in the culture war diverts activists from more immediate concerns like poverty or unemployment. As Teresa Ebert has recently argued, "politics, in this sense, then is a process without a product; it is a mode of semiotic activism."[61] Ebert's arguments typify that particular strain of Marxist reasoning in which words and images are seen as reflections of a pre-existing economic base, rather than factors that actually shape it. Besides promoting a shallow all-or-nothing binarism, these arguments weaken the left by limiting the terrain of activism. Political work is seen as taking place either in the library or in the street, but never both.[62]

Mistaken Identities

Cultural democracy has been frustrated by issues of identity. Although one might expect communities of color, age, gender, and sexual orientation to be the natural allies of groups on the left, an odd ambivalence toward cultural diversity has developed, which ironically parallels progressive shifts in conservative attitudes. In its xenophobic heyday in the early 1980s, the right labeled all unassimilated "minority" groups as potential threats to the nation's "common culture," often going so far as to blame immigrants (documented and undocumented alike) for such social problems as economic depression, teen pregnancy, illiteracy, urban violence, drug addiction. More than one analyst has concluded that for many conservatives the rainbow menace has become the new red menace.[63] Demands for such reforms as the revision of Eurocentric curricula and the implementation of multilingual education have raised outcries from those on the right, who believe that such efforts impede the integration of the foreign-born into U.S. society. In their most extreme arguments, critics of multiculturalism assert that the entire enterprise is a self-serving government-financed conspiracy, promoted by minority "special interest groups," to frustrate an otherwise peaceful process of assimilation. As Linda Chavez explains,

> Far from losing faith in the power of assimilation, they seem to believe that without a heavy dose of multicultural indoctrination, immigrants won't be able to resist it. . . . Younger generations must be trained to think of themselves as members of oppressed minority groups entitled to special treatment. And the government provides both the incentives and the money to ensure that this happens.[64]

This brand of extremist rhetoric was largely abandoned in the 1990s, when more moderate Republicans like Jack Kemp and Pete Wilson began to appropriate the language of "empowerment" and "equal rights" once thought to be the sole property of the liberal camp. Thus, the "principle" of equity became acknowledged by the right, but only in terms of "equal opportunity" for individuals.[65] Any government or legislative assistance in achieving it was to be blocked in a society in which all groups purportedly stood on an even footing. D'Sousa makes this case for individual rights over groups rights very clearly:

Democracy is not based on the premise of equal endowments, but of equal rights. It does not guarantee success, but it does aspire to equal opportunity. This opportunity is extended not to groups as such, but to individuals, because democracy respects the moral integrity of the human person, whose rights may not be casually subordinated to collective interests. Democracy requires representation, but in no sense does it mandate proportional representation based on race.[66]

Meanwhile, a different kind of reorientation was taking place on the left, reflecting a suspicion of the fragmenting tendencies of multiculturalism and political correctness. No less canonical leftist than Todd Gitlin recently exclaimed the "the long overdue opening of political initiative to minorities, women, gays, and others of the traditionally voiceless has developed its own methods of silencing."[67] Taking a somewhat broader view, Jeffrey Escoffier warned that while "the classical schemas of political representation in the United States have collapsed . . . the multicultural project offers only a limited possibility of providing representation."[68] Voicing similar sentiments, Barbara Epstein stated that in an era when "US culture is coming apart, that it is disintegrating into a series of disconnected and potentially warring fragments . . . the left barely exists anymore; it has been largely replaced by a collection of progressive forces with particular, limited concerns."[69] According to Epstein, the problem stems from the fact that one person belongs to many different identity groups simultaneously and for that reason may have difficulty finding a universal form of political agreement with others. In the absence of a universal program, identity politics may do more damage than good to the prospects of broad-based social change.

These arguments have proven some of the most divisive the left has ever seen, and they have led to a profound questioning of the very viability of the "left" as a unifying category. Offered instead has been a plethora of frameworks to promote political unity, from communitarianism to various forms of liberal, juridical, or radical democracy. Coming largely from white intellectuals, these prescriptions share the enlightenment vision of a universal program that bind groups together under umbrellas of ethics or rights, if not political agreement.[70]

Such approaches have been critiqued by people of color as unnecessarily rigid and totalizing. Among others, Cornel West has cautioned against reaching for "timeless criteria, necessary grounds, or universal foundations" in formulating social ethics. In West's formulations, "the only plausible candidates for the criteria, ground, or foundations in question would be contingent, community-specific agreements people make in relation to particular norms, aims, goals, and objectives."[71]

Drawing on the writings of third world feminists, Amarpal Dhaliwal has advocated an approach that eschews a simple "either/or" attitude toward identity politics in strategically utilizing elements of identity politics as they apply to particular situations. This notion of a "situated" or "differential" approach to political theory stands in stark contrast to the permanent and all-encompassing approaches advocated by most critics of multiculturalism. As Dhaliwal suggests:

> This requires constant critical reflection on the assumptions we are mired or embedded in, particularly assumptions displaying affinities with modernity or humanist frameworks and standards. This mandates that, instead of encouraging and valorizing the construction of a singular, static mode of resistance which is projected ahistorically and transhistorically, we devote attention to, as many have recommended, the creation of politics of specificity, mobility, and engagement.[72]

Despite the eloquence of these suppositions in theory, no widely held application of these views has materialized in practice. As a consequence, complaints persist within the left of identity politics as a diversion from a unifying political plan.

A unfortunate corollary to these complaints over fragmentation is manifest in the assertion that cultural identity only matters to people who can't gain access to genuine power.[73] As the argument goes, those who can't have an effect on the *real* politics of legislation and public policy shift their attention to the *symbolic* realm of texts. Not so coincidentally, these arguments are surfacing at exactly the time when certain oppressed peoples' stories are being heard for the first time. This privileging of material instrumentality over the politics of representation further forecloses access by women, people of color, lesbians, and gay men to suppressed histories and narratives of emancipation. From the right, this claim is typically used to suggest that cultural organizations are now overrun by formerly oppressed groups. But this assertion is contradicted by the facts. Although some small (and hard fought) advances have been made, the same groups that suffer discrimination and economic violence in society at large are victimized in the media and cultural realms. Mable Haddock and Chiquita Mullins of the National Black Programming Consortium explain that "the rumor of institutional privilege for people of color is propelled by those outside communities of color," adding that "white producers who get no money or less than they want propagate this myth most fiercely."[74]

Still, it is not unusual for the academic left similarly to criticize activists concerned with issues of racial or sexual identity by either trivializing their efforts (as irrelevant) or condemning them (as selfish). To some extent, this typifies a general historic tendency of radicals to not listen carefully to those they believe they represent. Yet it can also be seen as an indication of a broader ethnocentrism that has characterized the left as a whole. Despite the influences exerted on the New Left by women, people of color, lesbians, and gay men, the movement has remained largely defined by white male heterosexuals, who have tended to homogenize the concerns of diverse groups into a monolithic "leftism." Again, the link between identity and cultural exclusion is significant, for it has isolated this ethnocentric "left" from many potential allies.

In addition to ignoring potential allies, many groups on the left have discounted culture and media as legitimate sites of activism. By narrowly defining politics as economics, radicals have allowed liberals and conservatives to take the initiative in battles over public broadcasting, arts funding, and even school textbooks in certain regions of the country. These are major reasons why the left has been losing not only the cultural war, but the broader struggle over U.S. politics. By assuming that politics exists outside the talk, images, and writing about social issues, the power of information has been ceded to ATT and the Pentagon. This failure to effectively engage the mass media has contributed to the perception that the left, particularly its academic quarter, is out of touch with "mainstream" concerns.[75]

Contracts on America

Certainly, when the Bush government blacked out journalistic access to the Persian Gulf War, it wasn't underestimating the politics of representation.[76] By carefully regulating the ways the conflict was reported, the administration succeeded in reversing public sentiments firmly opposed to armed intervention. With news footage under near-total control by military sources, the Bush government was able to blur the line between televisual fact and fiction in a spectacle with the exoticism of *Lawrence of Arabia* and the futuristic pyrotechnics of *Time Cop*. The Gulf War coverage demonstrated a degree of media organization not seen in the promotion of government policy since the days of Ronald Reagan's "Star Wars" initiative.

Clearly, when the Republican National Committee published its "Contact with America" in *TV Guide* it wasn't overlooking the importance of America's most widely-read magazine. As academic liberals scoffed at conservative pandering and clichés, the GOP was engineering the biggest electoral coup in recent memory. Assisting this effort in no small way was the once-debased medium of talk radio. Of the dozens of conservative media personalities to grace the airwaves in recent years, undoubtedly the most influential is Rush Limbaugh. In just five years, Limbaugh has built a small empire—with a radio show boasting thirteen million listeners, a late-night television program, a newsletter read by 250,000, and pair of books topping the best seller list. With a flamboyant delivery and ultra-conservative message, Limbaugh regularly rails against muticulturalists, environmentalists, pro-choicers, the National Endowment for the Arts, and just about everything progressives stand for.

Most leftists dismiss Limbaugh's success without a second thought—a dangerously solipsistic stance at a time when fringe figures can so successfully exploit the national media. In the new electronic arena of the 1990s, logic is hardly as important as the affective appeal of feigned sincerity or strategic hyperbole (a strategy Bill Clinton seems to have grasped, incidentally). More than his counterparts, Rush Limbaugh uses satire to make his points. "If conservatism is out of fashion," Limbaugh recently quipped, "why do liberals think I'm the most dangerous man in America?"[77] More importantly, Limbaugh casts liberals as elitists who act as though "the average America is an idiot—stupid, ignorant, uninformed, unintelligent."

What is so worrisome is that all of this "talk" is beginning to have an effect on actual politics. Limbaugh, who now regularly appears as a guest on network news and variety shows, is credited with the ability to instantly shift public opinion polls— such as those conducted during the Zoe Baird hearings. His effectiveness underscores the uncomfortable truth that despite its populist posturing, the cultural left has always had an Achilles heel when it comes to addressing mass audiences.

This is not, of course, to suggest that progressive voices are totally absent from the mass media or that radical interventions are not made occasionally. But every *Thelma and Louise, Do the Right Thing,* and *Philadelphia* is counterbalanced by scores of misogynistic, racist, and homophobic productions whose producers have no qualms about exploiting their audiences' most regressive desires and fears. This ability to purposefully connect affective populism with political intent is a skill the left has lacked since the days of Depression-era movie makers like Charlie Chaplin and Willard Van Dyke. Regrettably, it is one of the reasons why so much discussion by the radical left of movies and television these days focuses on "media literacy" and "viewer response" rather than actual production. Like so many struggles over public life, the battle for media authorship largely has been conceded to the status quo.

Democracy Unfulfilled

The culture wars have done more than weaken an already splintered and debilitated left. They have further undermined the frail underpinnings of democracy throughout society at large. At issue in the relentless pursuit of managed consensus is its deleterious effect on the process of political representation. In a system where centrism is the highest good, radical disagreement is not looked upon with much tolerance. Undergirding the conservative (and liberal) backlash against pc has been a general delegitimization of opposing views. This exclusionary tendency has limited the sort of genuine debate so necessary in a healthy democracy. Operating under the guise of "civil argument," topics are ruled off limits or "too political" for proper discourse. As a result, entire regions of human experience are removed from critical examination.

These issues bear particular significance in the areas of education, public communication, and cultural expression. The chapters that follow will develop in more depth plans to restore an atmosphere of civic dialogue. Social theorists from John Dewey to Benjamin Barber have stressed the profound importance of schooling, first of all, as an institution that provides young people with the knowledge to make decisions as citizens.[78] But beyond that, education constitutes a primary site where students apply this knowledge in social contexts. For this reason, many theorists believe that school offers a crucial model for the exercise of democratic agency and civic participation. When the exploration of difference and disagreement is discouraged in education, skills of citizenship begin to atrophy and the ravages of social alienation begin to accumulate.

For the population at large, clearly the public media are the main purveyors of information from which political decisions are now made. The United States is one of the few industrialized nations in which so much of what citizens see and hear is produced by the business world. This has resulted in a two-stroke program to both exclude voices hostile to the market and promote the assumed virtues of abundance, freedom, and choice offered by the free enterprise system.[79] The successes of this program of "manufacturing consent" through the media have resulted in a narrowing of the voices and opinions available to the electorate.

Unfortunately the non-commercial alternatives to "mass culture" tent to err in the opposite direction. In attempting to compensate for absences in the commercial media, the non-profit spectrum produces reactionary exclusions of its own—in part because it must appeal to a class-identified audience of potential financial donors. Meanwhile, it appears that any motivations toward the representation of cultural diversity in either the profit making or subsidized arenas are motivated as much by demands for market segmentation and expansion as they are for any genuine commitment to difference. Within this increasingly polemic atmosphere, the range of civic dialogue becomes dramatically foreshortened. Is it any wonder that so small a percentage of the citizenry even bothers to vote in national elections?

These dynamics favor certain people and ideas over others by determining, not merely what can be said to whom, but also what kind of questions can be asked and through what structures discourse can evolve. Within this context the apparent "losses" felt in the culture take on war far greater significance than mere partisan squabbles. Something much greater is at stake when the exercise of political debate is undermined and the principles of civic reasoning are weakened. If the tides of the culture war are not soon reversed the price may be democracy itself.

three

Movies, Histories, and the Politics of Utopia

The 1990s may well be remembered as the decade when publicly subsidized culture came to an end. As conservatives and liberals battled each other to represent "real American" values, both parties yielded to the temptation to capitalize on the perceived distance of cultural producers from the "mainstream." In a scheme that paid off in the 1994 congressional elections, upstart politicians pandered to familiar stereotypes of writers, musicians, and filmmakers as somehow different from "average" citizens. Artists became prime examples of the many "special interests" unfairly claiming governmental perks, a perception encouraged by religious leaders promoting normative definitions of family and sexuality. Rev. Donald Wildmon of the American Family Association conveyed these sentiments well when he said that cultural workers see themselves as

> An elite group of people, superior in talent to the working masses, who deserve to be supported by . . . tax dollars . . . imposed on the working people of America. . . . We ask that the Senate stop all funding to the National Endowment for the Arts, or provide equal funding for all other groups of artists—carpenters, brick masons, truck drivers, sales clerks, etc.[1]

These remarks demonstrate the divisive character of current political rhetoric, which can quickly frame an opponent in extremist terms. Clearly such hyperbole works against any productive dialogue on the difficult social, moral, and political issues entailed in cultural philanthropy. Yet, rather than dismissing such discourse as strategic posturing, one might ask why it works. What are the ideological and affective chords that such populism strikes? This chapter will discuss these issues in relation to the divide that has emerged in attitudes toward the media arts. It will review the often problematic relationship of "the public" to both non-commercial and commercial works, with particular emphasis on the efforts of liberal and leftist groups.

I want to suggest that the failure of progressive media groups to connect with "the public" results in part from a genuine lack of contact with it. A recent survey sponsored by People for the American Way found that although ninety-three percent of the population opposed media censorship, most didn't care enough to do anything about it.[2] Another study by the federal government determined that the audience for arts organizations constitutes but two to four percent of the population, a group predominantly identified as educated, affluent, and white. Yet another study revealed the prime-time audience for Public Broadcasting Service (PBS) programming was an alarmingly low four percent.[3] Why don't more people go to art galleries or support public television? Because in their posture as "alternatives" these entities have created an exclusionary mirror image of the commercial world. To justify their existence as "public" institutions, subsidized media have become profoundly unrepresentative institutions.[4] How did this ironic reversal occur?

Living In The Material World

The elitism of progressive media is more than a matter of simple exclusion; it also results from the way cultural practices have evolved in material terms—most significantly in differing motivations of commercial and non-commercial sponsorship. This is hardly an innocent distinction, for it grew from a series of quite specific economic and political circumstances. The result has been the identification of subsidized culture with money and education, and non-subsidized culture with economic and academic poverty. Although this bifurcation of "low" and "high" registers contradicts the populist goals of both right and left, it is most damaging to the latter. While figures like Bob Dole and Newt Gingrich might decry the disregard of common citizens by a cultural elite, the right's political agenda is actually enhanced by a belief in social stratification, inherited values, and adherence to tradition. Within this reasoning, a politically loaded high culture (claiming to be non-political, of course) is the standard to which all people should aspire, but which only a select few will achieve. In contrast, the left's program of social equity claims to be at odds with rigid notions of cultural authoritarianism. The left would be expected to favor a more grassroots view. But many progressives have subscribed to the same condescending cultural attitudes as the right. In doing so they have replicated forms of address that reinforce social hierarchies and inequities, while draining the cultural realm of emancipatory possibility.

Both liberal and conservative media share certain fundamental attitudes about authorship. Despite much rhetoric about democratic decision making, most non-commercial media-producing entities have evolved around single individuals, whose "drive" or "vision" motivates the enterprise. Although much is made of the social conscience motivating liberal and left media, the same organizational hierarchies exist as in less high-minded efforts. Ironically, this auteurist focus on the maker replicates a Hollywood cult of personality that frequently overshadows the topic examined. In this scheme, the heroic documentarian is an outsider, entering the picket line, the riot, or the tenement to bring back evidence for a similarly distanced public. Along the way, this producer must compete with others for grants or journalistic assignments in an atmosphere that requires as much attention to career building and publicity as it does to political causes. In other words, competition enters the picture as in the commercial sector, and personal notoriety is frequently mistaken for political achievement.

Of course, the stakes in this arena of progressive media are different from their conservative counterparts. Or are they? Here, the emphasis on individual voice rather than collective sentiment is part of a long history of intellectual conceit, in which self-selected cultural authorities presume to tell the masses what to think. It reflects a legacy of vanguardism that lingers with particular virulence in certain segments of the left, a Leninist tradition of the professional intellectual revolutionary who creates an oppositional public sphere separate from what exists.[5] The affinity and frequent co-involvement of U.S. political activists in the 1920s and 1930s with immigrant artists and filmmakers from the European avant-garde partially explains this vanguardism. Indeed, one of the first proponents of media as a means of public manipulation was Lenin himself. "Of the arts," he stated in 1922, "film is for us the most important."[6] The tendency among left media activists to discount the critical abilities of ordinary people was further extended by the elitist Frankfurt School notions of a "false consciousness." To their credit, these arguments fostered a realization of the need to enhance public understanding of the conditions required for revolutionary change.[7] But implicit in the intellectualism of the Frankfurt School was the necessity of a visionary intelligentsia to provide a compensating "true consciousness." Many of these scholars fled Europe during World War II and assumed jobs in American universities, and their condescending views of media have held sway in certain circles ever since.[8]

Often motivating this vanguardism is a solipsistic moralism, licensing educated white activists to speak about and on behalf of all other "oppressed" groups. Conveniently overlooking questions of audience or demographics, many activists cast themselves in the role of the universal agent, able to embody any subject position or identity simply by virtue of being a scholar or a media producer.[9] In particular, the alternative film and video community has allowed itself to make an unlimited range of moral pronouncements about the world around it without having to account for its own ethnicity, class location, or position of privilege.[10]

The origins of these objectifying practices have little to do with liberal or conservative politics per se. Instead they hatched in the giddy environment of imperialism that coincided with the early decades of the entertainment industry. Indeed, nations most active in global colonization during the nineteenth century would shortly become the countries producing the most motion pictures. On one level, movies provided audiences with an unprecedented sensation of power and mobility (in both spatial and temporal terms), affording viewers unknown abilities to experience the world. In the estimation of theorist Christian Metz, the early cinema offered an enormous psychological attraction by fostering "a narcissism in that the spectator identifies with him/herself as a kind of transcendental subject." By prosthetically extending human perception, the apparatus grants the spectator the illusory ubiquity of the "all-perceiving subject' enjoying an exhilarating sense of visual power."[11]

In this sense, filmmakers and viewers acted in concert to consume the world in visual terms. Cinema historians attribute this drive in part to the changing demographics of moviegoing audiences. The popularity of film as entertainment paralleled the growth of large and crowded urban areas, where people quickly gravitated to the forms of escape afforded by the newly emerging movie palaces. By 1929, more than eighty million people went to the movies every week, a level of consumption that held constant for two decades. These viewers were looking for comfortable, yet exotic, spaces of amusement apart from the routine of daily life. To answer the demand, movie impresarios like Sid Grauman in Los Angeles and S.L. "Roxy" Rothapfel in New York opened opulent theaters with names like the "Egyptian," the "Metropolitan," and the "Chinese."[12]

This new form of public gathering performed an important social function as well for this newly established urban community. It provided a sense of identity and belonging with very specific nationalistic overtones. To Ella Shohat and Robert Stam, "the cinema's institutional ritual of gathering a community—spectators who share a region, language, and culture—homologizes, in a sense, the symbolic gathering of the nation."[13] Although it is important to resist overgeneralizing the effect of movies on different spectator groups, the sheer number of people attending the movies cannot be ignored. To the extent that movies were viewed on a regional and national scale, some writers have suggested that such imperialistic forms of entertainment actually helped divert public attention from domestic problems, serving to "neutralize the class struggle and transform class solidarity into national and racial solidarity."[14]

Depictions of Western civilization's proverbial "other" gained special popularity within the didactic travelogue genre that developed prior to 1920. Slide shows, short films, and lectures would appear between reels at commercial screenings to bring an "educational" interlude to an afternoon at the movies. Typical of the colonial mood of the era, these films liberally mixed fact and fantasy in the interest of "adventure" entertainment. The titles of works emphasize the exotic character of the subject matter: *Among the Cannibals of the South Pacific* (1918), *Head Hunters of the South Seas* (1922), *Hunting Big Game In Africa* (1923), *Trailing Wild African Animals* (1923), *Wild Beauty* (1927).[15] As Shohat and Stam explain,

> "Primitive" peoples were turned into objects of quasi-sadistic experimentation. This kind of aggression reached a paroxysm in the 1920s films of Martin and Ona Johnson, where filmmakers gleefully prodded Pygmies, whom they called "monkeys" and "niggers," to get sick on European cigars. In films such as *Trailing African Wild Animals* (1922) and *Simba* (1927), the Johnsons treated African peoples as a form of wildlife. The camera penetrated a foreign and familiar zone like a predator, seizing its "loot" of images as raw material to be reworked in the "mother land" and sold to sensation-hungry spectators and consumers, a process later fictionalized in *King Kong* (1933).[16]

Not surprisingly, the American frontier provided endless fodder for the emerging travelogue industry in similar films like *Camping with the Red Feet* (1913), *In the Land of the War Canoes* (1914), *The Covered Wagon* (1923). Actually, the practice of serving up western imagery had a venerable history dating to the mid-nineteenth century. During that earlier period, photographers like Alexander Gardner, William Henry Jackson, Timothy O'Sullivan, and Carleton Watkins found work by accompanying geological mapmaking expeditions. The resulting "scientific" documents quickly gained currency as exotic curiosities and later as high art. As critics Rosalind Krauss and Jan Zita Grover have pointed out, whether operating within the United States or around the globe, the intentions (conscious or unconscious) of imagemakers often have little to do with the ultimate use of photographic texts of this kind.[17] Certainly this was the case with the theatrical documentaries of producers like Robert Flaherty and Basil Wright. While tacitly anti-colonialist in their intention to present native cultures "untouched" by Western culture, Flaherty's *Nanook of the North* (1922) and subsequent *Moana* (1926) now stand as benchmarks in the commodification and sale of otherness to mass audiences.

These attitudes of condescending empathy became a progressive preserve as Hollywood's willingness to finance documentary features declined in the face of a steadily growing studio system. This forced many leftist filmmakers to make a choice between big-budget entertainment productions and independently financed political films. The new corporate consolidation in Hollywood marked the end of an era of relative heterogeneity.

Labor on Film

The drift of leftist filmmaking from its populist roots can be charted in the evolution of productions about work. The early decades of the twentieth century witnessed new configurations of labor and markets brought about by the continued shift from an agrarian to a manufacturing economy. Within this context of increasing management and control by employers, workers' movements grew in historical proportions. The rapid industrialization of the United States in the early 1900s produced unprecedented tensions between economic classes. In the realm of mass culture, these tensions became manifest in what have been termed "labor/capital" stories. Novels like Frank Norris's *The Octopus* (1901) and Upton Sinclair's *The Jungle* (1914) set the stage for a popular cinema of work-related films. These theatrical and non-theatrical works were sponsored by a wide range of labor and radical organizations, business and manufacturing groups, churches and religious organizations, as well as government agencies and philanthropic institutions. As Steven Ross has pointed out, "films emerged as class weapons, from the start and not, as some have argued, in the late 1920s and 1930s. Labor, capital, and the state quickly recognized the popularity and power of this new instrument and used it to present visual representations of their ideologies to the public."[18]

The majority of leftist works—with titles like *The Power of Labor* (1908), *The Strike* (1912), and *How the Cause Was Won* (1912)—were not produced as commercial or even theatrical entities, but as means of swaying workers at union meetings. The American Federation of Labor (AFL) began such work in earnest in 1911, the year after it had ordered a boycott of movie theaters showing "films that prejudice the minds of the general public against our movement by falsely and maliciously misrepresenting it."[19] Meanwhile, the business world was producing its own material for improving sales and boosting public relations. More often than not, the emphasis in corporate films fell on issues of modernization and safety, in efforts like *The Workman's Lesson* (1912) and *Crime of Carelessness* (1912).

The issue of technology is worth stressing, for within this modern order the machine became a powerful metaphor for progress, efficiency, and the control of workers. The infamous "scientific management" theories of Frederic Taylor specifically focused on ways to extract ever-increasing value from wages paid to employees. Henry Ford gained notoriety for the most celebrated institutionalization of these efforts in his assembly line for the Model T. Obliging workers to function as human machines, the Ford plant pioneered the endless repetition of actions determined by the pace of a constantly moving conveyor belt. Harvard philosopher Hugo Munsterberg discussed these principles in his book *Psychology and Industrial Efficiency,* in which he explored "under what psychological conditions we can secure the greatest and most satisfactory output of work from every man; and finally, how we can produce most completely the influence of human minds which are desired in the interests of business."[20] In some instances, film itself served as the technology to enact such "time/management" studies, as they were known. *The Cleveland Citizen* warned its readers of one such production, completed in 1913:

> Every detail of the work is performed by a first-class worker, who has been put on to a certain job, is reproduced on the film, while at the same time a stopwatch records the time employed for every move. The best films are afterwards shown to the other workers of the same shop, enabling them to imitate the time-saving performance of their best mate who, by the way, had been especially taught his task beforehand.[21]

Herbert Marcuse later commented that technology can serve simultaneously as "a mode of organizing and perpetuating (or changing) social relationships, a manifestation of prevalent thought and behavior patterns, and an instrument for control and domination."[22] Film accomplished a synthesis of these maneuvers by combining within a single narrative the benefits of technological innovation, centralized planning, and human potential.[23] The efforts of labor unions to counter these messages proved no match for the growing media monopoly.

At the end of the 1920s, the cost of producing feature films had priced unions out of the marketplace and the gap began to widen between smaller-budget leftist independents and the well-financed companies of the "movie trust." Social analysis became subservient to melodrama or comedy, as documentary was consigned to the superficial realm of entertainment newsreels. By the time of the Depression, films addressing political controversy were all but eliminated by a film industry bent on lifting the nation's spirits. This left documentary sponsorship in corporate and government hands, where production budgets would be lower and audiences more narrowly defined. Over time, the non-fiction feature film would all but disappear from the arena of popular culture. As a consequence, despite its historic commitment to notions of working-class entertainment, left media would pursue a more esoteric course.

Such a shift had already taken place in England, where government bureaucrats early on recognized film's potential for documenting the nation's colonial legacy. In the late 1920s and 1930s the Empire Marketing Board began underwriting productions intended to illustrate the benefits of British influence worldwide. John Grierson's *Drifters* (1929), about the international fishing industry, and the EMB's *Housing Problems* (1935) exemplify this genre. By 1939, the Canadian government had begun to produce similar material. Because filmmakers had to answer to political bureaucrats in both Britain and Canada, the status quo was rarely criticized.

Depression-Era Radicalism

In the United States, two related types of activist media activity emerged in this period: the first was the government-sponsored programs of the Roosevelt administration; the second was the output of the Workers Film and Photo League and related entities.[24] The government employment programs of the Works Progress Administration (WPA) produced a broad range of documentary projects, especially under the aegis of the Farm Security Administration (FSA) under Roy Stryker's direction. FSA projects recorded the conditions of the Depression and functioned as publicity for the Roosevelt administration—involving such artists as Walker Evans, Dorothea Lange, Carl Mydans, and Ben Shahn, among others. In addition to creating jobs, these efforts recognized the crucial role of government in sponsoring film and photography projects that the commercial media industry would not—or could not—support. As described by Don Adams and Arlene Goldbard,

> New Deal policymakers thought it vital to direct public support to initiatives that could never succeed in the marketplace despite their overwhelming importance—initiates such as documenting imperiled ways of life and dire social conditions, rescuing individual stories about to pass out of history

unnoted, encouraging artists to involve themselves with the great questions of
their time.[25]

Despite the huge scale of these government programs they were limited by the
liberal political motivations behind them. More pointed social criticism came
from government-sponsored cultural programs like the Federal Arts, Theater,
and Writers Projects. These programs provided sustenance to cultural workers
throughout the nation, including those in entities like the Communist Party's
New Theater League and the Arbeiter Theater (or Workers Theater Organization). Influenced by the work of such personalities as Bertolt Brecht, Harold
Clurman, and Lee Strasberg, participants in these and similar groups included
Elia Kazan, John Howard Lawson, Abraham Polonsky, Martin Ritt, and Robert
Rossen. The early-career government sponsorship of these artists and writers
helped launch many into the burgeoning film industry of later decades.

It also gave indirect support to members of more radical political organizations. The rise in socialist movements in the United States fostered the launching
of the Workers Film and Photo League in 1930, whose members included such
activists as Berenice Abbott, Margaret Bourke-White, Pare Lorentz, Ralph
Steiner, Paul Strand, and Willard Van Dyke. The Film and Photo League (as it
was later renamed) differed from the WPA programs in its commitment to the
development of a grassroots political movement. Like its European counterparts,
the league was committed to bringing "realistic" renderings of everyday life to its
audiences. During this period it provided a needed boost for a documentary
tradition quickly losing favor in Hollywood. (Over time, the industry's aversion
to non-fiction would grow.) Besides creating media productions, the league
offered film and photography classes so that working people could tell their own
stories. Due to this commitment to the collective process, the Film and Photo
League periodically was able to rise above the proselytizing that characterized
(and still characterizes) much activist media. Regrettably, its time and influence
were limited.

With the exception of a few anomalies like Lorentz's Dust Bowl documentary, *The Plow that Broke the Plains* (1936), and his later *The River* (1938), the
work of the New York City-centered league rarely reached mass audiences.
Explicitly seeking to counter the slick finish of Hollywood films, most Film and
Photo League productions never made it into commercial theaters, but were
shown instead at league meetings. Straightforward films with titles like *Workers'
Newsreel* (1931), *Unemployment Special* (1931), *Hunger* (1932), *Bonus March*
(1932), and *Taxi Strike* (1934) focused on the issues of everyday life that league
members felt Hollywood was ignoring.

What popular recognition the league attracted was often coopted by the establishment. By the end of the 1930s, growing public anxieties over the threats of war and fascism prompted the studios to reconsider their attitudes toward documentary. Soon huge sums were being spent on non-fiction and propaganda films. Over time, these changes produced tensions within the Film and Photo League as many members became attracted to the lure of bigger budgets and wider audiences. Meanwhile, as Hollywood embraced non-fiction a younger generation of leftists was moving toward fiction. Members of the league like Leo Hurwitz and Ralph Steiner argued for a broader approach to filmmaking beyond the stolid newsreels, even if it meant working in more theatrical genres. With Hurwitz as the main spokesperson, they argued that the league's old and dogmatic approach did little to persuade mainstream audiences. [26]These more liberal attitudes fit well within broader political movements. As the strain of the Depression years was lessening, Roosevelt had succeeded in weakening the appeal of the radical left. For many former socialists this meant joining ranks with the progressive wings of the Democratic Party. Some league members like Pare Lorentz caught the tide of a new generation of government propaganda efforts like the United States Film Service, launched in 1938. Others like Steiner and Willard Van Dyke departed from the league to form new production companies. From the activist Frontier Film group the two subsequently founded American Documentary Films, Inc. For many the lure of fame and career-building overtook their commitment to political collectivism. Soon the era of the protest film would be swallowed up in the rush of patriotic propaganda surrounding World War II. By the outbreak of fighting and the subsequent decline of the U.S. Communist Party in the Stalinist era, the activity of the league had all but ceased. The age of Hollywood liberal cinema was born.

Hollywood Interventions

Much of this chapter has addressed the troubling elitism that continues to characterize the cultural agenda of the radical left—an elitism that first became broadly pronounced in the divisions within groups like the Film and Photo League. As left media split into liberal and radical camps, the latter began to drift from its theoretical commitment to popular culture. Over time, the financial support of radical cinema from universities, the fine arts community, and other institutions further contributed to its distancing from the lives of ordinary people. The insistence by more dogmatic leftists on a purified "worker's cinema" rejected the possibility of subversion within the entertainment industry. This rejection of Hollywood in favor of simple, low-budget films indicated an ideological conflict to be sure. But it also represented a powerful denial of the very pleasure (scorned as "false consciousness") that made studio films so appealing to the ordinary people. This totalizing view of media as a conduit of harmful desire discounts the way that meaning develops in the communicative exchange. Much of this thinking is the product of outdated Marxist theory of ideological reproduction that refuses to acknowledge subjective agency on the part of the very "masses" it presumes to serve.

More recent scholarship in cinema studies has challenged these simplistic views of film politics, specifically addressing the role of movies in social history. One of the central themes in this revisionism has focused on the ways audiences actively engage films rather than passively responding to them. Scholars like Judith Mayne and Miriam Hansen have taken issue with the assertion that silent movies served a purely assimilationist function for newcomers to the United States. Arguing against the common logic that immigrants unproblematically internalized the behaviors they saw on the screen, Mayne suggests that movie theaters provided sites for immigrants to act out rituals of solidarity and community. Assembling themselves before the vast spectacles of consumption, viewers experienced the illusory splendor of a new "modern" culture, but they were also bound together in a more idealistic sense of mutual experience—and even resistance to what they watched. Statistics indicate that by 1910 more than twenty-six million people were regularly attending picture shows, approximately twenty-eight percent of the U.S. population.

Parallel theoretical thinking expanded this idea of a "proletarian public sphere" in the early movies, where viewers of the 1910s and 1920s forged new kinds of social bonds. In the view of historians Lary May and Roy Rosenzweig, the working class public may have looked to the cinema for an exotic escape, but it no longer associated moviegoing with the aristocratic trappings of European theater. Instead, this new inexpensive form of public entertainment came to function in much the same way as the tavern, lodge, or church. As audiences sat in these new theaters they would often watch films that offered them comforting narratives with nostalgic themes and resolvable tensions. Like those other popular institutions, the movie theater was a place of temporary respite from the pressures of school, work, or other forms of externalized authority.[27] Especially as the nation moved through the Depression and war years, movies consciously attempted to calm public anxieties.

These discussions of the emancipatory potential of movie viewing held great

significance in countering the overly pessimistic views of earlier Marxist film theorists. Yet one should not overly romanticize the abilities of early cinema audiences. Despite the periodic advances by socialist, communist, progressive groups, the United States remained a society very much committed to the capitalistic ideals of individualism, competition, and free enterprise. As Rosenzweig is quick to point out, working-class audiences may have possessed the capacities to formulate "alternative" attitudes to what they saw on the screen, but these rarely—if ever—reached a state of "oppositional" critique.[28] Hence, the experience of film viewing remained a complex and often contradictory experience— alternating between a skepticism about the ideologies of gross materialism and an acquiescence to the pleasures of the dream factory.

Certain movies themselves contributed to such resistance to material values. From the earliest days of Hollywood "labor/capital" films to the present era of "Clinton friendly" liberalism, the mainstream entertainment industry has tolerated a measure of leftist thinking. Typically, this has been less a function of conscious politicking than of seeking to satisfy particular market shares. In the years following World War I, the film industry responded to scientific management of Taylorism and Fordism with works like Charlie Chaplin's *Modern Times*, in which a hapless tramp struggles to adapt to the mandates of the assembly line. Audiences could easily identify with the tramp's experiences in an oppressive and sometimes dangerous workplace, where their work was extracted by overbearing supervisors. Chaplin used this basic theme in dozens of other films, in which the central character would emulate the experiences of his working-class audience, to make fun of the managerial class.

Hollywood's challenges to the values of capitalism got more serious in the Depression years, as the United States faced the twentieth century's most serious economic crisis. Influenced by leftist theater movements in New York City, films began to appear which dramatized the tension between values of individualism and collective action. Led by Warner Brothers, the major studios hired East Coast writers who focused film industry attention on contemporary social and political issues like poverty, crime, and unemployment. Often basing movies on leading newspaper stories of the day, Paramount established itself as the leading producer of gangster films with works like *Little Caesar* (1931) and *The Public Enemy* (1931). Typically these films depicted young men and women who turned to crime after being abandoned by a greedy society.

The focus on current events was hardly accidental. For many producers, the idea began to develop that filmmaking might supplant the printing press as the primary means of stimulating public debate over social issues. Noted documentarian John Grierson advocated a unique role for filmic media as a new means of mass education, writing that "cinema is neither an art nor an entertainment; it is a form of publication, and may publish in a hundred different ways for a hundred different audiences."[29] To Grierson, the powerful visual language of film should be directed toward one primary end: propaganda.

By the mid-1930s the Communist Party had assumed a role of relative prominence in Hollywood, taking leadership positions on issues of anti-fascism and the rights of working people. Hardly a marginal entity, the Communist Party had adopted the Popular Front policy in 1935 and had aligned itself with the coalition supporting the New Deal. Over time, the party had acquired significant influence within the Screen Writers Guild, and it counted among its members many of Hollywood's leading writers and directors, most notably Robert Rossen. At Paramount Rossen developed a series of successful films, typified by *They Made Me a Criminal* (1939), in which innocent "nobodies" are victimized by social circumstance and the greed of corrupt institutions. Still, like nearly every other popular film of its generation, *They Made Me A Criminal* ends with a validation of status quo values as its protagonist-gone-astray is vindicated in the courts and the "whole system of American Democracy" is reaffirmed.[30] Ultimately, the crisis of competition and individualism that so motivated leftist politics in the 1930s found expression in Hollywood only in the most diluted form. The emphasis on collectivity that formed the foundation of the anti-capitalist movements would soon be coopted in the spirit of national unity surrounding World War II. What remained was a distinctly American brand of grassroots populism.

The generalized failure of socialism in the United States has been attributed to many causes, including the absence of an aristocratic ruling class, the nation's extensive racial diversity, and the general well-being of the voting public.[31] In discussing Hollywood cinema of the 1940s and 1950s, Brian Neve has identified another key ingredient in the suppression of the nation's radical potential: the notions of popular sovereignty that yield a "pseudo-socialistic" character to American democracy. Neve suggests that the genuine structural reforms that socialism might entail have never been actualized because

> American political rhetoric has instead borrowed from the ideas and motifs of populism—both the particular tradition based on agrarian protest and the more amorphous cluster of ideas centered around the opposition of elites and "the people." More particularly, populism in the United States has historically been associated with the land, and with agricultural communities threatened by, and resisting, the processes of industrialization and urbanization.[32]

This form of populism embodies a suspicion of elitist culture and values, a contempt for displays of wealth, and a disapproval of excesses of any kind—including an excess of education and the specialist hierarchies that scholarship so often supports. In this sense, the politics of many Hollywood populist films have more to do with class antagonism than with articulated critiques of capitalism. Going hand and hand with populism have been the political demagogues promoting its values. From Huey Long and Senator Joseph McCarthy to Ross Perot and Rush Limbaugh, individuals have built constituencies based upon the common estrangement from power so widely experienced in this nation. The positive side of American populism is the healthy scrutiny it applies to institutions and leaders that may become estranged from the population they serve. The dark side of populism lies in the obsessive normativism that it so often implies. Who decides what constitutes an excess or an elite? From where do the mainstream values of populism emerge?

In an ironic reversal of circumstance, populists often portray themselves as outside the conduits of conventional power. Speaking on behalf of "the people" they argue for a new "common sense." But all too often this common sense degenerates into an orthodoxy that excludes and limits any subsequent reasoning. The rise of Huey Long (dramatized in the 1949 film *All the King's Men*) demonstrates the initial power of such populism in organizing people against exploitation and powerlessness. But it also demonstrates the consequences of a populism lacking any critical understanding of the way political power operates. The lesson of Huey Long lies in the way the mobilization of the Louisiana poor propelled its leader into a new regime of authoritarianism. "Populist leaders arrive in positions of power with a constituency, an enemy, and a mandate, but without—certainly in Long's case—an analysis."[33]

Needless to say, movies and television have long capitalized on this populist ethos. King Vidor's *Our Daily Bread* (1934) is frequently cited by film historians for the way it overtly promoted an agrarian communitarianism. Vidor's narrative depicts a young couple who find solace in a farm run by the downtrodden and the dispossessed. Rejecting the political ideology of "fancy words," the couple find happiness in a an edenic micro-society based on non-competition and non-individualism.[34] This is not to suggest that all manifestations of early populism made their points so directly. Rather than showing the benefits of life in the heartland, the popular genre of the screwball comedy often emphasized the excesses of the wealthy elite in films like *It Happened One Night* (1934) and *Philadelphia Story* (1940). As discussed by James Combs, such movies didn't directly suggest an assault on the rich, but they did imply that values of excess often promote irresponsibility and a lack of compassion. As Combs writes, "the rich are almost always degraded, but are capable of learning when confronted with the realities outside their domains, and often form private unions with 'streetwise' people who restore their utility and respect for the democratic folk."[35]

Perhaps more than any single director, Frank Capra promoted the values of American populism. Films like *Mr. Deeds Goes to Town* (1936), *Mr. Smith Goes to Washington* (1939), and *It's a Wonderful Life* (1946), among numerous others, villianized businessmen, politicians, and intellectuals, while celebrating the "underdog" persona of the average citizen, who is ultimately rewarded for his good character. In *Mr. Deeds Goes to Town*, the character of Longfellow Deeds is an otherwise unexceptional man (played by Gary Cooper), who inherits $20 million and wants to give it away to needy people. These philanthropic impulses seem inexplicable to the cast of big-city characters Deeds subsequently encounters, most notably a crass reporter (Jean Arthur) who tries to figure out what makes Deeds tick. Ronald Reagan was so moved by the story of *Mr. Deeds* that he incorporated the film's closing speech into his 1980 campaign to illustrate the virtues of voluntarism and good neighborliness. The film's message fit perfectly into the Reagan vision of privately financed charity, which formed the basis of "trickle-down" economics. Rather than a problem requiring a massive redistribution of resources, issues of poverty might be resolved by individual acts of generosity.

Melodrama and Democracy

After all, such a focus on individualism is a cornerstone of American liberal democracy. And it is part of what lent populist feature films their affective melodramatic appeal. As a genre, melodrama dates to the era of the French Revolution, and it is directly associated with liberal democracy. To John Belton:

> The melodrama supplanted the "elitist" vision of the tragedy with a more democratic worldview. Classical tragedy, which dies in the seventeenth century with Racine, could be seen as elitist largely through its concern for the fates of characters of a certain magnitude and/or social stature. But it was also aristocratic in its basic understanding of the essentially static relationship of individuals to the existing political and social order. The heroes and heroines of tragedy struggled to maintain the "natural" order of things.[36]

In this sense, films like *Mr. Deeds Goes to Town* and *It's a Wonderful Life* function to personalize what would otherwise be intensely political issues. As David

Grimsted puts it, melodrama subverted more radical political action in that it "reflected and supported what is perhaps the key element in democratic psychology: the sense which individual men have of their ability to decide, and hence of their right to participate vitally in the wielding of power."[37]

The melodramatic tension between populist individualism and communal impulses became most pronounced in the genre of westerns, where narratives of such iconoclastic "American" ideals as frontier discovery, invention, and independence were contained within a broader program of colonial conquest, domination, and exploitation. The frontier appears as a lawless territory where small towns constitute islands of virtue amid a sea of anarchy and evil. For example, in *High Noon* (1952), Gary Cooper is about to retire as the local marshal when he hears of a gunman returning to seek revenge upon him. Though he has good reasons for leaving town, Cooper's character feels a responsibility to stay and face the problem. As in many westerns, Cooper has no authority to whom he can appeal for help, no cavalry to call to the rescue. Bound by duty, honor, and a compulsive sense of community, he is the quintessential subject of American populism.

Perhaps not so coincidentally, *High Noon* has also been discussed as an allegory for the film industry during the cold war. The movie might have been billed as a western, but according to Carl Foreman, who wrote it, "What *High Noon* was about at the time, was Hollywood and no other place but Hollywood."[38] Foreman was referring to the way writers and directors had been abandoned by their associates when the House un-American Activities Committee (HUAC) conducted its hearings into presumed communist activity in the entertainment world. On one level *High Noon* is a western drama about a community whose sole protection is a marshal driven by his conscience. To Foreman the film presents a story of political courage in a nation where the authority of law was being seriously abused. Regrettably, unlike the metaphorical town in *High Noon* the embattled Hollywood left that had commanded so much influence in the 1930s and early 1940s would be forever fragmented by the forces confronting it. What once promised to be a unified force in the production of progressive media would shatter into so many market shares and differentiated ideologies. Themes of small communities pitted against a hostile world have retained their popularity ever since, although they have rarely carried the level of political innuendo attributed to *High Noon*.

The most telling episode in Hollywood's short-lived era of radicalism occurred just following the 1950 HUAC hearings. Studio executives flew into a panic when the conservative Hearst newspaper chain threatened to mount a boycott of leftist studios. Secretly convening in New York City's Waldorf-Astoria Hotel, the executives drafted a document—later called the "Waldorf Statement"— announcing an industry-wide agreement to deny employment, suspend, or otherwise "blacklist" film industry workers suspected of communist leanings. At the same time, the industry began producing a rash of anti-communist films like *The Iron Curtain* (1948), *I Was a Communist for the FBI* (1951), *Walk East on Beacon* (1952), *My Son John* (1952), and *Pickup on South Street* (1953). On a more allegorical level, sentiments of anti-communism found form in the new genre of science fiction. Movies like *The Thing* (1951), *Them!* (1954), and *The Invasion of the Body Snatchers* (1957) suggested that often unnamed external threats (visible and invisible) lay waiting to assault an innocent United States. These were soon followed in the 1960s by films depicting hidden threats of a more human character, in spy films of the James Bond variety. Meanwhile, the malevolence of science took a different ideological slant, as nuclear fears fostered a range of movies about the bomb. *Seven Days in May* (1964), *Fail Safe* (1964), and *Dr. Strangelove or: How I Learned to Stop Worrying and Love the Bomb* (1964) typify this latter genre.

Much has been written about Hollywood "political" films of the following decades. Although such works addressed a variety of activist issues, most fell within the ever-widening scope of a motion picture industry struggling to compete with the growing programming choices made available to viewers by broadcast television. But the depoliticization of Hollywood films is attributable to other social factors as well. During the 1950s and 1960s, the broader structure of American leisure began to change as the work week dropped from forty-eight to forty hours and as levels of affluence seemed to rise for certain groups. As Belton explains:

> Americans had not just stopped going to the movies, but they had begun doing something else instead. After the war, Americans grew disenchanted with passive entertainment and took a greater and greater interest in participatory entertainment—in gardening, golfing, bowling, hunting, fishing, and boating. The workweek dropped from a wartime high of forty-eight hours to forty hours in the postwar era.[39]

This growing competition for leisure dollars meant that movies had to get splashier—and as a result they got more expensive to produce . While the cost of a movie averaged approximately $400,000 in 1941, it had risen to $12 million in 1984. Eleven years later, the Kevin Kostner dystopian thriller *Waterworld* (1995) ran a budget of over $175 million. In Hollywood's early years this kind of financing was provided by major studios with long-term commitments to directors and particular visions. The organization of production has now returned to a pre-industrial model in which clusters of personnel assemble briefly around a single project. This shift toward more "independent" production had been set in motion in the 1940s, when antitrust legislation broke the vertical integration maintained by the studios. One would think that the resultant decentralization would have yielded a more heterogeneous field. Not true.

Although some studios still lend such support for favored projects, much of the financing for movies comes from investors in the multinational corporations that have taken their place. These partnerships, shareholder groups, and banks have little interest beyond a return on investment capital, and they tend to be quite cautious in the choices they make. The result has been a steady shift away from controversial or experimental films in favor of sequels, remakes, or formulaic works whose success is more certain. This creates a tendency among producers to appeal to the lowest common denominator among audiences. The result is a political void that independents increasingly feel compelled to fill.

Documentary and the (de)Politicization of Hollywood

Following World War II, the gap continued to widen between the highly financed productions of the entertainment industry and their poor relations in the independent sector. Like the Hollywood left, radical documentarians were dealt a serious blow by the HUAC. Beginning in 1947, the congressional hearings successfully put an end to groups like the Film and Photo League. As a consequence, independently produced activist films practically disappeared during the 1940s and 1950s. This coincided with falling box office receipts and heightened government censorship of the movie industry. Radical politics and formal experimentation were discouraged in a political atmosphere in which conservatives asserted that liberals had taken over then nation's cultural apparatus. The socially motivated films that were made tended to focus on individual problems, rather than national ones.

The climate began to change again in the late 1950s, this time due to the growth of a new technology: television. The emerging broadcast networks needed news footage and programs ,and as a consequence the demand for socially oriented, non-fiction films and productions began to grow once more. Typical works addressed issues of poverty, education, and crime—although very few did so with the radical verve of the Film and Photo League. One notable exception was David Lowe's CBS documentary *Harvest of Shame* (1960), depicting the exploitation and inhuman living conditions of migrant farm workers. Narrated by Edward R. Murrow, the film made a radical departure from journalistic convention by imploring viewers to contact members of congress about a pending piece of relief legislation. A few years earlier Murrow also launched his "See it Now" series, which produced the first widely circulated attacks on the McCarthy hearings.

Other influential independent documentarians of the period included Leo Hurwitz, whose *Native Land* (1946) and *Strange Victory* (1948) constituted two of the first serious critiques of racism and segregation. Both films shocked audiences with the directness of their coverage, an effect that alienated some viewers. Warren Miller comments about *Strange Victory* that its

> refusal to compromise with fact: the fact of the exploitation and oppression of the Negro people of America, the fact of anti-Semitism, of native fascism; and the disquieting idea that the recent war had indeed produced a strange victory, the values of the loser being adopted by the winner.[40]

Similarly direct in his ideology was George Stoney, who produced more than fifty films addressing issues of health, welfare, and race. Aside from his political radicalism, Stoney's films like *Palmour Street* (1950) and *All My Babies* (1952) departed from the documentary mainstream by mixing fictional and non-fictional elements. Stoney would later become a leading proponent of the community video movement to put cameras into the hands of citizens—an issue addressed at length in the next chapter. In working to break down distinctions between subjective and objective genres or between viewers and makers, Stoney recognized the importance of form as an issue in audience empowerment.[41]

Technical and theoretical developments helped forge new means of independent documentary filmmaking in the 1960s. The development of small, lightweight cameras and high-quality, portable sound recording made possible the development of a new cinema of human immediacy. The so-called "cinéma vérité" emerged from principles originally set forth by Dziga Vertov and Walter Ruttman, both of whom had sought to replicate lived experience by bringing the representational apparatus into the action being recorded. Unlike traditional Hollywood moviemaking, in which the presence of the filmmaker was hidden as much as possible, cinéma vérité accentuated such material elements as handheld camera movement and the grain of film stock. With the new portable technology, filmmaking was no longer restricted to the constraints of the studio; it could take place anywhere. These principles were taken a step further in the "direct cinema" movement, in which most directorial control over the action was surrendered to the unfolding narrative. Producers like Richard Leacock, D. A. Pennybacker, and Albert and David Maysles created numerous works predicated on the presumed "objectivity" of the direct cinema approach. Of course, the fallacy of films like *Don't Look Back* (1966) and *Monterey Pop* (1968) lay in their illusion of authorial detachment and journalistic purity. By the 1970s, the noble conventions of cinéma vérité and direct cinema had joined the lexicon of filmmaking as stylistic devices.

Like the independent productions of the period, mainstream movies sought to cover timely topics—albeit in a more restrained fashion. Films like *Alice's Restaurant* (1968), *Medium Cool* (1969), and *Easy Rider* (1969) typify the softcore politicization of films in which the central characters resist status quo values but lack a coherent program with which to replace them. When politics did become a focus of Hollywood films, it was generally secondary to other narrative elements. A case in point is *The Way We Were* (1973), which chronicles the lives of a student activist, played by Barbra Streisand, and her Waspish opposite, Robert Redford. The plot revolves around their on-again, off-again relationship from the 1930s to the 1950s, during which Redford becomes a Hollywood writer under assault by the HUAC. What might have been a biting indictment of the Hollywood blacklist was toned down in pre-release editing. Studio pressure to gear the film toward mainstream audiences obliged director Sydney Pollack to stage the highly critical screen play by novelist Arthur Laurents as a romance. Due in part to the box office appeal of the movie's two emerging stars, the $25 million film was an enormous financial success.

Woody Allen's *The Front* (1976) soft-pedals the McCarthy era in a similar fashion. In the film, Allen plays a nerdly screenwriter enlisted by blacklisted writers to "front" for them by putting his name on their scripts. The unwitting Allen quickly becomes a success and subsequently an object of HUAC investigation. Comic irony develops as Allen is investigated during the hearings. Lacking any political conviction of his own, the character is unable to comprehend the charges put before him. Due to its lighthearted portrayal of events, *The Front* was criticized broadly by critics on the left for underplaying the destructive implications of the blacklist. Like *The Way We Were,* the film made a healthy profit. Both films can be linked to a larger pattern of depoliticization in the entertainment industry, in which controversial projects are drained of their subversive potential.[42] In their own ways both films shied away from coherent political analysis—using romance in the case of *The Way We Were* and comedy in

The Front. They demonstrate the regrettable choices the entertainment industry makes when weighing difficult decisions about content against those of box office appeal.

Time and again the entertainment industry has demonstrated two primary tendencies in its political films of fictional narrative: personalization and trivialization. In the first instance, a purposeful inversion of the familiar dictum "the personal is political " becomes manifest as political struggle becomes neutralized as an individualized trait or an element of psychological makeup. Although such personalized activism is often portrayed as tacitly influenced by broader struggles or movements, it is more typically reduced to an element of heroic purpose or idiosyncratic character development. It reinforces the tendency within most mainstream movies and television programs to focus on a limited number of protagonists, around whom the storyline is drawn. As a result, political activists appear as isolated individuals, inexplicably "driven" by a cause. Such is the case of the activist Streisand character in *The Way We Were,* who appears early in the film at a demonstration where her fanatical ranting catches Redford's attention. Deemphasizing the collective vision of leftist anti-fascism of which she presumably was a part, the film depicts Streisand as a deviant nonconformist who eventually outgrows her radical politics.

A similar personalization of the political characterizes Jonathan Demme's *Philadelphia* (1993), widely touted as the first "big-budget" film to address HIV and AIDS. Tom Hanks plays a lawyer who sues a firm that fired him when it learned he had contracted the illness. Most of the narrative follows Hanks as he struggles to find evidence and hire a sympathetic attorney. Widely criticized for its medical inaccuracies, *Philadelphia* is perhaps most lacking in its portrayal of Hanks as a lone victim. AIDS activists appear only briefly in occasional protest scenes. In contrast to *Philadelphia* stands its low-budget precursor, the PBS American Playhouse feature *Longtime Companion* (1990). *Longtime Companion* followed a close-knit group of gay men in New York City through the 1980s, detailing a variety of HIV and AIDS narratives along the way. Opening with the first reports of the epidemic early in the decade, the film follows its characters as they come to form alliances and organize politically.[43]

Hollywood's trivialization of politics flourished in the Reagan years, when government policy and mass culture alike transformed brute ideology into popular fantasy. In this genre, conflict is either hyperbolized into a caricature or transformed into a non-issue. The former category includes films like *The Killing Fields* (1984), *Red Dawn* (1984), *Rambo* (1985), and the *Hunt for Red October* (1990), which constructed clearly identified enemies for the United States. The ideology of such films is well articulated by an excerpt from *Clear and Present Danger* (1994), in which the protagonist, played by Harrison Ford, is accused of "seeing the world in black and white." Ford replies, "It's not black against white, dammit; it's right against wrong."

Other films of political conflict stage their battles at the level of nostalgic or futuristic fantasy. Some argue there is little difference. This tendency to confuse media fact and fiction has become disturbingly frequent in recent years—a phenomenon demonstrated in the increasingly ambiguous language of news reporting. Although recent examples abound, one of the most far-fetched illustrations of such propagandizing involved the comical publicity campaign waged for a concept known as Star Wars. No, not the film fantasy of director George Lucas, but the political fantasy of Ronald Reagan. Inasmuch as both versions were popularized via the media, their differences became exceedingly difficult to discern. Interchangeable subject matter, terminology, and hardware blurred the line between science fiction and fact—and the Reagan administration took full advantage of it. Narrowing the gap between futuristic fantasies and world events permitted the reduction of complex international issues into a realm of simplistic figuration: Manichaean battles of light against darkness, tales of wilderness conquest and Manifest Destiny.

The Star Wars mythology was powerful medicine indeed, which president Reagan was able to translate into budgetary success. One might logically ask why the voting public was so willing to swallow so "unreal" an explanation for the expenditure of billions of dollars that might otherwise have served more humanistic purposes. In part the answer is attributable to the circumspect pathways that propaganda travels in Western society. As the sophistication of the film industry's illusionistic capabilities has pushed the public's fantasy quotient to all-time highs, the press increasingly encourages a language of euphemism and analogy—a distancing from the real.

Comparable narrative displacements were called into service to popularize the invasions of Panama, Grenada, and especially Kuwait. It is now well acknowledged that the Defense Department had prepared a media strategy for the Persian Gulf War years in advance of the actual conflict. The resulting spectacle of Pentagon spokespeople and computer simulation was sanitized and objectified into a video-game-like abstraction. In this vocabulary, war was not fought but "prosecuted," as civilian massacres were rendered invisible by terms like "collateral damage."

The transformation of political issues into entertainment narrative (or vice versa) found no more perfect a vehicle than in the 1994 smash hit *Forrest Gump*.

Here the film's main character and namesake is followed from his humble birth in 1940s Alabama to the present day, as he stumbles into nearly every major ideological confrontation of the postwar era. The film employs sophisticated computer imaging techniques to insert Gump into actual news footage of past events. The idiot-savant Gump peers over Governor George Wallace's shoulder as he attempts to bar black students from the University of Alabama, inadvertently joins Abby Hoffman leading an anti-war protest in Washington, D.C., and meets with Presidents Kennedy, Johnson, Nixon, and Reagan (not to mention Elvis) along the way. In *Forrest Gump* troubling events *literally* become stage dressing in a manner suggesting the irrelevance of politics itself. As J. Hoberman wrote in a review of the film, "This bleak, yet saccharin tale of simple goodness triumphing over retardation, amputation, assassination, exploitation, intolerance, child abuse, and AIDS embodies a sentimental populism that suggests Oprah as well as Capra. History really does dissolve."[44]

Everything Old is New Again

It's no surprise that Hollywood hasn't provided the political leadership to make serious political changes in the United States. The economics of big-budget productions are simply too imbricated in the fiscal and political conservativism of corporate America. This is not to say that spaces for intervention in cultural production do not occasionally appear in the entertainment industry, or that audiences are incapable of appreciating alternative media. Certainly the 1994 appearance of Michael Moore's newsmagazine program "TV Nation" on NBC and the widespread popularity of movies like *The War Room* (1993) by D.A. Pennybacker and Chris Hedges and *Coming Out Under Fire* (1994) by Arthur Dong suggest a degree of possibility within mainstream markets. With this in mind, it is important to stress that independent producers hold no exclusive franchise on radical idealism, a fact demonstrated by the many gestures of activism attempted from within the industry. It is important for left activists to recognize and support progressive movies and television productions when they are made, however limited the activism of such media may be. To do otherwise is to assume a naively separatist view of institutions, in which only an external elite is capable of genuine radicalism.

This is not to deny the significance of critical voices outside the marketplace. The role of such perspectives has become particularly important as groups formerly denied production and distribution opportunities are gaining such access, often for the first time. This critical ground needs special attention in the academic community, where poststructuralist arguments threaten to minimize the legitimacy of certain forms of political agency. Kirsty McClure has aptly summarized the argument of feminists and people of color who assert that:

> When marginal and oppressed groups are asserting their rights as political subjects is no time to deconstruct the categories. Indeed, to do so at the present is to become complicitous with a neo-conservative agenda, an agenda which aims precisely to restrict both the scope of such rights claims and the potential power of those actively beginning to advance them.[45]

Works like Robert Rodriguez's *El Mariachi* (1993), and Ang Lee's *The Wedding Banquet* (1993) do more than merely introduce "new" voices to audiences. They begin the important process of shifting the subjective frame of reference in journalism and entertainment from Eurocentric modes of perception that so dominate the industry. As most dramatically demonstrated in experimental documentaries like Trinh T. Minh-Ha's *Surname Viet, Given Name Nam* (1989) and *Shoot for the Contents* (1991), this shift has formal, experiential, and ultimately political implications. Trinh comments that no consideration of the political in filmmaking can exist without a consideration of the full range of institutional and linguistic parameters that encase the text itself. She asks in a recent interview, "Where does language start, where does it end? In a way, no political reflection can dispense with reflection on language."[46] Trinh points out the tendency within both Hollywood and avant-garde cinema to overlook or take for granted the formal parameters of language and style that frame any message and thereby limit its capacities. In this way she makes a compelling argument for external—in this instance, non-Western—perspectives to throw such solipsism into relief.

The danger in this reasoning lies in romanticizing the external perspectives at the expense of anything else. Such a vanguardist attitude has two serious political shortcomings: first, it validates the presumed invincibility of dominant institutions by assuming they cannot be subverted from within. In this way it consigns activists to the role of outside adversaries, who topple an oppressive regime by sheer force of numbers. This attitude is becoming increasingly unrealistic in an atmosphere in which major corporations are buttressing their capacities with mergers and collateral agreements. The very notion of an isolated institution has become an anachronism in an era of flexible management and multinational capital. Secondly, this condescending view of Hollywood liberalism discounts the validity of partial victories. It replicates an all-or-nothing view of politics in which subjectivity is always singular, unified, and unadulterated. Within this logic, consent is always total and immediate, with no shades of contradiction or indecision. If only life could be so simple!

These defenses of Hollywood liberalism aside, one would not want to subscribe to the brand of Clintonesque centrism recently debunked by Fred Herman in a letter to *The Nation* when he jokingly wrote, "The lesser evil is less evil than the greater evil and while it is not left, center remains to the left of the right."[47] As others have suggested, the center benefits too much from its own privilege to be expected to decenter itself.[48] For this reason it needs to receive education from the margins, which helps those in power to understand the logical—if not moral—bankruptcy of such a stance. Sharon Welch has well summarized the thinking of many feminist scholars who argue that any single perspective benefits from external viewpoints. Indeed, it is the very definition of solipsism to remain blind to what one does not know. Welch writes:

> The preference for unilateral action is dangerous for several reasons. One of the most troubling is a presumption of that preference, confidence in the rightness of one's views for all. Some political analysts assume that there are interests that are genuinely good for all and others that merely mask selfish interests. They assume, of course, that their nation, or they themselves, are the bearers of a wisdom that is universally valid, and that ideological blinders exist only in others. There is no recognition here that all perspectives are partial and that the creation of a moral vision and a strategy of moral action requires by definition the counterbalance of other groups and individuals. A single actor cannot be moral.[49]

More to the point, this critique applies to radical groups as well. No solitary perspective is appropriate or even strategically sound.

Regrettably, such pluralistic reasoning is often very difficult to keep in mind for groups caught up in the passions of political action. Historically, the very singularity of left causes has been blamed by some for the failure of a stable coalition. Others have seen the problem in the rigid universalism of "the left" as a conceptual model. Activists of that generation were brought together by the confluence of civil rights struggles, the women's movement, and anti-war protests, to create what felt like a novel resistance to ruling-class values and institutions. In fact, the lack of radical activism in the prior two decades gave many youthful proponents of the New Left the brash belief they had invented the movement that could encompass all other radicalism.[50] But while seeking to forge a new political imaginary such efforts often alienated more people than they persuaded.

Just as the right had oversimplified issues into convenient clichés, many groups on the left similarly collapsed all activist causes into a single category of dissent.

This presumption of an undifferentiated New Left failed to acknowledge the many factors of identity and interest that motivate people to act politically. The activities of the radical journalistic collective Newsreel in many ways typified this reactionary radical practice. Newsreel provided documentation of left activism (demonstrations, marches, and sit-ins) through grainy, hand-held films that took viewers behind the lines of protests, into occupied school administration buildings, and face to face with sometimes brutal police. But in focusing on the performative aspects of protest, the films often dramatized responses to inequity and injustice without offering explanations of their underlying causes. Most importantly, by focusing strictly on direct action, such groups overlooked the complex ways that political subjects are constructed *both* as bodies and representations.

Academic Questions

Not all activist media of the 1960s and 1970s was as extreme in its form or contents. Nevertheless, the work of Newsreel typifies the heavy-handed dogmatism that both defined and limited much cultural activism of the period. To segments of the population who were either past college age or for whom a higher education was economically unfeasible, much of the university-centered counterculture remained a mystery. Despite the concurrent activism by groups like the Young Lords and the Black Panthers, the New Left was largely a white male preserve.[51] Consequently, much cultural activism of the New Left was articulated in a vocabulary familiar to its suburban-bred constituents—but not to anyone else.

Although purporting to constitute a "people's cinema," Newsreel's vérité style spoke to a segment of the population acculturated to the formal conceits of avant-garde film. Indeed, the growth of university cinema studies programs, communications, and photography departments during the 1960s and 1970s contributed considerably to the training of activist producers and to the growth of audiences for their work. This movement originated in university film societies in the 1950s. In the absence of formal film programs within universities, these organizations developed on an ad hoc basis to offer screenings and discussions of documentary, avant-garde, and "foreign" films.[52] Supporting this growth were strong art-film communities in cities like New York and San Francisco, as well as nascent critical publications like *Film Society Review, Film Critic,* and *Film Culture.* Initially these entities geared their activity toward the connoisseurship of filmic "masterpieces," thus helping film gain a foothold within speech and theater departments. By the early 1960s, the film societies had gained sufficient acceptance to form their own confederated organization and to begin lobbying for a national institute to support their efforts.[53]

During the 1960s and 1970s, a confluence of three related circumstances solidified the position of film and media studies within the university. The first was the growing influence of linguistics as an academic pursuit, and along with it the importance of structuralism in disciplines ranging from anthropology to art history. Thus began an interest in "representation" as a critical (and political) issue in scholarship of many kinds. Secondly, communications became recognized as a vocational area on its own merits. This stimulated the growth of courses in broadcast media technique within programs formerly enmeshed in traditional print journalism and advertising. Finally, interdisciplinary programs began to appear in response to the failure of conventional disciplines to adequately address curricular needs. In this regard, media studies developed in an atmosphere in which women's-studies and ethnic-studies advocates had already done much of the political fighting to carve out new institutional spaces for teaching and research.

Regrettably, this growing interest in film, video, audio, and photography did little to advance the cause of leftist politics on campuses. In fact, the university quickly replicated the divide between activists and industry producers—a split with disturbing class implications. At the risk of oversimplifying this history, the programs oriented toward language and theory began to develop what might be termed a "cinema studies" model of scholarship. In the 1970s and 1980s, scores of such programs would develop, which offered MA and PhD credentials for middle-class students primarily interested in studying the entertainment industry from a distance. Although some of these programs would develop production components, they generally shied away from the actual making of films or television programs.

In contrast, departments oriented toward the vocational skills of media produced a "communications school" model stressing production or marketing techniques. These programs offered a broader range of certificate and degree programs for students seeking to enter the media industry for immediate career and income needs. When such programs engaged in analysis, it was generally from the uncritical perspective of market surveys or audience research. Despite the generalized endorsement communication schools offered the commercial media establishment, within larger programs occasional pockets of resistance would develop among younger faculty.

A more stridently critical approach to film and television emerged from interdisciplinary programs. This "media studies" model encouraged alternative approaches to production which did not necessarily conform to industry formulas. While the media studies programs were responsible for fostering a broad range of radical activity, very little of this work found its way to large audiences. Still, the media studies movement was largely responsible for the development of independent media centers, discussed in the next chapter, which supported a broad range of political and experimental production.

In the context of left activism, a profound irony grew from this three-way institutional divide. The two seemingly natural allies—the cinema and media studies contingents—remained (and still remain) divided along theory/practice dichotomies. This division is well described by Annie Goldson, who asserts that the "gap between production and theory is evident even when there appears to be the political will to unite them."[54] Goldson recounts her experiences at a conference intended to bring the two presumed allies together:

> On the one hand, the theorists present, most of whom teach at universities and write for academic journals, delivered papers that focused exclusively on commercial television . . . but there were no network television producers present who could contextualize, elucidate or defend broadcast practices. On the other hand, the producers who were present all worked independently and rarely, if ever, had shown work on network television. Confronting the gulf between theory and practice, the two groups-theorists and independent television producers—spoke at cross purposes and found little common ground.[55]

The Fine Art of Politics

Related to the separation of theory from production are a number of other factors that have conspired to divert non-commercial producers from their populist aspirations. Exacerbating an underexamined emphasis on production is the profound reverence for individual authorship, especially as it concerns the "alternative" text discussed earlier. Indeed, independent work is typically identified via an eschewal of bureaucratic affiliation, a characteristic nowhere made more apparent than in debates over government patronage centering on the Corporation for Public Broadcasting (CPB). Groups like the Association for Independent Video and Filmmakers and the former National Coalition of Independent Public Broadcasting Producers have repeatedly encouraged the CPB to adopt a definition of an independent as one "who is in complete control of the content and budget of a production."[56] The rhetoric of those financial discussions intensified during the Reagan and Bush years, as the CPB illegally continued disbursing the majority of its budget to network entities (PBS stations and consortia). The resulting capital squeeze on the independent enterprise drove attention back to producers and products. Competition in the grantmaking arena replaced competition in the market.

The fetishization of self-expression has been further exacerbated by the identification of non-Hollywood production as an aesthetic activity—evidenced by the prevalence of such terms as *media artist, media art,* and *media arts center.* Money for this stand of activity has come largely from the art market (acting in concert with the museum world), state and federal arts councils, and a few private foundations. Setting the tone for much of this activity has been funding from the National Endowment for the Arts, an agency from which many other philanthropists take cues in their grantmaking. Founded in 1965, the NEA has always been an object of suspicion to both conservatives (who suspected it would support cultural subversion) and liberals (who feared it promoted a "ministry of culture"). For this reason the NEA's founding legislation was intentionally vague about defining what constituted "art," leaving such matters to rotating panels of experts drawn from the very fields the agency supported.

Reasonable as this sounds, the "peer panel" system created a circular environment in which the arts community has sustained various strains of hot-house avant-gardism. Like the support for media within the university, government and foundation arts funding has simultaneously nurtured and limited the scope of activist film and video making. In the production guidelines for the NEA Media Arts: Film/Radio/Television program one finds the stipulation that grants must be used for "film and video projects which exemplify the use of these media as art forms" and that they are not for "productions whose primary purpose is instructional" or for "student media projects."[57] In recent years, major controversies have resulted within these agencies when attempts have been made to shift the locus of attention to audiences. Ironically, the initiatives for such educational incentives have come from conservatives. The right has recognized the tactical importance of cultural pedagogy as a means of instilling discipline and canonical values.

Auteurist dynamics notwithstanding, the mid to upper-level opportunities available through such entities as by the CPB, the NEA, the Independent Television Service (ITVS), the POV Series, the Rockefeller Foundation, the Sundance Institute, and certain programs of the American Film Institute have been responsible for the funding, production, or broadcast of numerous works during the past two decades by such producers as Chris Beaver, Ayoka Chenzira, Christine Choy, Michelle Citron, Lonnie Ding, Robert Epstein, John Greyson, Barbara Hammer, Judy Irving, and Renee Tajima—to name a few.

In this light it's worth remembering that the often-reactionary focus on individual voice that so characterizes the activist agenda is itself a very important response to a culture industry that tends to neutralize political controversy and homogenize cultural difference. Certainly films like Deborah Chesnoff's Oscar-winning *Deadly Deception: General Electric, Nuclear Weapons, and Our Environment* (1992) or Marlon Riggs's landmark documentary of inter-ethnic gay racism *Black Is, Black Ain't* (1995) would never have survived the scrutiny of industry bottom-liners. Yet the difficulties that such films had gaining access to the PBS airwaves bespeaks the ambivalence of "public" broadcasting to such material.

Clearly, many challenges confront activist media producers. Perhaps the most important of these lies in the need to recognize diversity—not merely among producer identities, but among the forms and constituencies of media work. Another challenge entails the issue of subjective address. It is a recurrent problem for many leftist media groups that even the most critically sophisticated fail to convey their radical critiques with an equally radical attitude toward the viewing subject. These are deeply political issues in that they involve the ability of citizens to speak—or not speak. But unfortunately, the left has rarely been able to capitalize on the potential of popular voice. As Andrew Kopkind has put it,

> The natural left—as opposed to small groups of self-conscious leftists—comprises an overwhelming majority of the world's population. It can't be that this force has no power to change things for itself, and for the better. For too long, however, the "talking" leftists have been telling the natural left (what used to be called the "masses") what to do and how to do it.[59]

Kopkind's comments point to the realization that what used to be called the "masses" can no longer be described (if it ever could) as a singular entity. One of the biggest impediments to political agency is the loss of identity implicit in such generalized thinking. It robs people of both the individual and the civic will (some would argue the self-interest) to act politically.

The question that begins to emerge is whether media can provide the impetus for people to develop the needed sense of political agency to rekindle a functioning democracy. Certainly, much commercial and non-commercial film and photography has augured against such development. This has largely resulted from forms of address that discourage dialogue and citizen participation in the making of media texts. As has been suggested above, television, cable, and videotape technologies have had significant periodic influence on the role of public media. Many argue that television exerts a determining role in contemporary politics. The next chapter will examine the development of television as an instrument of both failed expectations and democratic possibility. It will discuss the pedagogical implications of the medium in providing new spaces for public exchange and debate.

four

Video Culture and National Identity

More than sixty years ago, Walter Lippmann warned of the media's ability to "manufacture consent" and thereby undermine the workings of democracy. In Lippmann's view, the emergent technologies of print and film were controlled by a "specialized class" who threatened to distort the thinking of an unwitting public. He wrote in 1921 that "a revolution is taking place, infinitely more significant than any shifting of economic power," adding that "it is no daring prophesy to say that the knowledge of how to create consent will alter every political calculation and modify every political premise."[1] Of course, the concept of manipulated public opinion has been a central tenet of leftist cultural theory ever since. In the 1930s, Antonio Gramsci used the notion to explain how modern governments maintain what he termed "hegemony" without resorting to force. Later, Max Horkheimer and Theodor Adorno introduced a similar concept in their formulation of false consciousness.

More recently, the concept of manufactured consent has been resurrected by Noam Chomsky, Michael Parenti, Douglas Kellner, and Jeff Cohen, among others.[2] The idea has even become the title of a popular film (and book).[3] As discussed in chapters 2 and 3, the primacy of culture in political life is hardly any longer a matter of controversy. What remains in dispute is the extent to which occurs. These confusions are nowhere more apparent than in the contradictory moral address of the conservative camp. As liberal radio talk show host Tom Leykas observes,

> Conservatives say that violence on television and in rap music causes violence, and drug-oriented music makes people do drugs, but when the shoe is on the other foot and someone on the right is advocating violence, such as Liddy, they say, oh no, the media can't make them do that.[4]

In a diverse society, where people do not bring identical perspectives to the interpretation of media messages, the meaning of any given text can vary from individual to individual and group to group. These interpretive variations are further complicated by the complexities of media forms, institutional conduits, and reception contexts. If the media's manipulation is not always complete, to what extent do audiences exert agency over it? How far can viewers distance themselves from received patterns of image consumption? In what ways can these critical capacities be improved? Clearly, these are crucial questions for cultural democracy.

If such issues weren't complicated enough, it's also important to remember that people acquire much of their identities as political subjects through the media. Without doubt, substantial ingredients in the experience of citizenship are delivered through newspapers, magazines, movies, and most of all television, which bombards citizens daily. There is a growing sense that these media constitute the primary source of identity formation, supplanting roles formerly held by school, church, and the family. Not that the influence of media is necessarily bad. Rather than seeing this as a negative phenomenon, educators and parents should acknowledge the importance of media in social relations, and work to harness this power in productive ways. Like it or not, young people are as much educated, albeit informally, through daily encounters with media as they are in the formal environment of school.[5]

Some historians assert that the concept of citizenship is itself a product of media. This reasoning links the development of the modern nation state to the evolution of European "print capitalism."[6] Prior to the mass dissemination of newspapers, books, and pamphlets, people rarely imagined a collectivity on a broader than local scale. It doesn't take much insight to recognize the current role of network television and movies in constructing the illusion of connectedness among citizens thousands of miles apart. As Benedict Anderson puts it, "an American will never meet, or even know the names of more than a handful of his fellow Americans. He has no idea of what they are up to at any one time. But he has complete confidence in their steady, anonymous, simultaneous activity."[7]

It also should go without saying that the reach of contemporary electronic media is hardly bounded by a country's geographical borders. The ability to broadcast across national boundaries, even in the face of government resistance, motivated the electronic warfare waged by the U.S. Information Agency in nations around the world. Of course, media imperialism isn't always so belligerent. On the contrary, the mass marketing of U.S. productions throughout the world is customarily viewed as a positive function of the "free market." Due to the scale and technical sophistication of the American media industry, Hollywood films and television programs constitute the nation's second-largest source of foreign income, just behind aerospace technology.[8] Moreover, the mass dissemination of U.S. movies and TV abroad has helped provide an important context for the foreign consumption of American products—from MacDonald's in Russia to Marlboros in Thailand to Euro-Disney in France. Although this ability to profit in the media trade helps the nation's sagging economy, the massive influx of American media into other nations is not always viewed as a positive phenomenon. The now-familiar image of *Dallas* glowing on television screens throughout Europe, Africa, and Asia has triggered mass resentment about the transmission of Yankee culture throughout the globe. As a consequence, government-sponsored media education programs in nations that import significant amounts of film and television are far more advanced than in the United States. Foreign nations perceive the need to protect themselves from the boundless expansion of American capitalism.

Not that people in the United States are entirely thrilled by media either. Almost since the inception of television, a diverse assortment of educators, parents, and religious groups has warned of the corrupting influence of commercial media. Like critics of media dissemination overseas, domestic opponents believe it exerts an irresistible control over its consumers. Those on the right see media as the conveyor of moral depravity. On the left, media is believed to transmit oppressive ideologies. Both views are unified by their belief that media must be resisted at all costs.[9] All of these arguments against the media—both international and domestic—share several common flaws. They assign a range of social problems to the media that originate elsewhere. They make the error of believing that representations invariably correspond to outcomes and that viewers exert no license in the viewing process.

Most importantly in the context of cultural democracy, both conservative and liberal critiques of media emerge from a normative standpoint. In other words, both ends of the ideological spectrum share the belief that a single, correct perspective exists and that contemporary media diverts attention from it. This is not to suggest that there is any moral failing in preferring *Frontline* over *Melrose Place*—or vice versa. But democracy begins to suffer when the rhetoric of preference reaches the point of suggesting that selected options should be discontinued, defunded, or censored. Crude as it sounds, this is exactly what groups like Accuracy in Media, the American Family Association, and the Center for Media and Values often suggest.

In part these anti-democratic sentiments stem from a lack of understanding about how media are received and interpreted. Hasty conclusions get drawn about the effects of media messages, with little consideration of the technical, institutional, and social contexts in which the communication transaction occurs. Instead, intellectuals, parents, and clergy make judgments about the media practices of the less powerful. This results in a condescending series of assumptions about the capabilities of viewers to evaluate what they see. Two common threads run through all of these claims against media: that viewers lack a capacity for subjective agency; that media are inherently negative. The solutions to this perceived tyranny lie in turning off the tube or girding oneself to resist its mendacity. This has been the premise of media education, the rationale for the development of public broadcasting, and even the motivation for several United Nations resolutions. Obviously, such beliefs don't give viewers very much credit. They refuse to recognize that meaning develops in the relationship between text and reader, with readers actively comparing narratives to their own experiences. This position fails to consider the many ways that meaning is altered in the mechanics of information delivery. It also neglects to acknowledge viewers' abilities to accept portions of a text while discarding the rest. In short, this negative view of media insists that audiences are incapable of telling the difference between images and life itself.

In this chapter I will discuss media attitudes both at home and abroad, by raising questions specifically focused on issues of national identity. How do contemporary media define public perceptions of nationality? What role do media play in developing citizenship and collective agency? How do media influence relationships among global powers? Addressing these questions will entail both institutional and textual analysis of the way the nation has been constructed in an international context. Such analyses are particularly needed at a time when the United States is asserting itself as the only legitimate superpower in the New World Order. My central premise is that while the material and textual power of the communications industry is indisputable, the authority of media is clearly not absolute. Numerous opportunities exist for mediations in delivery, reception, and interpretation of media messages.

At the same time, it is necessary to concede that although audiences possess the ability to creatively mediate the texts they receive, they do not necessarily exercise that option with skill or consistency. Through a concerted media education program such capacities can be cultivated. Models for such pedagogies already exist, but they are few and far between. In an era in which schooling is increasingly driven by a corporatist agenda of basic skills, interdisciplinary studies like media are seen as both frivolous and subversive. Nevertheless, arguments for media education can be made that are both powerful and progressive.

Don't Try this at Home: Media and Democracy in the United States

It's difficult to discuss television in the United States without addressing the social function of technology in general. Throughout the history of media, successive technological developments invariably have been met with speculations about their abilities to alter human relationships. While it seems evident that media forms can indeed influence the way people live (as in the way people alter their schedules, the arrangements of their homes, and their social interactions in relation to TV), it remains unclear whether technological innovations precede or follow society's need for them. This question was considered at length by Raymond Williams in his paradigmatic work *Television: Technology and Cultural Form,* in which he discussed the role of broadcast media in public and personal life.[10] Significantly, he elaborated on the Marxist notion that capitalism continually adapts to changing social circumstances, reproducing itself anew in different forms of production and exchange. To Williams, new technologies always become the tools of those with the power to use them. As he wrote,

> The key question about technological response to a need is less a question about the need itself than about its place in an existing social formation. A need which corresponds with the priorities of the real decision-making groups will, obviously, more quickly attract the investment of resources and official permission, approval or encouragement on which a working technology, as distinct from available technical devices, depends.[11]

Within this scheme, dominant economic forces exert a powerful influence over any technology—and television is no exemption. Following Williams' argument, I want to contextualize the development of television in the United States by first examining the evolution of prior industries like radio.

Before World War I, radio was a relatively unorganized medium in terms of broadcasting, although a number of major corporations had already begun to dominate the manufacture of radio receivers: American Telephone and Telegraph (AT&T), General Electric (GE), British and American Marconi, and Westinghouse. During the war and the years immediately following it, radio gained in prominence due to its superiority over the telegraph for strategic and commercial communications. Radio's role grew even more in the 1920s, as the United States began to assume a dominant role in international markets and as mass production technologies at home began to make available new forms of consumer goods. In response to the growing importance of radio in the global and domestic economy, the major manufacturers of radio sets formed a corporate alliance in 1919 that led to the establishment of the Radio Corporation of America (RCA). Under the agreement, the new company was formed in large part from the resources of GE, which bought out the former American and British Marconi companies, while forging trade alliances with ATT and Westinghouse. In other words, the major corporations carved up the market.

The actual broadcast of radio signals began as a decentralized enterprise produced by schools, churches, department stores, and individuals. But the medium's commercial potential quickly became apparent to manufacturers of the telephone, telegraph, and radio equipment. Soon, new broadcasting companies emerged from these corporate giants to seize monopoly control of the market. By the mid-1920s, AT&T dominated telephone communications; RCA, Westinghouse, and GE produced nearly all radio equipment; Western Union controlled the telegraph industry; and NBC (later to launch ABC and CBS as subsidiaries) had monopolized radio broadcasting.[12]

Over time, the unregulated transmission of radio signals began to cause problems, which prompted the formation in 1927 of the Federal Radio Commission (FRC), the precursor of the Federal Communications Commission (FCC). The FRC initially functioned as a mere traffic coordinator that would issue broadcasting licenses to assure that competing signals didn't interfere with each other. However, under subsequent pressure from the communications monopolies the FRC soon assumed the role of kingmaker in the radio industry. Despite public outcries over the preferential treatment afforded the monopolies, the FRC began to assign the most favorable broadcasting frequencies (and, when necessary, reassign them) to companies with the largest commercial interests. In this way government actively colluded with the dominant interests of the radio industry to secure the corporate hegemony of the monopolies. Hence, today's broadcast industry structure of NBC, ABC, and CBS (challenged somewhat in recent years by UPN and Rupert Murdoch's Fox network) was put in place more than sixty years ago.[13]

Within this scenario the development of television was somewhat of an anticlimax. As discussed by media historian Brian Winston, although the physical technology to transmit visual images had been available almost since the beginning of audio broadcasting, the development of television was delayed by corporate greed and infighting.[14] At first, it was a simple case of the radio and movie industries hoarding financial resources. Television, they correctly understood, would present an unparalleled source of competition. Later the situation became more complex, as RCA used its monopolistic power throughout the 1930s to restrain the patents that could make television possible. As a consequence, the first regular television broadcasting did not begin until 1939, when NBC's service was inaugurated by President Franklin Roosevelt at the New York World's Fair.[15] Ironically, the onset of World War II would further delay the diffusion of television until the end of the following decade.

Network TV finally came to the American public in the late 1940s, amid a plethora of social changes. Military personnel returning from the war were eager to rekindle the hearth and home amid a new atmosphere of expanding consumerism. Manufacturing plants previously devoted to the war effort quickly adapted to the production of civilian goods. Not only did television fill an industrial need as a new commodity to be manufactured, it also fit perfectly into the family-centered culture of suburban leisure activity. From 1950 to 1957 the number of homes within the range of television broadcasts grew from three million to forty million.[16]

Following the model of radio, television development was dominated by the networks that still control most programming today. Also like radio, the new visual medium drew most of its financial sustenance from advertising sales. NBC president Pat Weaver described television advertising as a remedy to the postwar supply and demand crunches. Weaver wrote that "this and other solutions to steady demand means a new kind of selling—a complete change in emphasis— educational selling to wean consumers from old habits into new ways keeping with a new era."[17] Such noble intentions notwithstanding, this meant that television would not develop simply to deliver programs to audiences but rather to deliver audiences to sponsors.[18]

At the most basic level, this advertising orientation meant that to deliver the largest number of potential consumers television programs would seek to satisfy the lowest common denominator of viewers, thus excluding programming on marginal, difficult, or controversial topics. This is not to say that advertisers would directly dictate the contents of programs (although anti-capitalist programs are hard to find). Rather, as the industry developed and grew, subtle codes of "appropriate" content and self-censorship would begin to influence what types of material would even reach the initial stages of consideration.

Overt political discussion rarely entered the realm of "I Love Lucy" and "Your Show of Shows," finding expression instead in news reporting and occasional documentary programming during the 1950s. When political issues were raised, their coverage generally reinforced status quo attitudes toward foreign and domestic policy, with the exception of the renegade filmmaking discussed in the last chapter. Attitudes toward television began to change as the news itself became more complicated in the following decade. The 1960s brought the election of John F. Kennedy, the liberalism of "The Great Society," the war on poverty, civil rights struggles, urban riots, and the Vietnam War. Despite the unbridled promotion of consumer capitalism on the tube, the United States saw itself on television as a nation ridden with insecurity and self doubt. With these changes, television became a more dialogical medium, with both liberal and conservative factions seeking to influence programming on the new medium.

By the 1970s, conservatives had begun searching for scapegoats to blame for the nation's civil unrest and rampant anti-establishment sentiment.[19] Although television hardly constituted a hotbed of radical ideas, elements of subversion had begun creeping into prime time. Countering the rampant sexism and violence of much television of the era, programs like "All in the Family" and "Mary Hartman, Mary Hartman" drew public attention to often underacknolwedged patterns of prejudice and consumer capitalism, while other shows, like "Maude" and "Sanford and Son," began to address imbalances in representations of women and people of color (albeit in tokenistic and stereotypical ways).

Not everyone was pleased with the social changes television reflected. A corporate confederation assembled by David Rockefeller calling itself the Trilateral Commission concluded that the media had become "a notable new source of national power," and one aspect of a "reduction in government authority."[20] Its infamous report written by Samuel P. Huntington, entitled *Crisis of Democracy*, argued that education, business, and the legislature needed to restrict what it termed a "democratic distemper" to restore the nation to its former stability. In this way, the work of the Trilateral Commission in the 1970s helped lay the groundwork for the conservative backlash of the next decade.

The election of Ronald Reagan was more than a political reversal of fortune in the White House. It signaled the turning point in a conservative movement that had been gaining momentum slowly for over a decade. As movies from *Top Gun* (1986) to *Tank* (1984) glorified militarism at the box office, similar programs began to appear on television like "The A-Team " and "Blue Thunder." Facing increasing financial shortfalls, network news changed in two significant ways. To assure large audiences, Neilsen ratings, and advertising dollars, news programs became more like entertainment programs in content and form—focusing on general-interest stories (in major cities or affecting large numbers of people) and rapid-paced formats (necessitating superficial coverage). News organizations developed cost-cutting strategies to contain their expenses, most notably reducing their reporting staffs and beginning to rely on government spokespeople for material. Daniel Hallin has calculated that less than one-third of those appearing as spokespeople for issues in network news are citizens without some form of official position. "Washington controls the agenda for political reporting, and it is relatively difficult for a movement not pushing that agenda . . . to get itself taken seriously as 'hard news,'" Hallin asserts.[21]

The implications of the Reagan presidency ran far deeper than program content alone. Under the direction of presidential appointee Mark Fowler, the FCC undertook what may well constitute the most sweeping reorganization of pubic media in the nation's history. By 1984, Fowler's FCC had enacted the following deregulatory measures: removed all government limits on the number of commercials per hour, doubled the number of radio and TV stations a company could own, eliminated public service message and childrens' programming requirements, lifted waiting periods for sales or mergers of stations.[22] Later the FCC eliminated the Fairness Doctrine and the "equal-time rule," which had required networks to present opposing viewpoints on controversial issues. Most of these deregulatory actions still remain in effect.

To many commentators on the left, the 1980s marked historic era in the manufacture of consent. In response to what many perceived as a relatively open media atmosphere during the 1960s and 1970s, the Reagan administration helped return control of broadcasting to a corporate elite. Democracy suffered as a result. In the analysis of Douglas Kellner, the ubiquity of conservative imagery in the 1980s, along with removal of television from government oversight, resulted in a series of willful media misrepresentations to the public. Kellner argues that "television did not provide the information necessary to produce an informed electorate and that the media actively helped forge a conservative hegemony rather than impartially mediating among competing social forces."[23] Hardly an innocent set of circumstances, "television and the media were key factors in protecting the Reagan administration from complete collapse after the Iran/Contra affair in 1986–87 and in electing Bush president in 1988, thus preserving the conservative hegemony that the media had helped construct during the first half of the decade."[24]

An example of such collusion is cited by former congressional communications specialist Foote, who recounts the circumstances surrounding one of George Bush's final drug strategy speeches from the Oval Office. Following the address only one of the networks—CBS—aired the unedited rebuttal statement by Democrat Joe Biden. On what many would argue was a critical discussion of a problem facing the United States, both ABC and NBC opted to not carry the oppositional statement, rationalizing their decision as "business judgment." As

Foote observes, "others might choose to call it irresponsibility—or worse."[25] Such actions carry profound implications in a presumably democratic society. A further discussion of these issues as well as a range of possible alternative formulations for the return of egalitarian public sphere will appear in chapter 7.

The Big Picture: International Perspectives on Media Imperialism

As media giants were carving up the domestic marketplace, they were also shipping U.S. film and movies around the world. What began with the seemingly innocent export of commercial media products evolved over time into a global ideological offensive. Of course, U.S. business interests had long promoted American capitalism with a religious zeal. But it wasn't until the Cold War era that politicians and entrepreneurs like publishing magnate Henry Luce began urging Americans to spread the gospel of capitalism throughout the globe by accepting "wholeheartedly our duty and our opportunity as the most powerful and vital nation in the world and in consequence to exert upon the world the full impact of our influence, for such purposes as we see fit and by such means as we see fit."[26]

Complementing such attitudes was a U.S. diplomatic policy promoting a "free flow of information" throughout the world. This transparently self-interested stance was asserted as a protection against the resurgence of fascism and the outbreak of future wars. Yet it also represented a direct assault on the protectionism practiced by the Eastern Bloc. Such expansionist sentiments were well characterized by another influential publisher, Palmer Hoyt, who described the world in 1946 as headed for "destruction unless steps are taken to insure the beginning at least of freedom of news—American style—between the peoples of the earth. A civilization that is not informed cannot be free and a world that is not free cannot endure."[27]

This fusion of profit and politics fed a news and entertainment complex that was already the largest in the world—and one of the first domestic industries to restructure itself along transnational lines. In the 1940s and 1950s, U.S. wire services, magazine publishers, television studios, and movie companies quickly achieved global control. By the 1960s, concerns about American media hegemony had reached such a magnitude worldwide that the United Nations convened a special series of conferences to investigate the media market. Charges were made that the United States had stepped well beyond the realm of simple profiteering.

At one of those early meetings Finnish president Urho Kekkonen expressed the sentiments of many gathered when he asked, "could it be that the prophets who preach unhindered communication are not concerned with equality among nations, but are on the side of the stronger and wealthier?"[28]

As a consequence of the ubiquity of American product, UNESCO issued a series of policy statements intended to protect discrete cultural identities. Despite the non-binding character of such directives—and attempts by the United States to discredit UNESCO as "partisan"—the documents demonstrated the seriousness with which many nations viewed cultural imperialism. These concerns related to two fundamental tenets of national self-definition: concepts of limits (the ability to maintain clear boundaries) and sovereignty (the authority to govern within these boundaries).[29] Hence, a 1972 Free Flow of Information declaration pertaining to broadcast technology stated that nations must reach "prior agreements concerning direct satellite broadcasting to the population of countries other than the country of origin of the transmission."[30] In 1973, UNESCO issued the first of several statements of the New World Information and Communications Order, again calling for equity. These documents culminated in the 1980 report by the International Commission for the Study of Problems in Communication, known as the MacBride Report.[31] Nations like the United States ignored such declarations in part due to lack of enforcement, and both the United States and Britain subsequently withdrew from UNESCO.

In the years since the MacBride Report, matters have worsened. As borders continue to soften within the Americas, the European community, and throughout the world, the occurrence of cultural imperialism—led by a few dominant nations—continues to increase. A global economy may indeed open the door to an electronic global village. The question is, what can be done about this? Part of the answer lies in education, in the recognition that the cross-cultural exchange of media is not an inherently negative phenomenon. Old notions about the unilateral imposition of ideology from the strong to the weak need to be rethought. Understandings need to be developed of the complex and often contradictory ways that weak and strong powers enable each other. Assertions of cultural sovereignty are difficult to maintain in nations whose populations are clamoring for Madonna tickets. This is because typical cultural imperialism discourse fails to adequately theorize viewing/consuming subjects, their needs, desires, and pleasures. Instead of mediating the oppressive logics of capitalism and modernization, conventional cultural imperialism discourse offers a reactionary mix of humanism, chauvinism, and nostalgia. It fails to recognize how cultural imperialism works and what can be done pedagogically to help citizens resist it. For all of its good intentions, the UNESCO program was structurally incapable of exceeding a humanist appeal to universal merit. Implicit in this claim was the assertion of an essential sameness of all people in the "brother-hood" of nations.[32] This position was easily collapsed into the U.S. argument for universal trade rights in the presumed interest of international cooperation.

In the years since the UNESCO declarations, the United States has redoubled its cultural assaults. These efforts culminated in the passage of the 1989 Free Trade Agreement with Canada and its subsequent expansion to include Mexico.[33] In that accord, Bush and Clinton administration officials established what they considered a precedent-setting legislative rationale for limitless export. By legally affording "corporate speech" the same authority as "personal rights," transnational corporations received the authority to override any efforts to block, not only the flow of media, but also the flow of computer data, electronic communication, or commodities of any kind.

This has only increased long-standing worries about cultural imperialism among other allies of the United States. In Britain these anxieties have a long history. Since the end of World War II, values of "Americanization" were widely regarded as a threat to the purity of British national culture and tradition. Speaking of soap operas, George Orwell and Richard Hoggart both wrote of the erosion of working-class strength that might result from such a "feminine" medium.[34] To F. R. Leavis, the danger was less specified, but more sinister. Leavis pointed to "the rootlessness, the vacuity, the inhuman scale, the failure of organize cultural life, and the anti-human reductionism (of) the American neo-imperialism of the computer."[35]

Such criticisms of the media were justified but misdirected. In Leavis's comments, one finds a nostalgic yearning for authenticity that often characterizes cultural nationalism. This is a longing for common origins in a world seemingly run amuck with difference.[36] Racist innuendoes aside, such romanticism is patently anti-modernist—more pitted against notions of change than of media.[37] Like many cultural nationalists, Leavis was lamenting the threat to such traditions posed by an American media of rock and roll, fast cars, and plastic plates. Ironically, this disposable modern culture was a great deal more appealing to the British working class than the pastoral nostalgia it associated with British aristocracy. It wasn't Leavis's traditions that Britons found exciting, but the newness offered by icons like Elvis and Marilyn Monroe.

Similarly, it has been argued that much of what is customarily identified as cultural imperialism is really a function of change itself. John Tomlinson asserts that national identities defined purely in spatial terms fail to come to terms with the temporal character of culture.[38] Simply put, there is no such thing as a single national culture that remains the same year after year. Nations are constantly assimilating, combining, and revising their national "characters." Moreover, even spatial boundaries rarely correspond to the demarcations between racial and ethnic groups, speakers of various languages, and even families. Thus, the heterogeneous and changing nature of nations raises the question of who is authorized to speak on behalf of a nation. All of this seems to suggest that solutions to cultural imperialism are far more complex than the establishment of trade barriers and import quotas. The answers involve helping people to understand how and why media imperialism works and how it works on them.

Complaints and Theories

No one needs reminding that similar debates over media texts continue to be waged within the United States, as antagonists on both the left and right have recognized the capacity of images to assume a symbolic meaning in the national consciousness. This is a function of the way signs become unhinged from their references in the age of the simulacrum. The resulting slipperiness of meaning has been exploited by various groups—as in debates during the last decade over school books, motion picture ratings, and arts funding. By focusing on particular films or photographs as ideological emblems, public figures have used these discourses for political gain. But whether or not these critics have had an impact on the content of TV and movies is still an open question.

Bear in mind that recent advocates of media censorship were not initiated by popular outrage or scholarly concern but by religious extremists and headline-hungry politicians. Even though the potential has always existed for partisan misreadings of cultural signs, until the late 1980s the political incentive (and strategic wherewithal) was insufficient to elevate the practice above name calling. It took the catalyzing influence of forces outside the cultural mainstream to capitalize on domestic fears and to cast cultural workers as the terror of the heartland.[39] Religious fundamentalists and political conservatives linked their accusations of immorality to a populist resentment of artists, intellectuals, and the "minority" interests the cultural community represented. Rather than proffering an inherently "false" message, the right successfully linked its program to existing attitudes via a series of displacements that associated Martin Scorcese, Karen Finley, and 2-Live Crew with such perceived threats to traditional values as atheism, socialism, homosexuality, racial difference, and gender non-conformity.

While the conservative program makes surface appeals to a nationalistic populism, it simultaneously promotes a cultural elitism that excludes the identities and histories of most citizens. This is a function of the often contradictory deployment of power in contemporary society. As Homi K. Bhabha has suggested, the continuing renewal of national identity—the will to nationhood that is reaffirmed anew each day—requires an erasure of past origins, ethnicities, and places. The obligation to forget in the name of unity is a form of "violence involved in establishing the national writ."[40] It is a matter to which national subjects consent and with which they struggle.

Underlying the narratives of much of what appears in the media is an appeal to a peculiar form of national unity premised on exclusion. Nowhere is this rhetoric of national chauvinism and cultural purity more pronounced than in electoral politics. Republican presidential candidate Pete Wilson has been the most pernicious in his advocacy of California's now-infamous Proposition 187, which identifies foreign-born "aliens" as the purported cause of the state's economic problems. Within this discourse the social category of the "illegal immigrant" is counterposed to that of the "legal citizen." This parallels similar attacks by Ronald Reagan and George Bush on presumably debilitating "special interests" that threaten the coherence of civil society. As Noam Chomsky has pointed out, this rhetoric betrays a central bias: "If you look closely and asked who were the special interests, they listed them: women, poor people, workers, young people, old people, ethnic minorities—in fact, the entire population. There was only one group that was not listed among the special interests: corporations."[41]

The sustenance of academic and political conservativism lies in the consolidated corporate strength supporting it. No amount of theorizing by itself will place an alternative record album on a store shelf or an independent video on television. Those institutions are firmly under the thumb of an economic power structure that functions strictly in its own interest. Utopian speculations of the 1960s promised to replace alienating written texts with a humanizing electronic network. But such aspirations of technological determinism could not forecast that the mere exchange of medium would not disentangle the message from the capitalist order.[42] The realization of the unremitting presence of corporate agendas in the media, along with the continued paucity of credible alternatives to the entertainment industry has led many cultural theorists to rethink their ambivalence about the role of political economy. These sentiments are well summarized by Justin Lewis in his book on television, appropriately titled *The Ideological Octopus*:

For all its simplicity, there are elements of the Frankfurt School's grand cultural theory that strike a disturbing chord of truth. The deregulation of television
and radio that has characterized government policy in the U.S. and many parts
of Europe in recent years, does seem to suggest that free market capitalism will,
ultimately, suppress cultural innovation and diversity. There is also no doubt
that the age of television, like the age of religion, provides us with a common
cultural currency, a set of ideas and images that most of us share. This gives
television the power to create a degree of ideological conformity, whether
about a soft drink, a politician or a social issue, with greater speed that ever
before.[43]

Not that this is a simple process. Further analysis has recognized that media
tend to address what has been termed an "ideal spectator" who possesses a particular set of interpretive capacities and preferences. The appeal to an ideal spectator is made in the form of a "preferred reading" that asks the viewer to identify
with particular values and beliefs. These preferred readings rely on "dominant
codes" of semiotic meaning. As a subset of this process, television has its own
special forms of address, related to its ability to communicate to national and
international audiences.[44] This address assumes four basic functions in national
identity formation. First, it replicates and thereby reinforces hierarchies of capital
within a given society. Major media networks are owned and controlled by a
small elite who dispense information to multitudes. Second, television is structured into what Raymond Williams termed a "flow." This is the tendency of
viewers to watch a chain of programs, commercials, and news without switching
from discrete program to program. Over time, this flow creates the impression of
a unified theme. Third, television's direct address to viewers (who are often isolated) positions them as "the public" looking over a commentator's shoulder.
This positioning implies a controlling gaze through which viewers survey and
control a world of difference. Fourth, television often depicts "ordinary" people
in a fashion that implies populist consent to this controlling gaze. Recognition of
this power within the media led the United States to seek an alternative to commercial broadcasting—but with a peculiar ambivalence.

Public Television in the United States

With the exception of the United States, most industrialized countries take the
stewardship of their national airwaves very seriously. To such nations, assaults
on governmentally sponsored programming like those waged by congress in

1995 against PBS and the Corporation for Public Broadcasting would be unthinkable. Throughout Europe television is still regarded as a precious resource, too important simply to be ceded to the will of the market. This results in part from the limited broadcast originating from these nations and in part to the presence of the American system—as both a negative model and a potentially overwhelming presence. Within the United States, the diffusion of television during the 1940s and 1950s was met with general enthusiasm, with any grumblings about the detrimental consequences of the medium confined to the realms of academics and political dissidents.

The mainstream critique of television emanated from government itself in the persona of FCC chair Newton Minow. The FCC, it should be remembered, had the legislative charge of ensuring the fair and democratic use of the airwaves—although it had often functioned at the whim of corporate interests. In 1952, the FCC had set aside 242 television channels nationwide for noncommercial educational broadcasting. But without a mechanism for the funding and distribution of programming for the nonprofit channels, such channels tended to be locally focused and poorly administered. In 1961, Minow made his now-famous "vast wasteland" speech to the National Association of Broadcasters, in which he decried the "squandering" of what he termed the "public's airwaves." [45]Describing the role he perceived for the FCC, Minow presented a set of philosophical principles, beginning with the idea the "the people own the air. They own it as much in prime evening time as they do at 6 o'clock Sunday morning. for every hour the people give you, you owe them something."[46]

Prompted by concerns about commercial TV and by growing speculation about the social potentials of video technology, the Carnegie commission on Educational Television convened in 1965 to prepare a study on the medium. Two years later, the commission concluded that the nation needed a coherent system of public television programming and distribution. Conceived in an era of liberal social investment, the Carnegie Commission envisioned a system that was locally oriented, federally funded, and shielded from bureaucratic meddling. This model was given life in the Public Communications Act of 1967, calling for a system to offer an *alternative* to commercial broadcasting, and to provide a *diversity* of programming.

In this way public broadcasting represented exclusionary attitudes from its inception. Liberal policy makers successfully framed the commercial media as a barren wasteland of "false consciousness." The public needed a compensating "true consciousness" in the form of non-commercial media. Utilizing a rhetoric of diversity and egalitarianism, liberals (joined ultimately by many conservatives) fashioned a national institution with a range of unacknowledged biases concerning education and economic class, among other issues.

To implement this agenda a pair of new entities were developed during the next two years: the Corporation for Public Broadcasting (CPB) would support programming; the Public Broadcasting Service (PBS) would provide distribution for the material. Like many new federal projects, both liberals and conservatives were leery of the potential political abuses of the newly formed entities. Although many legislators strongly supported the concept of a federally sponsored system free from commercial pressures, others remained committed to the marketplace as the appropriate arbiter of quality and cultural worth. These arguments were tempered by anxieties that public television (and radio) might devolve into a pawn for whichever political party held power. For this reason, congress structured CPB and PBS as non-profit subcontractors to the government, rather than federal agencies. Without government staff or direct oversight, CPB and PBS would be shielded from political pressure and would avoid the appearance of an official "ministry of culture." Charged with the sponsorship of programming, CPB also would remain a step outside the process by not directly producing programming. Instead, CPB would delegate the work to individual stations or producing collectives. PBS also would stand at a remove from government. Similarly free from direct government ties, the system would be owned and administered by a national network of stations to circulate material using satellites and other means.

The late 1960s represent the honeymoon period of public broadcasting; during its first four years the system received ninety percent of its funding directly from congressional budgeting. This primacy of federal sponsorship changed forever in 1972, however. Responding to increasing pressure from conservatives, Richard Nixon vetoed authorization legislation for the CPB. Among other arguments, Nixon asserted that the oil crisis of the early 1970s had resulted in a windfall for big oil companies in the United States. Within a year, the president successfully levered a massive infusion of support for public broadcasting from these new corporate sources. This shift from public to private sponsorship produced considerable ire among public broadcasting advocates, provoking some to dub PBS the "Petroleum Broadcasting Service" or the "Pro-Business Service."

By 1976, the percentage of federal support to public television had fallen to twenty-nine percent, where it remained for the next few years.[47] With the Reagan and Bush administration came further cutbacks. By 1990, Washington's contribution to the system stood at a meager sixteen percent. As reported by William Hoynes, while federal support decreased the importance of business and subscriber support grew substantially. From less than four percent in the early 1970s, contributions from corporate philanthropists rose to seventeen percent by 1990. Subscriber contributions similarly rose from seven percent to twenty-two percent.

Politicians often rationalize this shift of funding from government sources by looking at viewer demographics. As indicated in chapter 2, by some estimates the prime-time audience for PBS programming stands as low as four percent of those watching TV, an audience perceived as an educated, affluent elite. Why shouldn't these people pay for what they're getting? Hoynes and other public broadcasting advocates argue that such figures are misleading, citing PBS's own sensitivity to such charges. "Who watches public television?" asks a PBS brochure. "A small, select audience? Only the well-to-do? Quite the contrary. Public television has grown to become what its founders intended, a truly public television service."[48]

Honan asserts that PBS audiences are difficult to track because they vary from program to program and from one locality to another. Citing "four-week cume" statistics, Hoynes states that eighty percent of U.S. households tuned in to PBS at least once a month in 1992—up from fifty-nine percent in 1978. Figures on income are similarly murky. Although more than one-third of those viewing shows like the *MacNeil/Lehrer NewsHour, Frontline,* and *Wall Street Week* have incomes above $60,000, the number of lower-income families watching them stands at approximately the national average. Likewise, PBS claims that seventeen percent of viewers of a show like *Frontline* have not completed school degrees, compared to twenty-two percent of all citizens. These variations make it problematic to generalize about a consolidated "audience." More focused research might begin to locate the various *audiences* that public broadcasting serves.

More recent critiques of public television have addressed program content and the role of PBS in relation to new distribution technologies. Censorship occurs at several distinct levels, although only one of them receives much public attention. In the category of visible censorship, protests of local communities and boycotts organized by groups like the American Family Association have successfully kept programs like Marlon Rigg's *Tongues Untied* (1992) from airing on specific local stations. Beyond this, headline-hungry politicians and corporate sponsors have on occasion pressured PBS into keeping programs off the air, like Judy Irving and Chris Eagle's anti nuclear film *Dark Circle* (1984). The case of the Academy Award-winning *Dark Circle* is noteworthy, for it was rejected for its lack of what PBS officials termed "journalistic objectivity." After outcries from independent producers, PBS has since softened its position on documentaries that make particular arguments about divisive issues.[49] One way PBS has dealt with this issue is by airing the current "POV" series, which explicitly warns viewers that its independently produced segments will be presenting biased "points of view."

Corporate sponsors rarely interfere directly with program content. As with shows on commercial networks, the process of censorship is far more insidious and indirect. On one level, only programs on fundable topics ever get considered by the large PBS producing stations like Boston's WGBH, New York's WNET, or San Francisco's KQED. Because these stations must gather support for expensive programs by appealing to numerous agencies, foundations, and corporations, they are especially conservative in choosing what they will pursue. Here self-censorship becomes an issue once again. Moreover, until relatively recently most CPB funding was available only through large grants awarded through what was termed the Station Programming Cooperative (SPC). Not only were SPC monies allotted in large chunks, but because they exclusively went to PBS stations, they effectively excluded independent producers from the system.

Beginning in the 1970s, independent producers had protested the increasing insularity of the CPB/PBS system. Independents asserted that the entire system had become an elitist preserve that increasingly failed in its professed mission of providing diverse programming and an atmosphere of democratic dialogue. As will be discussed in depth in chapter 6, the independent community organized itself during the 1980s largely under the auspices of the Association for Independent Film and Videomakers (AIVF). Through a series of well-planned legislative lobbying campaigns (generally timed to coincide with the CBP's reauthorization or budget hearings), independents successfully argued their case before congress. These efforts resulted in the 1988 establishment of the Independent Television Service, a separate funding source for public television producers outside the PBS system. Although some activists within the independent community have recently criticized the ITVS for itself becoming too mainstream, the service has helped to return a measure of diversity to public television. Yet, in an era in which commercial movies often cost as much as $40–100 million, the relatively small $6-million budget of the ITVS greatly compromises its activist potential.

The Wired Nation Revisited

One of the last great hopes for cultural democracy on television came with the cable revolution. Video theorists of the 1960s foresaw a utopian communications era in which viewers would have access to scores of channels from a diversity of commercial and non-commercial sources. Using newly available video porta-paks, audio decks, and other inexpensive production equipment, it was expected that a new generation of television would be produced by community organiza-tions, schools, political parties, arts centers, religious groups, social clubs, hob-byists, and other providers. Beyond this, early cable visionaries envisioned what Ralph Lee Smith termed in 1970 "an electronic highway" of two-way communi-cations not unlike the "information superhighway" of today.[50] Even in its earliest stages of development, cable possessed the capability of incorporating a "return bandwidth" to allow subscribers to talk to central switching mechanisms, data storage facilities, and electronic mail systems.

No one needs reminding that things didn't turn out according to plans. Although early cable legislation enabled municipalities to require operators to provide open channels for non-commercial use, the development of such "com-munity access" programming failed to gather much momentum in most commu-nities. Rather than the grass-roots diversity envisioned by cable visionaries, a new generation of commercial networks sprang up instead—CNN, TBS, MTV—along with a host of premium offerings ranging from HBO and Cinemax to the Playboy Channel. Subsequent deregulation during the Reagan era allowed cable operators to further shirk their responsibilities to provide diverse programming, while at the same time exploiting their local monopolies through rate increases.

The ubiquity of cable in the current era has made many advocates lose sight of the fact that it is a metered service. One of the major conservative rationales made during 1995 for the proposed elimination of PBS is that cable has super-seded the need for such an "alternative" government television service. Ironically, cable may indeed represent an excellent argument *in favor of* public television. As Hoynes puts it, "the rise of new technologies does not make noncommercial media obsolete," because the emerging technologies are organized around the same principles of the market (and owned by many of the same multinational conglomerates) as the old ones; "new technologies that are developed for com-mercial purposes may make noncommercial media even more important; they may serve as an oasis for the use of these technologies in an environment partially insulated from the market."[51]

This relationship points to the profound logical flaw in the presumed corre-lation between competition and diversity. Although capitalism is frequently described by the apologists of free enterprise as a progressive force in new product development and market segmentation, the experience of the media industry demonstrates the opposite tendency. The same economies of scale that limit the risks of Hollywood moviemakers have constrained the creative potential of network television. Moreover, corporate mergers and interlocking directorates have contributed to a system of rigid uniformity. Even in the so-called "free" environment of VCR use, where tape renting, home recording, and program "time shifting" have presumably liberated viewers from the mandates of network decision making, the old Marxist dictum still holds true, that people "make history, but not under conditions of their own making."[52]

Grassroots Alternatives

No contemporary discussion of television's changing cultural infrastructure would be complete without a consideration of grassroots media groups. In their diversity of forms, interests, and organizational structures, these groups offer great potential for the growth of a cultural democracy. Made possible by technological advances in portable production equipment, this activity continues to grow among the ranks of political activists, artists, businesspeople, and hobbyists. The proliferation of small-format production began in earnest after more than a decade of commercial development. With the introduction of the low cost ($1,500–$2,000) porta-pak in the 1960s, this technology was immediately seized upon as a way to decentralize TV and invert production hierarchies. Although it became apparent over time that camcorders alone could not democratize the television industry, the idea of independent production encouraged the founding of scores of media organizations nationwide.

Paralleling this material decentralization was an intellectual shift in the way media were understood. Much of the impetus for the early enthusiasm about video technology came from Marshall McLuhan. While in residence at New York's Fordham University during the late 1960s, McLuhan attracted a quasi-religious following based on his vision of a global telecommunications network designed on biological (and therefore "natural") principles that would undermine all hierarchical structures.[53] As in the early days of photography, a belief became commonplace that the new video technology would democratize television because everyone could become a producer.

From this era two basic camps emerged, both of which stressed decentralized media production: "guerrilla" television and community television. Associated with the guerrilla TV movement were entities like Ant Farm, the Videofreex, Top Value Television, and Global Village."[54] Stridently iconoclastic, these groups eschewed any clear ideological identification with the New Left.

Working on the street, from roving "media buses," or in schools, guerrilla media groups tended to be more enamored with the apolitical utopianism of the period. As Raindance founder Michael Shamberg wrote, "power grows from computer printouts, not the power of a gun.[55] In this spirit, the guerrilla television movement—along with the installation and conceptual art movement in the art world—was among the first efforts to put video cameras in the hands of poor people, children, people of color, and the elderly.

Nevertheless, the guerrilla TV movement lacked the democratic focus to effect broad-based social change. Its periodic outreach efforts to disenfranchised groups occurred only occasionally, and as a consequence, guerrilla TV failed to garner much of a following outside the student legions of the counterculture. As described by media historian Martha Gever, "all revolutionary allusions aside, the prominent figures among the first generation of video activists were almost all white, middle-class, and male, with most women, Blacks, Latinos, Asian-Americans, etc. playing supporting roles."[56]

Setting the standard for more concrete political work with video was the Canadian National Film Board (NFB). During the 1960s, the NFB initiated a series of experimental programs that had profound implications for media activism. As part of the NFB's "Challenge for Change" program, producers used film and video to enable local groups to communicate to government leaders with minimal third-party mediation. Based on earlier *cinéma vérité* and "consent film" efforts by producers like John Adair, Colin Low, George Stoney, and Sol Worth, NFB units confronted the paternalistic notion that filmmakers could make objective statements about those photographed. They did this by engaging community members in the process of their own documentation—much in the way anthropologists conduct "participatory research." Dorothy Hénaut and Bonnie Klein applied these principles in a series entitled "VTR-St. Jacques" (1969) that involved a French-speaking community near Montreal. St. Jacques residents scripted, acted, shot, and critiqued a series of programs describing the issues facing their neighborhood. Hénaut and Klein found that citizens quickly gravitated to the idea of producing a tape about their civic concerns.

As the project moved to other Canadian towns it quickly demonstrated the enormous potential in creating new forums for popular speech. In group after group, it became apparent that vast storehouses of ideas and expression had been waiting for release.[57] Speaking of similar efforts, bell hooks has suggested that this process of "coming to voice" can be an important initial step in instilling political agency. If, as hooks puts it, people can "talk back" to the media, they may be moved to challenge other forms of authority.[58]

In a nation polarized between a corporate media monopoly and large-scale government production entities, the idea of decentralized production has clear political implications. For this reason the development of an alternative media infrastructure in the United States has been fraught with difficulty, especially when government money has been involved. During the 1970s, two new institutional forms came into existence: the local phenomena of cable access facilities and the nationwide network of regional media arts centers.

Getting Wired

Long before the promise of a "wired nation" was realized, counterculture advocates of cable television predicted yet another democratization of the media. Not only would cable increase the number of channels tenfold, more importantly local communities would gain the capacity to select and produce their own television. FCC regulations enacted during the 1970s required cable operators to provide channels dedicated to local use. Beyond this, many towns bargained with cable companies to build free community access studios as part of their municipal franchise contracts.

The actual gains of the cable access movement proved more modest than initial speculation. While many local cable outlets did indeed permit community organizations, labor unions, and youth groups to gain spots on the television dial, the audiences for such programming proved to be minimal. This is partly attributable to the inherent "narrowcasting" of programs intended for specialized audiences. But it also results from the inability of cable producers to replicate the visual pyrotechnics of commercial studios and also, in most cases, from the failure of program listing services to publicize access programs.

Despite these shortcomings, a range of successful models have emerged in the past decade, many of which focus on the use of media for educational purposes. One highly regarded cable access collective, the shoestring Paper Tiger Television Manhattan cable series, critiques magazines and newspapers in its weekly programs. With makeshift sets and a comical wraparound, each weekly episode opens with the question, "It's 8:30. Do you know where your brains are?"—a spoof on a local Group W news program that asks, "It's 10 pm: Do you know where your kids are?" Paper Tiger episodes feature scholars or artists (commentators have included Myra Bain, Brian Winston, Serafina Bathrick, Joan Braderman, Alexander Cockburn, Herbert Schiller, and Ynestra King) deconstructing periodicals like *Cosmopolitan* or *The New York Times.* Consider this excerpt from Murray Bookchin's reading of *Time* magazine:

Time makes time disappear. Everything is the same. There is no history . . . The essence of *Time* is that it destroys the present, the past, and the future. Just like the hands of a clock keep turning around and around and give you no message, no perspective, no coordinates, no sense of direction. What *Time* does is relax you in time.[59]

In addition to discussing the contents of the periodicals, Paper Tiger programs also provide information about the economic structure of the publication, its reader demographics, the composition of its board of directors, and so on. In this way, Paper Tiger Television explicitly addresses issues of viewer interpretation and the ability of people to make informed decisions about the media. Their productions suggest that the meaning of a media text is not a stable substance that flows unproblematically from message sender to receivers, but something that emerges in the relationship between them. Because meaning is made in this fashion, audiences can assert a degree of autonomy in viewing.

Beyond specific projects like Paper Tiger Television, a broader level of collective strategizing is needed to effect large-scale political reform. Generally speaking, this means strengthening legislative mandates for public accountability and the decentralization of media ownership. One might begin by more tightly regulating the standards of access and program diversity that holders of broadcast licenses and cable franchises are supposed to meet. Antitrust laws could be reinvigorated and applied more stringently. Regrettably, during 1995 the business-friendly congress has shown a reluctance to enact such measures, with House Speaker Newt Gingrich even going so far as to urge boycotts of media outlets that criticize the free enterprise system.[60]

In the meantime, media groups need to continue the organizing strategies that have worked so well in the past. This will entail the establishment or strengthening of alliances among those groups that have always been the backbone of progressive politics: trade unions, student groups, churches, ethnic coalitions, peace and justice collectives, and environmental organizations. Models for large-scale media organizing are relatively few, particularly when funding agencies encourage only the most bureaucratic and politically ineffectual of such structures. Yet one entity developing from the cable access movement seems to hold promise.

The "Deep Dish" cable satellite network was developed to structurally correct the stumbling block of narrowcasting that plagued cable access from the beginning. The project began in 1986, when members of Paper Tiger in New York City and Boston began renting time on the Westar Galaxy 1 television satellite (which also carried such services as The Nashville Network and the Disney

Channel). With grant support to help publicize the initial hour of programming, Deep Dish suddenly put community access (in the form of thematic programs gathered from producers nationwide) onto scores of cable networks and into the homes of over eleven million satellite dish owners. In offering a program of subsidized transponder time, Deep Dish has provided activist videomakers and community groups with a national system for cable access and home dish reception. Although the impact of its current one hour of weekly programming should not be overstated, the effort offers an important model of intercommunity exchange outside the realm of corporate authorization.[61]

Grassroots Media Centers

Multi-purpose media arts centers were established to provide shared pools of equipment, distribution resources, and non-commercial screening facilities. Beginning in the late 1960s with start-up money from the National Endowment for the Arts, and the Rockefeller and Ford Foundations, the number of such facilities grew to 200 within a decade. Regrettably, the legislative mandate of the NEA to stay out of politics by supporting "professional" artists (as opposed to amateurs, students, or community groups) limited the populist potential of such centers. It also tended to skew their programming toward the fine arts.

Despite these difficulties, the network of regionally based media organizations has remained intact and remarkably politically active—due in large part to the activist commitment of the independent film and video producers they serve. Taken together, these groups constitute the closest approximation of a democratic cultural civil society that the nation currently has. In most cases, these entities have survived because they offer specific communities the means to produce, exhibit, or distribute media. Such groups include Appalshop in Kentucky, New York City's Women Make Movies, the Rocky Mountain Film Center in Colorado, the Southern California Asian American Studies Central in Los Angeles, and the San Francisco International Lesbian and Gay Film Festival. Lobbying under the umbrella of the Association for Independent Video and Filmmakers (AIVF), media centers and their members have repeatedly pressured the stodgy PBS and the Corporation for Public Broadcasting into more diverse and politically pointed programming. In this way, the AIVF has worked to counter the anti-democratic tendencies of both corporate and state bureaucracies.

It's worth reiterating that these advances have occurred in an atmosphere of inconsistent (and frequently antagonistic) sponsorship. Often combining income from commercial and non-commercial projects, these media centers demonstrate the potential of a democratic project that embraces cultural inclusion and genuine constituency involvement. By enabling diverse peoples to gain access to the tools of video and film, media centers have made an important departure from the monolithic and one-directional address of prior producers on the right and left. In this dialogic approach to audiences, the regional media center movement has proven its centrality in the future of participatory politics.

The strength of the movement was demonstrated in the development of the Independent Television Service (ITVS). In 1988, Congress responded to complaints from independent producers about the commercialized and unrepresentative character of public television. Lawmakers created the ITVS to receive $6 million in production funds formerly administered by the Corporation for Public Broadcasting. Now quietly functioning, this entity has been specifically designed to create alternative models of media discourse. This means working as much on the development of audiences as on the production of new programs. As described by ITVS board member Lawrence Daressa, the entity is an endowment for viewers who do not yet exist: "Instead of naturalizing a single point of view, it makes point of view its overt subject matter."[62] Daressa's statement succinctly articulates the responsibility facing democratic media artists: to create an environment in which diversity and contest are encouraged rather than suppressed. Obviously, this is not a new task, for cultural democracy has always entailed a struggle by the disenfranchised to gain voice. But what is often overlooked in contemporary media work is the power of those voices when drawn together. That the ITVS could be brought into being is evidence that such structural revision is indeed possible.[63]

The need for models like Deep Dish and the ITVS is becoming all the more important as the nation moves closer to fiber optics cable (carrying up to 500 channels), direct broadcasting satellites (transmitting directly into homes), and the Internet computer communications superhighway. One needn't be a technophile to understand that the way information is distributed is again about to change dramatically. As in the past, the commercial communications industry is anxious to maintain its hegemony. Media activists Jeffrey Chester and Katherine Montgomery assert that

> Technological innovation has triggered a power struggle of unprecedented proportions. The country's giant communications industries are locked in battle over which will control telecommunications in the 21st Century. . . . These developments will have a significant impact on the future of independent video

and filmmaking. Depending on the outcome, independents would either have new opportunities for access and funding or find themselves pushed further to the edges of the electronic media system.[64]

The future of cultural democracy lies in the unified efforts of media activists to work together, across the boundaries of individual struggles, to meet its challenges head on. These issues assume a heightened urgency in an era in which public gatherings and social rituals are increasingly undermined by the isolation of home-based culture. They take on even greater importance at a time when cultural difference advances to the front of the political agenda. Democratic activism can no longer limit itself to exclusionary and hierarchical forms of one-directional address.

Similarly, at a time when political ideologues increasingly criticize institutions and government in the name of "individual" solutions to social problems, proponents of cultural equity need to emphasize the positive capacities of collective action. Citizens may be disillusioned with the idea of bureaucracy, but they still very much support the services that bureaucracies provide in assisting the disadvantaged, protecting the environment, providing a physical infrastructure, and in ensuring diverse cultural perspectives. The challenge facing the United States is to reinvent the means of accomplishing these tasks.

five

Fantasies of Power on the Information Superhighway

No one needs reminding that communications technologies are rapidly transforming the world. Cyberspace, virtual reality, and the "information superhighway" represent but the latest in a series of technological advances promising to restructure daily life on a local and global scale. Every day more than 2.5 billion people turn on 750 million TV sets in 160 nations.[1] Most recent political changes have been mediated by these technologies. Think about student manifestos from Tiannamen Square, the "TV war" in the Persian Gulf, the technicolor spectacle of the L.A. uprising, and the O.J. Simpson trials beamed by satellite into nations of the former Soviet Union. Add to this cash machines on every corner, teenagers carrying beepers, telephones on airplanes, laptop computers and fax machines seemingly all over the place—and the growing centrality of communications technologies in everyday life become apparent.

Freedom and equality are frequently evoked in discussions of these emergent public media, as new technologies prompt a seemingly endless cycle of hope and disappointment over their ability to help citizens enhance communication, develop forms of community, and gain control over their lives. With each successive invention, from the printing press to the radio to the technologies of television, satellite, and computer, every advance has generated fresh waves of speculation over new social potentials. Such is the myth of scientific progress ever-advancing in human improvement

Technology and Society

The democratic application of technology will hinge on the synthesis of two opposing attitudes: what might be termed *instrumental* and *determinist* categories.[2] Instrumental theory offers the common-sense view of technologies as tools (whether new or old) that extend the capacities of their users. In this sense,

105

a technology simply supports the interests of its user; a tool has no intentions of its own, but is simply a formal device. Marshall McLuhan, classic instrumentalist, used the example of a light bulb to illustrate a technology that does not discriminate in the workings of what surrounds it.[3] It simply does its job, whatever the social context, without bias or political motivation. Rational and neutral, it replicates this scientific detachment in every situation and thus can be considered universally applicable. As *Wired* magazine editor Kevin Kelly comments, "the solution to bad technology is better technology."[4]

Determinist views see technology as a social system premised on control. Rather than a neutral instrument, technology moves through history manipulating humankind and nature. Hence, each successive scientific advance is perceived as effecting people's individual autonomy and interpersonal connectedness. Jobs grow more routinized, the environment is altered, and an entire network of social institutions evolves to regulate and monitor human behavior. In the view of some, technology eventually takes on a life of its own, perpetuating its own dominance and excess.[5] People no longer watch television simply for information or entertainment, but because it has taken over their lives. Technology becomes an addiction.[6]

Instrumental and determinist views of technology mark two ends of a continuum strangely devoid of cultural and ethical dimensions. Both theories tend to abstract technology from the values and belief systems in which it operates. Technology is regarded as either passive or aggressive, with little discussion of the purpose to which it is applied. Social issues are politely ignored or deeded outside the realm of technological discourse, and as a consequence the power relations beneath the workings of technology remain unchallenged.

This failure to fully address the connection of technology to human need and purpose is not unlike difficulties political parties are having in connecting with the American people. Public opinion polls indicate that the right is only slightly ahead of the left in finding solutions to public concerns over economic instability and the crisis of government. Echoing an instrumentalist view of technology, conservatives promote the freedom of individuals in a neutral society purportedly cleansed of inequity or injustice. A determinist position is put forth by liberals, who argue for the advancement of common equality in a world overrun by selfishness and discrimination. These extreme positions fail to acknowledge the importance of both of instrumental and determinist analysis, of freedom and equality in a democracy.

Exacerbating these polarizing tendencies are the ways each of these new technologies is linked with its own (sometimes novel) form of power: to purchase, to communicate, or to observe. On one level, this power creates hierarchical relationships between its subjects and objects, between those who act and those who are acted upon. Often this results when novel communications technologies simply extend the capacities of institutions like banks, utilities, and government. On another level technological power separates people according to levels of knowledge, expertise, and access. In this scenario, economics frequently influences who may use or control communications technologies

Free-market apologists view these tendencies as healthy extensions of the logic of business. In fact, the very creation of post-Fordist economies of multinational capital and flexible management is made possible by electronic communications, high-tech manufacturing, and the localization of labor enabled by computerized production and distribution. This view credits technology with the ability to continually expand and maximize efficiency, yet it fails to acknowledge what Martin Heidegger discussed as the "will to control" that drives the machinery of technology. It further fails to examine the economic or political interests that motivate this controlling impulse.

From the left, attitudes toward technology remain similarly focused on technology's presumed ability to improve life and extend social relationships. McLuhanesque visions of a 1960s "global village" find new life among proponents of hypermedia and the Internet, who make claims about the potentials of new media to decentralize authority and empower human communications. On another level, leftists see their mission as that of building an oppositional edifice of alternative institutions to combat their enemy. Often these activist cultural organizations and media groups are motivated by the Marxist dictum to "seize the means of production" in the battle against false consciousness and capitalist expansionism.

Typically, these approaches have yielded little success because they fail to adequately take into account the social structures, political motivations, and moral principles that guide technology. Communications media are not isolated phenomena that exist outside relations of production, exchange, and use. They are firmly embedded in the culturally inscribed meanings people assign to them. Most progressive activists have failed to understand these crucial contextual relationships. Perhaps most importantly, they have failed to recognize that the contemporary degradation of work, leisure, and the environment is rooted not so much in technology per se as in the antidemocratic values that inform technological development.

These phenomena are evidence of powerful impulses that communications technologies seem to satisfy: people's desire for control and human connectedness. Much of this book has addressed the lack of control that people often feel toward the very institutions that exert the most influence over their lives. In the presumably democratic society of the United States, which is so intent on the global export of "freedom," average citizens perceive the government, law, media, and education as monolithic structures beyond their control or influence. Rather than a quality to be actively exercised, freedom can become negatively rationalized as the ability to go about one's business or to lock one's own door. Although technology cannot be blamed completely for this state of affairs, it often has been used by powerful political and corporate interests to consolidate their dominance. Such was the monopolistic story with radio, television, and cable industries discussed earlier, and it threatens to become the case with the emerging information superhighway. The consolidation of media technologies in the hands of a small number of multinational corporations has placed them beyond human scale.

This concentration of ownership has only reinforced hierarchies that further remove control from the realm of the everyday. Within this scheme ordinary citizens are regarded as incapable of participating in decisions that require specialized knowledge. This attitude promotes a circular relationship in which fields of knowledge become restricted to ever-narrowing groups of specialists whose discourse only includes other specialists. Before long, expertise takes on a life of its own, as the advance of disciplinary progress becomes detached from its social moorings. As important as specialization can be, this perception of expertise run wild is shared by millions of citizens increasingly distrustful of pollsters, scientists, and politicians. As public communication becomes increasingly technologized and transferred to the function of experts, the meaning of democracy is destroyed.[7]

It is important to acknowledge as well that this movement toward bureaucratic expertise is hardly an abstract occurrence. Replicated within many hierarchies of specialization are the very relations of gender, race, and ethnicity that have been deployed to sort, classify, and rank citizens for centuries. These methods of categorization become manifest in the very "real" worlds of work, education, law, and government.[8] Who historically has been permitted access to training, funding, and roles of authority in these domains? What assumptions and criteria have been used to influenced these matters?

As suggested above, the development and dissemination of new technologies rarely proceeds in the interest of democratic ideals. Egalitarian principles have always found themselves secondary to the need for state expansion or corporate profits. Technology may always empower someone, but it can only empower those who possess it and who have access to it.[9] More to the point, these new configurations of empowerment are changing at an ever-increasing pace. As *Newsweek* recently explained it, in a special issue that seemed to celebrate these accelerating changes, this revolution is "outstripping our capacity to cope, antiquating our laws, transforming our mores, reshuffling our economy, reordering our priorities, redefining our workplaces, putting our Constitution to the fire, shifting our conception of reality."[10]

Contrary to the views of techno-apologists, this reshuffling is not advancing along the lines of some neutral natural order. This does not mean that media technologies are forever destined to replicate social inequities. Yet it does suggest that the ways to reverse these tendencies will never be purely technological in character. New attitudes need to be forged and new social relations developed where public communications are produced and received. Indeed, the effects of oppressive regimes are never as absolute as the representations they project. Even the most authoritarian power structures exist in a relationship between the dominator and the dominated, with one enabling the other. Therefore, the process of dismantling such relations frequently begins with the mobilization of the marginalized, who work at a grassroots level to unlearn the pedagogies of oppression.[11]

Much of this chapter will discuss ways this political work can be executed. Modern circuits of power are discontinuous and disbursed through everyday institutions like the school and the office. Rather than exclusively seeking a centralized source of political conflict, strategic infiltrations and interventions become possible when exercised at these local levels. In this way the pedagogical endeavors generating emancipatory attitudes toward communications media can be applied in a variety of institutional contests. Although considerable pessimism exists about the presumed corporate future of multimedia and the information superhighway, control of these technologies has not yet been ceded to ATT and IBM. A range of citizen groups, special interest organizations, and transnational coalitions is quietly taking shape to contest the co-optation of global communications by the media monopoly. Some even argue that the very ontology of hypermedia precludes its centralized control by business interests.

Such utopian speculation notwithstanding, any comprehensive approach to media technology must grapple with basic assumptions and motivations that drive scientific development in Western capitalist societies. All too often, modernist compulsions for progress, efficiency, and ever-increasing profitably stand at odds with democratic precepts of equality, justice, and mass participation. Needed is a new democratic imaginary based on moral principles of mutual dependency and the common good—principles that seem increasingly distant in an era consumed by individual desire and civic alienation. This democratic imaginary needs to be linked to concrete reforms in the way communication technologies are structured and financed. In the final analysis, these issues must enter the profoundly political realm of public policy.

Whether the topic is the latest computer interface or such commonplace vehicles as the newspaper, pamphlet, or book—the hunger the people have for collective engagement is increasingly channeled through media representations. From local to national levels, it is often argued that political identity itself constitutes a product of media's ability to construct illusions of connectedness among citizens across the street or the nation. As Benedict Anderson puts it, an individual may have no idea what other citizens "are up to at any one time. But he has complete confidence in their steady, anonymous, simultaneous activity."[12] Given the importance of film, television, and computer interfaces in constructing a sense of national identity, one would expect to see a vital popular interest in the maintenance of a democratic media infrastructure. Yet public communications in the United States have evolved in a particularly non-egalitarian fashion due to the monopolistic hold gained by corporations and large public broadcasting interests.

Fantasies of Control

When particular groups' access to the civic discourse has been frustrated, these citizens have devised alternative means of entering. Historian Anne Freidberg has described the circuitous strategies devised in the eighteenth and nineteenth centuries by women forbidden from association outside the home.[13] In one circumstance this need for social connection found form in shopping, which functioned as a cover for public mobility. In other instances the desire for transport was only achieved via the displacements afforded by such representational contrivances as dioramas and panoramas. These pre-cinematic forms of entertainment offered illusions of travel and association unavailable by other means. With the emergence of motion picture technology at the beginning of the twentieth century, a new virtual public arena became available as a site of fantasized experience (viewing the films) and actual assembly (gathering as an audience). In a now-famous quote, Walter Benjamin described the exhilaration of the early cinema goer:

> Our taverns and our metropolitan streets, our offices and furnished rooms, our
> railroad stations and our factories appeared to have us locked up hopelessly.

Then came film and burst this prison-world asunder by the dynamite of the tenth of a second, so that now, in the midst of its far flung ruins and debris, we calmly and adventurously go traveling.[14]

In this sense, the early cinema satisfied public desires for a variety of imaginary experiences for women—and men as well. The travel fantasies of exotic painted diorama backdrops soon gave way to travel films, which in turn encouraged parallel institutions of vicarious experience such as the amusement park and the museum. The pleasures of shopping would find contemporary articulation in the elaborate commercial "worlds" of the arcade and the department store. Both of these entities would come to provide cinema-like versions of public space, complete with staged tableaux and theatrical lighting. Not unlike the experience of viewing a film, observers would change scenes by moving among displays and shop windows. This ability afforded by movies and shopping malls for subjects to move about a virtual public sphere, satisfied a number of psychic needs. As Freidberg explains, "the mobilized and virtual gaze of the cinema answered not only the desire for temporal and spatial mobility, but for gender mobility as well. . . . The spectator-shopper—trying on identities—engaged in these pleasures of a temporally—and spatially—fluid subjectivity."[15]

The use of technology for such forms of virtual travel or social interaction has advanced greatly in recent decades. On one level, television offered audiences greatly enhanced control in determining what they watched, where, when, and in what contexts viewing would occur. These capabilities were greatly extended by the broad-based availability of cable, which, despite its failed promises, nevertheless dramatically altered the production and reception of television. More recently, a device as commonplace as the video cassette recorder has greatly extended the capacities of viewers to exercise agency in their media usage by renting particular programs, recording shows for later use, viewing selected segments repeatedly, or combining segments of programming in new combinations or sequences. Perhaps romanticizing these abilities somewhat, Paul Virillio wrote the "the machine, the VCR, allows man to organize a time which is not his own, a deferred time, a time which is somewhere else—and to capture it."[16]

The negative side of this equation lies in the economics of much communications technology. Not only are costs associated with both hardware and programming, but the seemingly free choices exercised by individuals remain circumscribed within the range of options preselected by television executives, cable operators, and computer network hosts. Perhaps the most ironic twist in the evolution of interactive video is the widespread current application of the technology for TV home shopping. For networks like the Quality Video Channel (which in 1994 nearly completed a merger with CBS television), "talking back to your television" means the ability to pick up the phone and buy a bracelet or a food dehydrator. Entities like QVC make a great deal of the empowerment this new form of "dialogue" offers to viewers—and they are quite correct. After decades of passive programming viewers are responding to the interactivity of home shopping channels with considerable relish. As the information super-highway permits ever-more elaborate ways for people to select entertainment and respond to electronic cues, the popularity of interactive media will undoubtedly grow. Audiences clearly are attracted to the participatory qualities of these new video offerings—even if the interactively is largely illusory. The question is, how will these new systems be envisioned and for what purposes? Certainly this promising technology can be applied to more democratic ends.

Virtual Campgrounds

In the now-classic book *Neuromancer,* William Gibson coined the term "cyber-space" to describe the fantasized landscape of virtual reality and computer telecommunications.[17] The concept of cyberspace extends to computer users cin-ema-like capacities for virtual travel and identity transformation. Although one's body never leaves its place behind the keyboard and screen, with a little imagina-tion cyberspace explorers can make friends, attend parties, join clubs—and in more outlandish applications fight dragons, pilot spacecraft, or pose as coun-terespionage agents. Gibson's book helped shift the image of the computer hack-er from isolated nerd to reckless adventurer, brazenly travelling the cyberspace world battling international criminals and spies. Mobility remains a central fas-cination in its genre, as evidenced in the following passage.

> Program a map to display frequency of data exchange, every thousand megabytes a signal pixel on a very large screen. Manhattan and Atlanta burn solid white. Then they start to pulse, the rate of traffic threatening to overload your simulation. Your map is about to go nova. Cool it down. Up your scale. Each pixel a million megabytes. At a hundred million megabytes per second, you begin to make out certain blocks in midtown Manhattan, outlines of hun-dred-year-old industrial parks.[18]

For Gibson and a growing list of cyberspace authors, the Internet is no longer an illusory place created by phosphorescent light; viewers feel they are really "there." More significantly, users can move around and act within this world. A decade ago cultural theorists spoke of the way our understandings of experience had become increasingly mediated by representations. In what has become a postmodern manifesto, art critic Douglas Crimp wrote that "we only experience reality through the pictures we make of it. To an ever greater extent our experience is governed by pictures, pictures in newspapers and magazines, on television and in the cinema. Next to these pictures, firsthand experience begins to retreat, to seem more and more trivial."[19] The cyberspace image on the computer screen has become a reality on equal footing with any set of concrete artifacts.

Most cyberspace writers celebrate this new era with unbridled optimism. Indeed, the rash of books, periodicals, programs, and software promoting virtual worlds has exploded in the last few years. As with the other technologies discussed in this chapter, the rhetoric surrounding cyberspace typically focuses on representations of power (the imagistic capacity to control a situation, travel somewhere, or make something happen) and interactivity: (the electronic means to communicate, transact business, or form a group).

Rarely examined are the underlying philosophical and political issues of what happens in the interface of machines and human beings. If one can set aside for a moment the delirium over the "newness" these technologies project, it is important to remember that the next great technological fix always promises to be hiding just around the next bend. Yet anticipation of its arrival tends to divert attention from the material and ideological contexts in which it will appear. The liberating "cyborg" model that Donna Haraway discusses as a vehicle for crossing borders and expanding human possibilities also has a dark side. For all of the "transgressed boundaries, potent fusions, and dangerous possibilities which progressive people might explore," there also comes a danger.[20] When we engage technological devices do we extend our capacities or risk ceding their control to unseen forces?

This might seem a Luddite caution if the interests of corporate enterprises were not so firmly entrenched in cyberspace. One of the most prescient aspects of *Neuromancer* is that its roguish hero finds himself caught in a battle among multinational software barons. Certainly one needs to look no further than the pages of magazines like *Wired* and *Mondo 2000* to see the role of IBM, Apple, Intel, Sega, and Nintendo in the development, promotion, and marketing of utopian ideas involving their products. In this sense, the simulated realities of cyberspace constitute simply another technology of knowledge. These representational technologies always convey forms of power in their ability to shape perceptions, transform subjectivities, and limit the possibilities of human imagination.

In its more negative manifestations, the lure of digital technologies is motivating the coalescence of affinity groups that resonate with arrogant elitism. This is exactly the sort of cultism that the new digital magazines seem to promote. Instead of emphasizing the potentially inclusive and participatory aspects of the computer age, the appeal of technical mastery devolves into a self-important libertarianism. As stated in a recent *Wired* editorial, "technology has given us powers with which we can manipulate not only external reality—the physical world—but also, and much more portentously—ourselves."[21] Who exactly is this "we?" For readers of publications like *Wired,* it is a group defined by those it excludes. As explained by Gary Chapman,

> If hyperbolic optimism were all that *Wired* represented, it would be a modestly interesting, if sometimes howlingly brainless, gazette of our times. Unfortunately, the magazine and its popularity among the young, urban elite also seem to present something darker. *Wired's* inside-outside dichotomy has the taint of contempt for the poor and the uneducated, people not using computers now and not likely, in the near future, to find a reason to use them. The disadvantaged haunt *Wired* by their absence, like a negative space that can be seen but can be accounted for. *Wired* frequently exhibits resentment toward any kind of civic obligation that might divert resources from life on the net.[22]

This story doesn't need to be so one-sided. New communication technologies are not yet lost to democracy, because they still exist in a fluid state. Although corporations are quickly moving to consolidate their grip on virtual reality, multimedia, and the Internet—spaces for progressive change still exist on many levels. In the most populist terms, cyberspace subversion is carried out by "hackers" who assault the computer networks by cracking access codes, planting viruses, breaking into databases, and stealing network or telephone time. Mostly the work of white middle-class adolescents, hacking constitutes a classic form of negative resistance. Its youthful perpetrators assert themselves against overwhelming sources of authority, while still leaving the structures of that authority in place. Hackers become virtual renegades, who make surface disturbances on the periphery of an industry whose domination they resent but do little to unseat. This form of resistance is very important in articulating the powerlessness felt by individuals increasingly subject to the regulation, surveillance, and control of computer-based information systems. Yet by failing to address the larger issues of class, gender, and race of technological ownership and control, hackers actually reinforce the very authority that they oppose. They play by the rules of the system itself. Needed instead are positive plans.

Certain examples of such productive work can be found in the burgeoning networks of conferencing systems made possible by the Internet. Most of these services work like endless electronic bulletin boards, on which one person writes a message (usually in text), below which another individual can write a response, to be followed by yet another comment, and another, and so on. Long-standing conferencing systems like Whole Earth Lectronic Link ("The WELL") have developed elaborate listings of such ongoing conversations on topics ranging from radical politics to childrearing. An unabashed advocate of the social potentials of these "virtual" encounters, Howard Rheingold asserts that "people in virtual communities do just about everything people do in real life, but we leave our bodies behind."[23]

It goes without saying that the virtual crowd also leaves behind such bodily inconveniences as hunger, poverty, and violence in the pursuit of electronic comradeship. Yet in a vision of simulated experience worthy of Jean Baudrillard, Rheingold sees the gap between virtual faction and physical reality shortening. As he puts it:

> Not only do I inhabit my virtual communities; to the degree that I carry around their conversations in my head and begin to mix it up with them in real life, my virtual communities also inhabit my life. I've been colonized; my sense of family at the most fundamental level has been virtualized.[24]

This is where things get interesting. Rather than focusing on the binary opposition of virtual/non-virtual worlds (or to put it another way, representation and reality) these two spheres can be viewed as mutually informing. Each reflects and shapes the other.

In this sense, the notion of a virtual community need not be regarded so much as an end in itself, but rather as one of many "spaces" where dialogues can emerge. *Whole Earth Catalogue* founder Stewart Brand describes the virtual meeting place as being much like the public sphere:

> There's always another mind there. it's like having the corner bar, complete with old buddies and delightful newcomers and new tools waiting to take home and fresh graffiti and letters, except instead of putting on my coat, shutting down the computer, and walking to the corner, I just invoke my telecom program and there they are. It's a place.[25]

For obvious reasons, the idea of virtual communities has become attractive in certain political circles. This was the fundamental premise behind Ross Perot's vision of national "electronic town meetings" for conducting instantaneous votes on public policy issues—an idea more recently advocated by House Speaker Newt Gingrich. This notion of a giant national conversation holds enormous popular appeal, for it satisfies both the affective desire for an inclusive community and the "common sense" thinking that such a unified common culture is possible and advisable.

Of course, the very premise of elected "representation" was intended in part as a buffer against the faddish indulgences of unbridled populism. Indeed, Washington's current reliance on focus groups and instant polls provoked a writer in *Time* magazine to comment that the federal government "isn't dangerously disconnected from the people; the trouble may be it's too plugged in."[26] These sentiments are echoed by Jonathan Gill, special projects coordinator for the White House Office of Media Affairs, who is particularly leery of the growing media frenzy over making democratic decisions in cyberspace. Gill fears that such capacities may in fact do more harm than good if not deployed with restraint. "Democracy requires dialogue, reflection, learning growth, and the ability to evolve," Gill recently wrote in an e-mail message, "all of which require time and not channel-clicking."[27]

Fears of populist excess notwithstanding, this was the fundamental reasoning behind McLuhan's utopian vision of a "global village" in which national and international conflict (in particular the threat of nuclear war) would be eliminated. At the core of McLuhan's program lay a concept of media as "information without content"[28] that defined international turmoil as the result of failed communication rather than ideological confrontation. The flaw in McLuhan's technological determinism stemmed from his tendency to dehistoricize innovation and remove it from specific social contexts.

Of course, the global communications network that McLuhan envisioned was still decades from realization. During the 1960s, the system we now know as the Internet was but an abstraction, waiting to receive initial form the following decade from the Defense Department. In the 1970s, the U.S. military established the Advanced Research Projects Agency Network (ARPANET) to facilitate the exchange of technical data among weapons scientists. The premise of ARPANET was developed by the California-based RAND Corporation, a private think tank hired by the government to study issues of national security. ARPANET had been originally designed as a fail-safe communication system to be used by the government in the event of a nuclear war. The ARPANET system primarily remained the domain of academics until the 1980s, when personal computers and modems began to expand consumer access to this *free* service.

The exponentially expanding market for equipment meant that before long electronic bulletin boards and conferencing systems seemed to be springing up everywhere. In 1987, the Internet counted 10,000 "hosts" (organizers of electronic conversations); by 1992, the number had risen to 740,000, a number that has increased exponetially in recent years.[29] Unfortunately, this delirious expansion of the Internet was not accompanied by comparable increases in government expenditures. In 1987 the Reagan government moved to privatize management of the Internet by contracting certain of its its operations to private contractors. This was followed in 1993 with the award of Internet directory services to ATT. Although most simple uses of the system are still subject to only the cost of the connecting phone call, during the last few years companies have been clamoring to develop fee-for-service information, communication, shopping, and advertising offerings with gold-rush zeal.

In 1995, a further move toward privatization shifted electronic traffic from the federally subsidized NFSNet onto four privately run network access points run by Pacific Bell, Ameritech, Sprint, and Metropolitan Fiber Systems. The companies received a franchise through the year 2000 to compete with each other to carry the Internet business previously subsidized by tax dollars. So far, the shift to private providers has not effected the price of Internet service, although it likely will mean that free speech on the Internet will soon be a thing of the past.[30] Of the approximately $100 million required to keep the system going, the government had chipped in only $11 million. But in exchange for this subsidy, rates had been held at a consistently low level. This is in keeping with the scientific and research-oriented purpose for which the original APARNET had been designed. Many college employees and students receive what they perceive as "free" Internet access for unlimited usage, although their schools pay up to $100,000 per year for the service. In contrast, subscribers to commercial services like America on Line or Compuserve pay $10–20 per month for a package of metered services that includes the Internet. Educational users fear that the privatization of the Internet will constrain non-commercial use. Like long-distance telephone service, one's ability to communicate would depend on one's capacity to pay. Lacking federal regulation to maintain open access, the egalitarian character of the Internet is diminished

In the face of such increasing corporate management, many cyberspace free-speech advocates suspect that before long the promises of an electronic public sphere will go the way of radio and television. These concerns have prompted the formation of a range of public service organizations dedicated to citizen involvement in the Internet. These entities range from local networks like the model Public Electronic Network (PEN) Action Group in Santa Monica, Cal., to the

International Institute for Global Communication (IGS), to the plethora of advocacy and special interest groups like the Electronic Frontier Foundation (EFF). Like the media centers described in the last chapter, these groups are gradually forming a new type of civil society on the Internet—and they will continue to do so if their existence is not foreclosed by economics.

Santa Monica is one of a growing number of municipalities to recognize the potential of electronic networking in improving communication between citizens and city officials. However, it is important to point out that the proposal for a community Internet system originated from a group outside the government. In 1990, the PEN Action Group—an organization that had been long active in local issues concerning unemployment and homelessness—petitioned for a system to enable on-line conversations on topics of community concern. The Santa Monica city council complied by placing free-access terminals in homeless shelters, libraries, schools, and other publicly accessible sites, as well as offering accounts to citizens to a municipal conferencing without charge. The system enables residents to monitor information bulletins from the city, exchange e-mail with officials or each other, participate on municipal conversations on subjects like zoning and the environment, or establish public exchanges on other topics. And it is used by thousands of residents who now hold accounts. Like most commercial Internet systems usage varies from user to user. The success of the PEN model has demonstrated that individual citizens are willing to overcome the immediate technological hurtles to gain a means of civic interface. The idea of such community systems is growing, especially in areas where other forms of public exchange are difficult.

The IGC was founded in 1982 with funding from Apple Computer Corporation and the San Francisco Foundation to encourage worldwide discussions of environmental issues. The result was the formation of the now well-known EcoNet, which was subsequently complimented by a similar network called PeaceNet dedicated to conflict resolution. Emphasizing the potentials of the Internet for international dialogue, the IGC has established numerous branches and alliances with similar networks in such nations as Brazil, Canada, and Great Britain—and more recently in countries like China, Nicaragua, and the countries of the former Soviet Union. The significance of the IGC networks has already demonstrated itself repeatedly in times of international crisis, when direct transmissions from Bosnia-Herzegovinia or the Persian Gulf nations preceded and at times contradicted the mainstream newscasts from CNN and the major networks.

These efforts aside, wide-scale growth of an international civil society has been slow in developing. In part, the lack of impetus may be symptomatic of the anarchistic fragmentation that characterizes the Internet. More significantly, however, this lassitude may be attributable to the material difficulties that impede the poor and marginalized from gaining access to such technologies. As suggested in the earlier discussion of *Wired* magazine, when the digital generation does get political it generally does so around conservative issues of freedom more than liberal concerns over equality. A case in point is the much-ballyhooed Electronic Frontier Foundation (EFF), an entity founded in 1991 by Apple computer co-founder Steve Wosniak, Lotus development co-founder Mitch Kapor, and Grateful Dead lyricist and prominent Republican John Barlow, among others. The rational for EFF was the purported infiltration of the Internet by FBI agents and the Secret Service. In a now-apocryphal story, an assortment of innocent on-line characters with names like Captain Crunch and Acid Phreak were routinely harassed by government agents searching for corporate saboteurs and communists. In response to these real or imagined intrusions, the industry-oriented EFF group developed a non-profit organization dedicated to privacy and free speech. The concerns of EFF are well summarized by Rheingold, who participated in group's founding meetings:

> People in cyberspace are citizens, not criminals, nor do citizens tolerate criminals among them; however, law enforcement agencies have a commitment to constitutional protections of individual rights, and any breach of those rights in the pursuit of criminals threatens the freedoms of other citizens' rights to free speech and assembly. The constitutional government of the United States has proved to be a flexible instrument for two centuries; but cyberspace is very new and we are now moving into it quickly. Any freedoms we lose now are unlikely to be regained later.[31]

While no one would question the importance of privacy "rights," the intrusion of any governmental big brother into Internet conversations has proven far less of an issue than the degree to which entities like banks, credit card companies, and other corporate interests use computer telecommunications to monitor citizen behavior. But the quiet ubiquity of such corporate information gathering lacks the cops-and-robbers appeal of more dramatic scenarios, and as a consequence gets little attention from groups like the EFF.

Readers and Writers

The growing consolidation of technology in commercial hands mitigates against the extension of democratic ideals discussed throughout this book. The addition of economic roadblocks to the existing distance between people and technology further worsens the sense of powerlessness that feeds civic alienation and passivity. Fortunately, the story doesn't end there. In addition to grassroots efforts like the PEN Action Group, a growing number of theorists are pointing to new potentials in the organization of technology to unseat the monoliths of corporate control. George P. Landow asserts that the postmodern decentering of monolithic forms of authority is embodied in the new forms of information exchange and organization enabled by computers.[32] Landow explains that hypertext constitutes a form of "non-sequential writing—text that branches and allows choices to the reader, best read at an interactive screen. As popularly conceived, this is a series of text chunks connected by links which offer the reader different pathways."[33] Emphasis is placed not so much on the main text as written, but on the reader's ability to reference supplementary texts in varying configurations. "We must abandon conceptual systems founded upon ideas of center, margin, hierarchy, and linearity and replace them with ones of multilinearity, nodes, links, and networks," Landow writes.

The principles of hypertext are actualized in the evolving capabilities of computer writing, especially when authors can be linked to databases, libraries, and other authors via such telecommunication technologies as the Internet. Telecommunications networks facilitate forms of collaboration in the creation of texts, which previously took great amounts of time and effort. Not only can writers easily retrieve and integrate supplementary paragraphs, imagery, maps, video, or audio accompaniment to their work, they can conceive of jointly produced works such those emanating from electronic bulletin boards or conferencing networks. In these latter contexts any number of individuals can take turns adding information to an ever-expanding body of exchanges on a given topic.[34] Such relationships create a web of communication, which works against the centering of authority around individual authors or canonical bodies of knowledge. No longer must readers satisfy themselves with books as written. The new capacities of hypertext permit the realization of literary potential envisioned by Michel Foucault when he wrote that the "frontiers of a book are never clear-cut," because "it is caught up in a system of references to other books, other texts, other sentences: it is a node within a network."[35] This intertextuality allows the reader to become more than a partner in the creation of meaning; it begins to throw into question the category of authorship itself. In this way the arbitrary character of such a subject position is revealed, along with the institutional frameworks holding it in place. As Foucault explains,

> The "author-function" is tied to the legal and institutional systems that circum-
> scribe, determine, and articulate the realm of discourses; it does not operate in
> a uniform manner in all discourses, at all times, and in any given culture it is
> not defined by the spontaneous attribution of a text to its creator, but through
> a series of precise and complex procures; it does not refer, purely and simply,
> to an actual individual.[36]

This suggests some intriguing political possibilities. By casting doubt on such categories as copyright and originality, the very premise of literary authority becomes undermined. Subverted by extension are the hierarchies of knowledge that support such institutions.

In literary and film studies in the early 1990s, similar ideas of empowered readership became popular in academic circles. Theories were advanced that touted the native abilities of audiences to contest intended meanings of films and television programs—or to make up new interpretations of their own. With added education, it was argued, viewers could further gird themselves against the manipulations of advertisers while also developing richer means of enjoying entertainment. The flaw in this discourse lay in the absence of any empirical grounding, for little scholarship could document the political claims of its propo-nents.[37] Rather than illustrating any substantive activism, such work would often dwell on the resistant activities of "Quantum Leap" or "The X Files" viewers, who would use existing texts as points of departure for personal fantasy. Worse still, like much unchannelled rebellion, this behavior was often less than enlightened in its orientation. It would as frequently replicate popular stereotypes of race, class, and gender as it would challenge them. This point is conceded by fan club analyst Henry Jenkins, who states that "readers are not always resistant; all resistant readings are not necessarily progressive readings; the 'people' do not always recognize their conditions of alienation and subordination."[38] As discussed earlier, this somewhat superficial articulation of politics led many skeptics to view reader-response theory as armchair radicalism or mere "semiotic activism."

The Rules of the Game

Partly in response to such criticism, more recent analysis of high-tech cultural forms has begun to integrate thinking from the social sciences. A growing body of research on video games reveals this interest in infusing cultural scholarship with principles from educational research and developmental psychology.[39] One doesn't need an advanced degree to recognize that the lure of video games from *Pong* to *Teenage Mutant Ninja Turtles* stems directly from the need for mastery and control. Not only does such amusement provide an important way for children to develop and test their own capacities, but it often encourages kids to creatively extend the principles of the "game" in other areas of their lives. Looking beyond the regressive role modelling and occasionally violent behavior that video games have recently been accused of engendering, one might speculate about how these games also foster cooperation, joint learning, and such productive activities as storytelling and drawing.

According to Jean Piaget, a child's experience as an active subject in the world is a key element in cognitive development. Piaget writes that "in order to know objects, the subject must act upon them, and therefore transform them."[40] Through this act of transforming external phenomena, the young subject is also changed. Growth occurs as a consequence. For this reason "play" becomes an important activity for very young children. In this context the very act of manipulating buttons, joysticks, electronic signals, and screen representations has a primary pedagogical function in congitive and emotional development.

Prior to the development of video games, the Hollywood entertainment industry could only satisfy this need for interactive play by offering images of interaction or by selling other kinds of toys. Television programs like "Pee Wee's Playhouse," "Sesame Street," or "Muppet Babies" often would depict children manipulating levers, operating cameras, or pushing buttons in mock-TV studios—encouraging viewers to imagine they had production roles. At other times, these programs would feature segments emulating adult game shows like "Jeopardy" or "Wheel of Fortune," in which home audiences could "play along" in a form of virtual participation.

In its more crassly commercial manifestations, industry producers exploited the interactive impulses by offering program-related toys. Such product tie-ins were made possible by the deregulation of children's programming enabled in 1984 by the elimination by the Reagan Federal Communications Commission of a ban against product-based programs. This afforded kids access to their favorite Saturday morning television characters through toy versions of "Dink, The Little Dinosaur" and "Beetlejuice." These participatory impulses gained a more direct outlet in the late 1980s with the emergence of video-game versions of shows. Nintendo, the industry leader in this field, currently offers interactive games based on television programs, and also on such popular movies as *Total Recall, Dick Tracy, Who Framed Roger Rabbit, Robocop,* and *Indiana Jones.* One recent

Nintendo promotion exhorts young fans to "step into Arnold Schwarzeneggger's shoes by assuming the role he played in the movie . . . *Predator.*"[41] Extending the virtual reality of movie-related video games yet another step has been the phenomenal growth in popularity of Hollywood-inspired theme parks. Using state-of-the art techniques of robotics, video projection, surround-sound, and flight simulation, visitors to the growing chain of Disney, Universal, and Paramount theme parks can place themselves inside the action of movies like *Jurassic Park* and *Back to the Future.*

Needless to say, the regressive content and blatant commercialism of much of this material can only be partially rationalized through its benefits to cognitive growth and the development of childhood agency. Whether or not one believes in a correlation between representational violence and the real-world variety (certainly little concrete research exists to support the connection), there can be no doubt that media and computer imagery create a staging ground for aggressive fantasy. Moreover, this background imagery is framed almost exclusively in terms of male spectatorship.

Although the replication of gender stereotypes by the entertainment industry should come as no surprise, video games offer a more focused application of these roles than conventional passive media. As educational researcher Marsha Kinder points out, "the fact that video games were introduced into the United States at a time when fewer households include a father may have contributed to their oedipalization. Video games provide an appealing surrogate against which a son can test his powers."[42] She adds that "even in those homes (such as my own) where the father is present and nurturing, the games can help boys deal with their rebellious anger against patriarchal authority."[43]

If video games offer ways for children (primarily boys) to work though issues of personal autonomy and power, do they serve the same purpose for adults? Certainly the popularity of particular games suggests that issues of mastery and control do indeed have a comparable appeal for many age groups. Here, the symbolic economy of interactive gaming takes on a more serious tone, because in the grown-up world matters of dominance and submission become blatantly political. Although this generally translates into reifications of patriarchal authority, certain video amusements are premised on issues of race. Such is the case with the popular *SimCity 2000* game, which allows participants to create a fantasized human community of the future. Simply explained, *SimCity 2000* permits players to become urban planners, each of whom constructs a model of a city complete with businesses, infrastructure, and zoning districts. Once cer-

tain parameters are put in place, the consequences of the plans actualize themselves: utilities function or fail, traffic flows smoothly or becomes congested,
neighborhoods thrive or decline.

Implicit in *SimCity 2000* are a variety of ideological assumptions about
urban life, premised primarily on modernist values of capitalist growth, efficiency,
and, most importantly, order. Within *SimCity 2000,* values of utopia and
dystopia quickly surface—and along with them a range of racial implications.[44]
One "loses" in *SimCity 2000* when one inadvertently creates urban poverty
zones, implicitly identified as racial ghettos, in which crime and riots represent
the ultimate consequence. A "winning" environment is defined by stability, profit, and lawfulness. In this way, utopian visions of order, control, and chaos go
hand in hand with images of the sort of urban future that is desirable (white) and
undesirable (non-white). The important point in analyzing such games lies in
the excavation of the often unacknowledged dimension of race in popular media
and high-tech entertainment. Technological systems have proven especially
adept at disguising their racial coding.[45]

Lessons of Power

Not that one needs to study video games to experience technology's hidden
mechanisms of control. Some of the these systems of control have become so
commonly accepted in daily life that they no longer are challenged for the
oppressive institutions they have become. Complicating matters further is the
particular function of contemporary representational technologies to deny their
implication in the construction of ideology—to cast themselves as somehow
neutral. Medical imaging is a good case in point.

What could be more objective than an x-ray or a CAT-scan? Such a simple
question seems to imply an equally simple answer, but one is not available. It is
impossible to consider such matters without also considering "the broad cultural
technologies with which medicine and science legitimate their own cultures as
they diagnose, survey, and document other sites ranging from the inner body to
outer space."[46] Although women have been the object of medical imaging as frequently as (or more so than) men, they historically have been excluded from
positions in the sciences. For this reason, the gendered character of science has
become a matter of great recent interest to feminist researchers.

Control is a primary issue in the medical encounter. All too often those
receiving treatment are either directly or indirectly excluded from decisions

involving their own care. Although a sensitivity to "patient rights" and empowerment has become a standard part of much medical training in recent years, physicians and other health care providers must still negotiate the internalized power asymmetries that patients and care-givers bring to their relationship. The threatening presence and imposing capacities of medical imaging technologies to survey the body have only exacerbated the inequities between those on either side of this relationship, mitigating against the notion of patient and doctor as a team addressing a problem together.

A pilot program at Dartmouth College is currently seeking to reverse the alienating role of imaging technology by giving patients a more active role in the treatment process.[47] Recognizing that patients are often uninformed about the full range of their choices, the Dartmouth Interactive Laboratory's Shared Decision-making Program focuses on education and participation. The program's key technological element are interactive video disks, to which patients are referred by their physician. Keyed to the patient's specific illness, each disk describes a range of procedures and treatments, likely consequences or side effects, and the range of possible outcomes. Due to the interactive character of the video, patients are free to explore the disk at different rates and to view the material in any sequence. Not only can a viewer repeat sections for clarity or select "learn more" options for more detail, but choices also exist involving the benefits ("good news") or drawbacks ("bad news") of various treatments.

An important goal of the Dartmouth project is the emphasis on "the lack of a 'right' answer based on clinical information alone: instead, the right decision for each patient is one that takes into account the patient's personal preferences."[48] Another aspect is the incorporation of information deemed important by former patients who faced the same decisions. By placing access to information in the hands of patients, the Dartmouth program begins to undo the debilitating relationship that medical imaging so often puts in place. The deployment of information in this way begins to validate the assertion that technology is not the villain in such relationships, but an instrument within a broader social context. As with many of the media literacy projects discussed earlier, this broadened view of technology plays an important pedagogical role as well. In unsettling the primacy of a single valid answer and in decentering the expertise of the physician, technology is revealed as a social construction. Perhaps more importantly, as the mutable meaning of the technological system becomes evident, new spaces are opened for agency on the part of the lay observer. The result is a more participatory and egalitarian relationship for all involved.

Such a synthesis is required to overcome the alienation and feeling of powerlessness that discourages civic involvement. Democracy is a process that depends on participation—the willingness and belief that the actions, voices, and votes of individuals can have an effect on the collective totality. In part, this constitutes an exercise in political imagination; in part it is a consequence of positive agency that convinces an active citizenry that its constituents are their own rulers. To a large extent, what makes this process of democracy work is a faith in its fairness, in a belief that participation is unstymied by inequity and injustice. This is what gives the practice of democracy its moral character. Not a belief in a common culture that supplants all others, not a faith in an unproblematic form of patriotism that blindly follows symbols, not a reverence for a dehistoricized heritage.

This democratic practice is both the means by which the oppressed come to know their oppression and the vehicle through which they struggle to find methods for change. Similarly, it is clear that groups on the left can no longer afford to insist that issues of identity and representation have no place in material struggles. Overcoming these attitudinal problems will mean recognizing the reciprocal role of media as both reflective and constitutive of social formations. In other words, materialists and textualists need each other to build a viable program of social transformation.[49]

six

Problem Youth:
Pedagogies of Representation

"Couldn't the baby boom pick on a generation its own size?" begins a recent *Newsweek* article. "Boomers are bashing twentysomethings with startling relish these days," the essay adds. As a result the twentysomething generation is having an identity crisis. "They're all sleeping in their clothes, moaning about the national debt they've inherited, and pining for Greg or Marcia Brady."[1] By now the nation is painfully aware that yet another youthful scourge has been identified by a writers anxious to label and periodize groups into convenient sound bites. Add a few inflections of race and sexuality and the picture is complete. Not that this is a novel occurrence. From James Dean to Easy-E, adolescent alienation has made good editorial copy to inflame the anxieties of the middle aged and the middle class. Like most generations of demon youth the so-called slackers, baby-busters, or posties are a fictional construct, comprised partially in fact and partially in fantasy. Compressing a plethora of differences into a single demographic, *Advertising Age* referred to Generation X as "that cynical, purple-haired blob watching TV."[2] *The New Republic* chimed in that "these kids today. They're soft. They don't know how good they have it. Not only did they never have to fight a war, like their grandparents, they never even had to dodge one."[3]

Reading such statements, one would get the idea that the current generation of youth is completely bankrupt of social concern, political commitment, or capacity for action. These perceptions are far from accurate, yet they reflect the all-too-familiar capacities of mass media to homogenize social groups into artificial totalities and to demonize those that are not easily understood. If the current generation does indeed have a unique identity, perhaps it lies in the degree to which it has been written about and labelled. In a recent anthology, Andrew Ross comments that the early 1990s mark a time when "with the cessation of Cold War antagonisms and an uneasy interregnum in effect, the full force of media punditry had come to be trained on the new postboomer sensibilities. Youth, in this context, would be analyzed as a symptom of this or that prophetic comment about the near future."[4]

To correct a number of misconceptions: Generation X is not the white, disaffected, collection of dropouts depicted in such disparate works as *Slacker* (1991) and *Reality Bites* (1993). Actually, the thirty-eight million twentysomethings are one of the most racially diverse groups to date (seventy percent white and thirty percent African American, Latino, Asian, and Native American). Contrary to some impressions, the much-publicized "grunge" ethos, while popular, doesn't account for the taste of all young people. Certainly it doesn't include the $800 million in recordings sold in 1995 by rap and hip-hop artists—approximately half of which were bought by whites. In terms of employment and community involvement, seventy percent of post-boomers reported that they were "somewhat or completely " satisfied with their jobs, and forty-eight percent of those between eighteen and twenty-four are engaged in some kind of volunteer work.[5] In short, "it's the stereotyping of Generation X, not the reality, that bites."[6]

Actually, the real factor that sets Generation X apart from others is its *resistance* to categorization, its complete lack of a single identity. *Rolling Stone* rock critic Eric Weisbard called it the "post-you-name-it" generation, in that it lacks the sort of cultural anchor of its predecessors: an arms race, a civil rights movement, or a war.[7] Instead, it embodies an atomized range of interests and concerns that will not go by a single name. Just as this refusal to be categorized has frustrated commentators, the slackers' decentered subjectivity has become its own ethos. As Weisbard puts it,

> Un-generation means resisting being homogenized into a generation. It's become a bit clichéd to note that the subcultural has replaced the countercultural, but in fact, as thirteeners, as Generation X, or more specifically as hip hop nationalists, slackers, riot grrrls, and queers, we incorporate notions of racial, cultural, gendered, and sexual difference—ideas that earlier generations battled to institutionalize, but we've grown up with—into our very identity.[8]

This pansexual, multicultural resistance to a single identity is laden with implications. A trigger-happy theorist might jump on baby-busters as the first postmodern generation. The fragmented, decentered, multiple identity might well be construed as living proof of the end of the modernist tradition of grand master narratives, common culture, and universal truths. And indeed, this eclipse of Enlightenment humanism seems validated by recent public opinion surveys that indicate that more than seventy percent of Americans believe that the United States is experiencing a loss of national unity and a "crisis of values"— a statistic duplicated in exit polls from the 1994 mid-term elections.[9] Without rehearsing the now-overblown complaints over the "fraying of America" brought on by identity politics, one can fairly observe that the nation's real or imagined singularity of purpose now seems diminished.

This failure of engagement and loss of purpose is manifest in a widespread disaffection from prior forms of community: the decline in organized religion, the loss of commitment to political parties, and the waning of such common entities as local social clubs and neighborhood organizations. These changes are reinforced by the growth of massive state bureaucracies and corporate hierarchies. Without a doubt, these views are manifest in the rise of anti-establishment sentiment that swept Bill Clinton into office on a mantra of "change" and just as quickly decimated the Democratic Party two years later. Behind such political forces are other factors. Rapidly expanding networks of technologies and media have drastically reorganized relations of work and leisure, redrawing the landscape of choice and creativity. Despite the utopian hype about virtual reality and the information superhighway, huge numbers of people are being written out of the new communications revolution. Others are being sold a high-tech illusion of control. We many not all be hip hop nationalists, slackers, or riot grrrls, but for many Americans the alienation produced by a postmodern electronic frontier feels palpable. Always consigned to a position of relative powerlessness in society, young people in particular are affected by this narrowing of options.

What are the prospects for cultural democracy in such an environment? Undoubtedly the most authoritarian institution of enlightenment to which young people are exposed is education. After all, the real job of public school is to sort and regulate students into manageable categories of discipline and control. Henry A. Giroux asserts that "as thoroughly modernist institutions, public schools have long relied upon moral, political, and social technologies that legitimate an abiding faith in the Cartesian tradition of rationality, progress, and history."[10] As a socializing institution with very particular rules and regulations, school fosters in many students—both those who achieve and those who don't—a widespread reluctance to express opinions or question authority. To most who experience it, school contradicts the very principles of liberty, diversity, and freedom of choice that America purportedly values most. As a consequence, many young people leave school with the belief that their actions don't matter, that they can't make a difference. Is it any wonder that both young people and old feel a broad-based disaffection from the very notions of democracy itself?

Hence, a fundamental tension exists between the postmodern multiplicity of the slacker generation and modernist monoliths of school, work, and state authority. Although many a conservative would willingly force the "un-generation" into a convenient mold, such a move has disturbing implications for the future of our already weakened democracy. Consider the current state of affairs. Beyond its conflict with the normalizing institutions that confront it, post-boomers face a nation whose egalitarian values seem in growing contradiction with the its actions. If democracy means a fair chance at a prosperous future, Generation X is faced with a government that has already mortgaged its future with a limitless deficit. If democracy means popular participation in civic decision making, the wide-scale resentment toward public officials (and the rise of fringe personas like Ross Perot and Oliver North) indicates a growing alienation from their common government. If democracy means freedom of the press, Americans are faced with media that is increasingly owned by a small minority of corporations. And if democracy means the enfranchisement of all voters, the election of President Bill Clinton by the smallest percentage of voters, and the participation of less than thirty-eight percent of the electorate in the 1994 balloting, signals the disinterest of most of the population in the democratic process.

Each of these examples suggests the perversion of democracy in a society whose dominant institutions have long ago lost touch with its meaning. This is nowhere more manifest than in the opposition between twentysomethings and the gigantic technologies of social control they confront. Due to its prime role in this arena, this chapter will discuss education as one of the most useful means of restoring the lost senses of connection, purpose, and civic possibility. Not only the conventional schooling that goes on only at particular places and at particular times of the day, but the broader forms of education that each of us experiences in multiple forms every day. Teaching and learning—in their active definitions— provoke forms of engagement in which people participate. Education can function as a model for broader forms of democratic practice or it can act as a participatory sphere in its own right. Moreover, education in its broadest sense should validate exactly the kinds of decentered subjectivity and multiple identity that the baby buster generations seems to represent. This isn't a particularly new idea. Throughout U.S. history education has been held as the great enabler of such democratic ideals as equality, liberty, and individual freedom. Focusing on the United States during the postwar period, I will emphasize how schools have served as barometers for the nation's aspirations and anxieties, its accords and disagreements.

Always a politicized activity, education functioned in the nation's first 150 years as an instrument of assimilation, normalization, and class stratification. Its meritocratic reward structure reinforced the desire of an increasingly industrialized society for workplace conformity and productivity. As the United States advanced to its role as an international superpower, schools were regarded as a source of burgeoning military and economic strength. This was reflected in the massive resources committed to science education and research in the cold war years. With the social reforms of the 1960s, education was called upon to resume its role as an equalizer—as curricula were revised to promote diversity and racial fairness. By the 1980s, these trends had all but reversed. The nation is still grappling with the effects of those changes as the Clinton administration struggles to formulate new politics. With each successive turn disagreements have arisen over the definition of human needs, societal goals, and the proper place of government—yet in a healthy democracy such disagreements should be a welcome part of collective decision making. An important function of education (some would argue the most important function) is to encourage forms of critical thinking and dialogue that make such exchanges possible.

Regrettably, neither conservative or liberal approaches to education do very much to promote this kind of democracy. Both rely on weary Enlightenment social engineering that would have citizens defer to the mandates of an idealized political order. While purportedly working for the good of the electorate, the overarching purpose of the state is the perpetuation of itself and the interests supporting it. In this scheme, any extremes of disagreement are neutralized and dissent is delegitimated. As a result, democracy is stripped of its dynamic quality. What is needed are ways of reopening conversations and rekindling a spirit of public debate. Generation X may not be the answer, but its multiple voices point to a solution. The nation should listen. In the words of George Lipsitz, "At a time when oppressive social hierarchies preserve parochial interests by controlling access to discursive and physical space, young people who don't know 'their place' might be the very people most suited to letting us know what time it is."[11]

A Hard Turn to the Right

For much of the past two decades, the conservative reform movement has set the tone for educational policy in the United States. Although slightly restrained by the centrist Clinton administration, the general premises of social reproduction and worker preparation continue to define the meaning of schooling. With the economic downturns of the 1970s and 1980s, supply-side analysts blamed schools for the nation's inability to compete in world markets—while, ironically, arguing for reductions in federal education spending. This resulted in intensified ideological intervention through curriculum changes and corporate management techniques. A renewed emphasis was placed on course content—specifically content that would reinforce conservative subjectivity. As Lynne V. Cheney argued, the biggest "culprit is 'process'—the belief that we can teach our children how to think without troubling them to learn anything worth thinking about."[12]

The approach to schooling currently touted by conservatives, which would suppress (or neutralize) difference and dissent, is a common threat to all disenfranchised groups. It offers a model of an unchanging social order that perpetuates existing hierarchies of power and privilege. Similarly, the right's program of education reform reintroduces bureaucratic control, measurement, and ranking in the service of a capital-driven curriculum of basic skills. It promotes an unquestioning view of authority and cultural heritage. As such, it represents the antithesis of a pluralistic democracy, focusing instead on techniques of social stratification and discrimination. As discussed by Samuel Lipman:

> What is necessary are definitions of culture and democracy based less on the muddling of definitions and more on their clarification, less on inclusions and more on exclusions, less on finding similarities between conflicting realities, concepts, and goals and more recognizing the differences between them.[13]

These efforts to maintain order and enforce traditions reveal the anxiety of a dominant regime faced with instability. It is the sign of an aging monoculture coming unglued in the face of increasing racial and sexual diversity—not to mention the burgeoning "post-you-name-it" generation.

As discussed in chapter 4, at an earlier political juncture thirty years ago, when elements of diversity and social change were gaining momentum, such circumstances were termed "an excess of democracy" by the Trilateral Commission. Assembled by a corporate confederation led by David Rockefeller in the wake of another era of activism by students, women, and people of color, the commission's "Crisis of Democracy" report argued that unbridled freedom breeds anarchy, loss of common purpose, and, more to the political point, economic decline.[14] Couched in terms of social moderation and cooperation, the report presented a program to perpetuate the rule of the business leaders by cracking down on students and other unruly groups.

Three decades later, the cultural right again has directed these dusty arguments at education. Rather than acknowledging the democratic potential in multiple, conflicting viewpoints, the conservative program's pessimistic view of human agency brands such diversity a danger to educational coherence Regrettably, this program has held sway over the major institutions of the United States due in large part to the economic scapegoating applied to liberal social and educational programs following the Vietnam War. This revolt against the progressive educational reforms of the 1960s and 1970s (many of which were quite effective, in fact) made possible the virulent attacks of the Reagan and Bush administrations on cultural pluralism and public programs.

Liberal Alternatives?

As recent political campaigns have pointed out, liberal arguments present equally problematic attitudes toward education, democracy, and difference. Rather than accepting the inequities produced by unbridled capitalism, liberalism constructs a model of a normative middle class to which citizens should be economically reconciled. Differences are obstacles to be overcome or "tolerated," as citizenship is collapsed into a single category. While expressing tacit concern over issues of social inequality, this rhetoric fails to acknowledge systematic oppressions related to gender, race, and sexual orientation that install people within relations of wealth or poverty. Where conservativism advocates the unbridled "opportunity" of the individual, liberalism places more emphasis on the compensatory capacities of the state, which is envisioned as an independent and apolitical ground on which to build civic consensus.

To achieve these monolithic visions of national community, liberals have often joined conservatives in criticizing as divisive the proponents of multiculturalism or identity politics.[15] Ignoring historically entrenched power asymmetries among social groups, they have argued that such "separatist" and "ethnocentric" views subvert the potential of a national accord.[16] They similarly have been intolerant of the apparent indolence and lack of commitment of Generation X. Promoted instead is a monolithic definition of citizenship, which dismisses the specificity of human variety as either irrelevant or selfish. Ironically, much of this is carried out in the name of a "freedom" that would claim to protect each citizen from interference by others while leaving intact the mechanisms through which that freedom is selectively denied to certain groups.

These criticisms of notwithstanding, the approach of liberal humanism to education deserves certain credit. By posing crucial questions about power and the state, liberalism has identified key issues in the relationship of education to democracy. First, it is important to distinguish between the philosophies of liberal schooling and their occasionally flawed applications. As mentioned above, the United States has always regarded education the key to the American Dream. In the 1960s era of desegregation, urban renewal, and other liberal initiatives, standard pedagogies and tests were recognized as culturally biased. Based loosely on the thinking of John Dewey, theories of "educational formalism" were introduced into many schools as a means of de-emphasizing differences of race, gender, and class. Stressing student experience over rote mastery of detail, these programs regrettably often also entailed a degree of anti-intellectualism. The unfortunate consequence was that many poor and disadvantaged children never gained the basic skills in language, math, and science that they desperately needed. Because of this, progressive reformers became easy prey for conservative critics.

In many ways, Dewey's attitudes exemplify the worst and best of liberal educational thinking. In institutional terms, Dewey was an unabashed proponent of the liberal state that responded to "man's distrust of himself" by providing ground "to get beyond and above himself."[17] In this respect Dewey tended to view institutions in utopian terms, which blinded him to their political dynamics and power asymmetries On the other hand, Dewey's much-discussed advocacy of "learning by doing" signaled a profound departure from conservative attitudes toward learning. In contrast to the view of students as passive recipients of knowledge, Dewey recognized the importance of student experience. The key to this process was not the separation of theory from practice (as it is often interpreted), but the necessary integration of the two for genuine learning to occur.[18] Most importantly, Dewey recognized that for a democracy to function it must embody the Jeffersonian ideal of an informed citizenry.[19]

Radical Critiques

In the 1960s and 1970s, political economists like Samuel Bowles and Herbert Gintis began pointing out the ways that both conservative and liberal schooling replicated the economic base by teaching students to assume worker/manager roles.[20] This so-called "reproduction" or "correspondence" theory of education was later refined to critique not only the contents of books and curricula, but the "hidden curriculum" that taught students how to behave.[21] In this formulation, schools not only legitimated certain kinds of knowledge and expertise at the expense of others, but they also obliged young people to acknowledge particular forms of authority and reward. In this way, the structure of the school was regarded as preparation for management and compensation relationships in the workplace.

Important as this analysis was, it failed to acknowledge the role of human agency, much as did the Marxist cultural analyses of the Austrian Frankfurt School. To the Frankfurt School theorists, culture was perceived as little more than an advertisement for capitalism, and thus directly reflected the manipulative interests of the market. Max Horkheimer and Theodor Adorno, among others, described a system in which the masses were systematically duped into lives of servitude and consumption. Within such apocalyptic logic, cultural objects functioned as propaganda, and the citizenry was incapable of resisting the seduction of the dominant "culture industry." Although useful in the broad mapping of ideological reproduction, this totalizing position refused to grant makers or audiences any autonomy whatsoever. Unabashedly elitist in its views of "the masses," the resulting "reflection theory" readings of art and entertainment invariably produced predictable evidence of existing class inequities.

Alternatives to these ideas date to the 1940s, although until recently many were unknown to wide audiences. Some of these works emphasized the independent character of educational and cultural practices, apart from the presumed overdetermination of the economic base. Others focused on audiences. Louis Althusser's work in particular sought to undo myths of unproblematized transmission and reception. In his essay "Ideology and Ideological State Apparatuses (Notes Toward an Investigation)," he argued that subjectivity is socially inscribed in the relationships *between* individuals and organizations.[22] Institutions like the school and museum constructed systems of meaning that install people in imaginary relations to the real situations in which they live. Identity was recognized as a fiction upon which various forces exert influence.

More significantly, Althusser proposed a revision of reflection theory that assigned a quasi-autonomy to texts. No longer mere superstructural manifestations of the economic base, curricula and media were seen to operate in a complex dialectic with students and audiences. In other words, a space was acknowledged between the oppressive institutions of the state and the consciousness of individuals. Within this space, resistances could form that were capable of destabilizing ruling power structures. These sentiments were echoed in the writings of Herbert Marcuse, who likewise argued against the classical Marxist doctrine that material relations alone were responsible for producing consciousness. Emphasizing the role of human agency, Marcuse said that "radical change in consciousness is the beginning, the first step in changing social existence: emergence of the new Subject."[23]

A further refinement of Marxist cultural theory came in 1970 when Hans Magnus Enzenberger proposed in his "Constituents of a Theory of Media" that the left had been misguided in its understandings of how mass communication actually works. He suggested that instead of tricking people into a web of false desires, media actually found ways of satisfying real (but often unconscious) desires. This position was later elaborated upon by poststructuralist Marxists like Frederic Jameson and Roland Barthes, who further considered the negotiable possibilities of signification. If cultural signs could be interpreted variously, their meanings assumed a "floating" character as individuals assigned them different readings. From an understanding of the contingency of meaning has evolved a complex discourse on the many forces that struggle to influence it. The very way one sees the world becomes a matter of strategy.

These analyses were incorporated into the British cultural studies movement, which sought to ground cultural theories in the practical context of schooling. An initial means to account for student aberrations and failures took form in the development of "resistance" theories as elaborated by researchers like Stuart Hall, Angela McRobbie, Valerie Walkerdine, and Paul Willis.[24] Taking cues from reader response theorists, leftist educators recognized that not all parties respond to ideological transmission in exactly the same way.[25] This work afforded students a hitherto unacknowledged agency in rejecting school authority, even if this behavior did little to change their class positions. Rather than a purely negative attribute, this willful ignorance was recognized as a positive manifestation of students' desire for power. From this realization evolved a range of ideas emphasizing the ingenious ways that suppressed student energy found release: vandalism, drug abuse, sexual promiscuity, radical dressing, and gang violence. Teachers were to seek ways to harness this often self-destructive power.

Largely a reaction to the monolith of reproduction theory, the early resistance thinking often locked itself into a debilitating polarity. In emphasizing student response to authority, it failed to adequately consider the complex ways that students make culture of their own. Later work began to address the formation of student identity, as suggested in the title of Dick Hebdige's 1979 book *Subculture: The Meaning of Style.*[26] However, most of these efforts focused on what students did outside of school. As useful as this thinking was in suggesting ways that education could be considered wherever it is found, it went too far in neglecting the issue of institutional formations. It also largely left unaddressed the ways that adults and young people, teachers and students, might constructively engage each other in an educational dialogue.

A turning point came in the early 1980s, as educators began to recognize the potential for channeling resistant impulses in positive ways. Rather than simply accepting lessons as given, students would be encouraged to bring their own insights to the pedagogical encounter. No longer did texts need to be interpreted as intended by their authors or manufacturers, they could be revised, combined, or contested according to the reader's interpretive capabilities. This led to broadened considerations of the many issues that contextualize culture and education. Factors hitherto subsumed within base/superstructure objectivism like history, social formation, and class struggle began to be examined in relation to language, identity, technology, and power. Moreover, this discursive expansion challenged strictly aesthetic definitions of culture by reading into the very fabric of all political and social relations. Because cultural works are subject to multiple readings, meaning became a matter of contest on the broad terrain of politics.

Crucial to the evolution of radical education were the theoretical developments of what has been termed "critical pedagogy," an amalgam of radical philosophies that first gained wide recognition in the 1970s through the writings of Brazilian expatriate Paulo Freire.[27] As practiced by Freire in countries throughout the third world, the doctrines of critical pedagogy were used by colonized citizens to analyze their roles in relations of oppression and to devise programs for revolutionary change. To Freire, this analytical process grew directly from a process of dialogue among disempowered people, rather than from the top-down dictates of an intellectual vanguard. The notion of dialogue was the ideal antidote for citizens who had always been told what to do by oppressive leaders. Rather than subordinate "objects" in a one-directional address from dominant figures, participants in a dialogue become "subjects" who could jointly share ideas.

The political implications of this philosophy derive from its related emphasis on "praxis"—the linkage of theory to action. As Freire puts it,

> A revolution is achieved with neither verbalism nor activism, but rather with praxis, that is, with reflection and action directed at the structures to be transformed. The revolutionary effort to transform these structures radically cannot designate its leaders as its *thinkers* and the oppressed as mere *doers.*[28]

Freire and his colleagues aggressively advocated the extrapolation of this program for revolutionary action into a range of social contexts and political institutions. In this way the concept of critical pedagogy became synonymous with a variety of interventions both inside and outside the classroom. During the 1970s and 1980s, the philosophies of critical pedagogy were adopted throughout the industrialized world as a means of addressing power imbalances there. Significant in this regard are the writings of such scholars as Michael Apple, Henry Giroux, Peter McLaren, and Ira Schor, among others.[29]

Much of the movement's vocabulary of "empowerment," dialogue," and "voice" has entered the lexicon of Western social reform movements. At the same time, the principles of critical pedagogy have undergone significant modifications that adapt them to the needs of contemporary technocratic societies. In a world that is rapidly redefining relations between its centers and margins and questioning the legitimacy of master narratives, critical pedagogy's analytical strategies have been modified with theories of postmodernism, feminism, gay and lesbian studies, postcolonial theory, and youth culture.[30] In different ways each of these discourses has advanced the concepts of critical pedagogy by challenging it to be more self-reflexive and attentive to its own internal biases, hierarchies, and solipsisms.

Because critical pedagogy stresses the importance of human agency, it is sometimes faulted as a "motivational" practice that exaggerates the importance of education in political life. Its emphasis on subjective empowerment has been accused of romanticizing political struggle while doing little to alter power imbalances within school itself. These arguments have become particularly pointed in suggesting that, despite Freire's intentions, certain academic strands of his theories have broken loose from their practical origins and taken on lives of their own.[31] While such claims identify important issues in the inevitable institutionalization of knowledge, critical pedagogy has proven its continued significance. As it has evolved and changed in recent years, critical pedagogy has located itself in a dialectical relationship between such overdetermined influences as capitalism, sexism, racism, and homophobia and the subjective autonomy of the individual. This self-conscious repositioning of critical pedagogy in relation to other discourses has helped sustain its relevance for successive generations of educators. However, its identification with the critical tradition of the Western Enlightenment has led some analysts to question its universal application in all circumstances. This has led certain radical educators to abandon critical pedagogy in favor of approaches with more diverse origins.

The New Literacy Wars

Conservatives are rarely so divided in their cultural convictions. As liberals and leftists continue debating the perils of totalizing narratives, the right has been turning such retrograde ideology into best-selling literature. Witness the small fortune (estimated at $5 million to date) made by former Bush administration drug czar William J. Bennett with his anthology *The Book of Virtues: A Treasury of Great Moral Tales*.[32] With several million of those volumes in print, Bennett continues to promote the same cultural rhetoric he did as Reagan's Secretary of Education. To Bennett, "the greatest threat to the humanities lies within" American society—a threat to be eradicated by the "great books."[33] Bennett, whose platitudinous approach to education has gained astonishing publicity in the 1990s, is specifically concerned with the failure of non-reading parents to convey a proper interest in literature and culture to their children. Like a growing list of conservative ideologues, he prescribes a method of social reproduction in which parents concentrate on exposing their kids to the "best" of American thinking. Unfortunately, the question of cultural literacy is hardly that simple, for determinations of *what* should be read and by *whom* are bitterly disputed. To the extent that literacy determines one's role in society, one's relationship with language(s) can function as both social empowerment and ideological oppression.

But exactly what is behind all the recent fuss about reading? In many ways, the issue really isn't about illiteracy but about good old-fashioned social control. Although no one disputes the importance of communication skills, most recent literacy incentives cast negative implications on the nation's disadvantaged. For this reason we should question the attitudes of public policy makers who directly attribute social dilemmas to a lack of English competence. Although conservatives readily draw connections between illiteracy, unemployment, poor health, welfare dependency, and mental illness, the notion that illiteracy might result from economic inequities (rather than cause them) is rarely considered. Consequently, most government programs have difficulty attracting students.

A major factor in this dilemma is the low regard students hold for education in general. Recent statistics indicate that more than 4.3 million young people drop out of school each year, and that in major metropolitan areas like Los Angeles, Chicago, and New York the numbers can exceed thirty percent of those enrolled.[34] After years of negative experience with the system, young people come to view academic achievement and compliance with school regulations as socially repugnant. Students see schools as oppressive institutions that promise little in terms of genuine reward. One of the main planks of the conventional literacy programs is their focus on "proper" literature. Yet many students (regardless of ethnicity, nationality, or sexual orientation) find the works of Poe, Wordsworth, and Longfellow irrelevant. Young people are alienated by the disparity between the type of literacies sanctioned in school and the literacies they practice in their daily lives. Missing in most school curricula are notions of *active* writing, whereby individuals tell their own stories or explore community concerns. Experiences of popular culture or personal history are rarely given credence. Instead, normative standards of achievement are set forth, against which any inability to conform is equated with poor performance. This creates a chain of failure that brings students to blame themselves rather than question the system. The result is a situation in which students know full well that schools are racist, sexist, and generally unfair, yet they nevertheless fault their own lack of discipline, intelligence, or will. As a result, students are forever left with confused impressions of school failure.

The New Media Go to School

Media constitute an extremely effective means to link student experience to school curricula. But although television entered the classroom in the decade following World War II, critical viewing was the furthest thing from its proponents' minds. As the first wave of the baby boom hit the classroom in the 1950s, video became recognized as a means of increasing teacher productivity. By simply eliminating the need for duplicate presentations, video was credited with reductions in labor of up to seventy percent.[35] It was also recognized as a powerful tool for observation and evaluation.[36] Concurrent advances in computer and telecommunications industries prompted more elaborate speculation.

This idealistic vision of new technology fit perfectly into 1960s educational reformism, while also complimenting U.S. cultural policy. In a domestic atmosphere of desegregation, urban renewal, and other liberal initiatives, efforts were made to eliminate the biases inherent in standard pedagogies. As a means of de-emphasizing differences of race, gender, and class, theories of educational formalism were introduced into many schools to stress the structure of learning over culturally specific content. Educators uncritically seized upon photographic media as tools for directly engaging student experience. They developed concepts of "visual literacy" to compete with what some viewed as oppressive print-oriented paradigms.[37] As one educational textbook of the era explained, many students "demonstrate a lack of proficiency and lack of interest in reading and writing. Can we really expect proficiency when interest is absent? To what purpose do we force students through traditional subjects in traditional curricula?"[38] Within this movement, many teachers adapted photography and video equipment to their purposes.

Problems resulted from the inability of educators to reconcile their new methods with existing curricula. Meanwhile, with the economic downturns of the 1980s and the ascendancy of the Reagan/Bush government came sweeping indictments of liberal programs. Conservative reformers blamed schools for the nation's inability to produce competent workers and to compete in world markets. Because they often required expensive equipment, media programs were terminated in the name of cost reduction, as renewed emphasis was placed on a "back to basics" curriculum. This did not mean that television disappeared from the classroom, only that its more complicated, hands-on, applications were replaced by simple viewing.

The type of media that survived the reform movements of the early 1980s differed greatly from its utopian predecessors. Stripped of any remnant of formalist ideology, video was reduced to its utilitarian function as a labor-saving device. This redefinition of "television as teacher" paralleled distinct shifts in media production and distribution. These were outgrowths of large-scale changes in the film and television industry brought about by the emergence of affordable consumer video cassette equipment. For the viewer, home recording and tape rental allowed hitherto unknown control over what was watched. The same was true in the classroom. For the instructional media industry, the hitherto costly process of copying 16mm. films was quickly supplanted by inexpensive high speed video duplication. The entire concept of educational media products began to change, as films could be mass produced on a national scale (in effect "published") like books. Market expansion in this type of video was exponential. So profound was the technological change that 16mm. film processing labs from coast to coast went out of business over night.

Outside of school, this video proliferation yielded great benefits to consumers, along with the profiteering business interests who serve them. Beyond making available a wide variety of materials—from Hollywood movies to aerobics tapes—the VCR revolution has afforded viewers an unprecedented degree of autonomy. With the options of time shifting, editing, and even producing video tapes, the average television user has become significantly more involved in TV culture. The creative potentials of orchestrating video within family life, building tape collections, documenting important programs or personal activities are all active gestures of cultural production. They are practices that media educators can encourage as means of promoting citizen agency and voice.

Within the classroom there also has been a negative side to the VCR boom. Beyond obvious arguments that pit time efficiency against human interaction lie the more subtle issues of subjective address. Unlike home viewing which affords a degree of flexibility and choice, the use of educational media does indeed position students as passive receivers of information, while at the same time validating an intellectual process based on stereotyping.[39] This replicates the most conservative forms of transmission learning and teacher-centered pedagogy. Such an approach is typified in the flood of slickly produced and moralistic videos for the school market from such entities as the Children's Defense Fund, the Center for Humanities, and Guidance Associates, among others. These latter organizations offer an enormous range (the current Guidance Associates catalogue lists more than 500 filmstrips, slide series, and tapes) on topics from drug abuse to "values clarification," all stressing a prescriptive and normative ideology.

This marriage of normative content with authoritarian form stands in direct contrast to the principles of cultural democracy in that it couples a radical denial of difference with a suppression of dialogue. As the influence of Christian fundamentalists on government grows—especially at the local school board level—educational policy seems increasingly bent on merging the normative framework of the nuclear family with that of the nation.[40] Indeed, the correspondence between home and country as "domestic " regimes becomes literalized in the figure of the motherland: chaste, dutiful, and maternal.[41] Like other tropes of nationalism, this identity of woman-as-nation is determined as much by exclusion as inclusion. This nation is not the motherland of aggressive sexuality, homosexuality, or sex outside the legislated precincts of marriage.[42]

In some of the more extreme versions of this moral proselytizing, educational media producers construct a normative national subjectivity for young women based on fear and coercion.[43] One of the most insidious examples, by the Children's Defense Fund, evokes the dual specters of teen pregnancy and HIV contagion as consequences of sexual transgression. In such materials, both adolescent sexuality and homosexuality are equated (metaphorically or literally) with illness, humiliation, crime, poverty, or death—as in this excerpt from a Children's Defense Fund report: "Teen pregnancy affects everybody's family, community, neighborhood, and region. Like the prospect of nuclear war, illegal drugs, and Acquired Immune Deficiency Syndrome (AIDS) and other sexually transmitted diseases, teen pregnancy is becoming an equal opportunity threat."[44] Clearly, the intended reading of this message is one of intimidation. Since AIDS and teen pregnancy are presented as immoral sexual practices (homosexuality and sex between "children"), both are referenced in terms of "epidemics" or "crises" that threaten personal well-being and the social totality.[45] Clearly, such media materials do more than simply teach students about the consequences of unprotected sex. They constitute elements of a broader mechanism of social control in which young people are socialized into specific belief systems and institutionalized behaviors.

For both practical and political reasons, electronic media will continue to grow in school, in the workplace, and at home—with the proliferation of videocassette equipment, added cable channels, home shopping networks and computer information services, telecommunications link-ups, interactive texts and games. We should not delude ourselves that these new technologies by themselves have the capability of changing social relationships or economic structures. As quickly as a new gimmick is developed, Madison Avenue finds a way to turn a profit from it. Yet these new tools offer potential for innovative use and subversion, for the establishment of new forms of alliance, and for the creation of new strains of cultural production.

Reception and Identity

The key for an emancipatory use of media in the classroom lies in helping students to locate progressive readings of the materials offered. Particularly in settings with students from diverse backgrounds, it is important to stress that culture isn't limited to what is legitimated in books and other instructional materials. It is also "ordinary."[46] Culture is a sociological substance produced every day by each of us. This is especially true with everyday texts, and it is what makes a static view of national identity problematic. People's narrative relationships are constantly in flux—both those we find in books and the diverse narratives we encounter in such items as movies, television, clothing, appliances, food, and housing. Understandings of these texts are always partial and incomplete, always in need of some revision to adapt them to change and circumstance. As people continue to adjust and adapt their interpretations, they are making the meaning that is culture.

In radical circles of education, a growing body of literature has developed in recent decades to contest hierarchical models of schooling.[47] Partly informed by critical pedagogy and cultural studies, the new "media literacy" movement (as opposed to its older "market research" counterpart) is an amalgam of reader response theories and institutional analyses. While acknowledging the persuasive properties of images, practitioners of media literacy emphasize ways that viewers use media in individualized ways. Moreover, because moviegoers and television watchers can recognize the artifice of representation, they need not always be fooled by it. The concept of literacy is central in this pedagogy, as explained by Cary Bazalgette, "every medium can be thought of as a language. Every medium has its own way of organizing meaning, and we all learn to 'read' it, bringing our own understandings to it, and extending our own experience through it."[48]

In this sense, the media literacy movement holds political significance. Not only can it help viewers to "decode" complex sign systems, but it also can connect theory and practice—often by attempting to literally explain (or demonstrate) complex theories to young people. By doing this it diplomatically reconciles opposing concepts of the viewing subject. In textual terms, the media literacy movement argues that our abilities to mediate dominant readings and spectator positionings media can be improved with study and that these skills can be taught to children regardless of age or grade level. One can teach young people to use the media for their own ends by actively interpreting how it functions and choosing how to read it. Put another way, the movement proposes to begin identifying strategies for contextual reading, thereby suggesting changes to the "institutional structures" that condition spoken and interpretive norms.[49] This is done by encouraging viewers to look beyond specific texts by asking critical questions like "Who is communicating and why?," "How is it produced?," "Who receives it and what sense do they make of it?"

In an exercise conducted in Northern California by the Race, Representation, and Youth Project, students contrast media images of teenagers to those they produce themselves.[50] By making visual comparisons between "90210," "Fresh Prince," and themselves—teens are asked to ponder "which is real?" Of course, the answer is none, because depictions—private and public—are fictional. Through this exercise, youngsters begin to learn not only how they are interpellated by the forces of media mythmaking, but also the ways they have internalized normative narratives of race, nation, and sexuality. Again, the lesson is that children are not part of a unified "national family" but many different communities and affinity groups. By drawing attention to their own attitudinal biases and stereotypes the lesson underscores the relationship of self to image.

Media education can also interrogate the very concrete ways that television, radio, and movies structure audiences and their material surroundings. For example, the address of TV has evolved in part to cater to a domestic audience and to encourage certain patterns of television use within the home. It serves as breakfast entertainment, evening family ritual, or weekend sports gathering. These functions have influenced the layout and use of spaces within the home as well as appointments within individual rooms. Consequently, TV has both a direct and an indirect impact on a broad range of commodities—a point hardly lost on the merchandisers of goods ranging from popcorn poppers to easy chairs. John Fiske has written of the way people employ television to modulate the "texture" of living environments, which people create and alter as a means of laying claim to social space: "Television is used to increase, enrich and further densify the texture. It is typically left on all the time, adding color, sound and action to apartment life; it is used to frame and cause conversations, to fill gaps and silences. It can provide both a means of entering and intensifying this dense everyday culture and a way of escaping it."[51] Again, use becomes a matter of strategy and intent.

Regrettably, media literacy curricula are rarely so critically grounded. All too often in conventional pedagogies such emancipatory forms of media literacy are discounted as inconsequential, banal, or unhealthy. Offered instead is a program of viewer "empowerment," suggesting a free-market attitude of audience "choice" in which viewers become reconciled to the options available to them. This has been the rationale of numerous recent prescriptions from the mainstream educational establishment, as typified in both conservative and liberal "inoculation" approaches to media literacy that promote a single, "good," standard of visual literacy to which all Americans should subscribe. Again, the overall implication in this approach is the production of a national identity of verisimilitude, wherein all citizens share the same competencies, values, and rights.

Another cause for the paucity of media education on a national level results from the unwillingness or inability of many localities to integrate media into their curricula. In part this is due to the relative intransigence of North American education markets and to the economic difficulties many school districts face. Also, as an interdisciplinary field largely devoted to popular culture, media studies is often dismissed by school administrators as an educational frill. Such courses are vehemently opposed by "back to basics" advocates, who claim that they undermine traditional culture and values. (The difficulty, of course, is that the popular appeal of mass cultural texts comes largely from their *anti-educational* character.)

It hardly goes unnoticed that media courses are by definition student-centered and subversive in their critiques of capitalism and patriarchy. The result is a form of institutional control that limits the extent to which criticism can be raised or even discussed. When media literacy does find its way into the school curriculum it generally takes one of two forms: a form of vocational education, or an enhancement of an existing course in another discipline. As media education is introduced in a vocational context, it is generally driven by a job-preparation mandate lacking in any critical consciousness. This is not to deny the very real benefits that such a curriculum can offer in terms of skill development, role modelling, and collaborative practice. it is only to point out that most such models promote an unexamined image of commercial media and journalism. The media landscape usually is presented as an inherently even terrain, where choice is open and access unstymied. Little acknowledgment is given to the extremely unequal positions from which people enter this terrain, the continuing discriminations they suffer, and the power structures that benefit from these arrangements. Instead, these issues are smoothed over and ignored.

As enhancements to existing courses, studies of television, movies, or print media are most likely to be found in English, art, or social studies classes where textual reading and production already have a footing. Unfortunately, this atmosphere is often locked into canonical regimes that can stultify critical thinking. Speaking of media education in English classes, Len Masterman has suggested that "an emphasis upon links and parallels with literature and a reliance upon student response via the limited form of the literary review suggest that the realities of curricular life . . . may act as a brake upon achieving the fullest potentials for media education."[52] As media education has been constituted as an add-on to existing courses, it has been extremely limited in its ability to challenge forms of identity—national or otherwise—perpetuated in schools.

Teacher, Teach Thyself

Perhaps the most underacknolwedged impediment to the media literacy movement is in its focus on curricula rather than institutional infrastructure. One place to correct this is within schools of education, where teacher preparation continues to reproduce very traditional attitudes toward media. The introduction of media literacy into other courses need not rely on special texts or instructional materials. Like other critical pedagogies, it hinges more on the way a teacher handles existing materials. On a primary level, media education within a given curriculum entails a greater attention to photographs, films, or videos as producers of meaning. Although there is nothing new about this emphasis on media, the media literacy approach involves a greater emphasis on the way this meaning is made.

This entails abandoning assumptions that particular readings are self-evident or that the medium itself is a neutral carrier of information. Such views are rooted in the same subject/object dualisms that foster transmission theories of teaching. In contrast to these views, it needs to be pointed out that truth does not pass perfectly through a video to a student, nor knowledge through a teacher. Both require the engagement of students in receiving the messages and making sense of them. Therefore, beyond attention to course content and the forms of its delivery, emphasis needs to be placed on developing competencies of reception that permit students to make choices and exercise agency in learning.

In their recent book, *Unthinking Eurocentrism: Multiculturalism and the Media*, Ella Shohat and Robert Stam describe these competencies as a process of "reading from the margins."[53] Shohat and Stam explain that media literacy is not so much a matter of deciphering true or false messages, as it is an issue of understanding the discourses from whence messages emerge. For example:

> Within this perspective, it makes more sense to say of *The Gods Must be Crazy* (1984) not that it is untrue to "reality," but that it relays the colonialist discourse of official White South Africa. The racist discourse of the film posits a Manichean binarism contrasting happy and noble but impotent Bantustan "Bushmen," living in splendid isolation, with dangerous but incompetent mulatto-led revolutionaries. Yet the film camouflages its racism by a superficial critique of White technological civilization.[54]

This form of media education capitalizes on what students already know about the vocabulary and syntax of media, while encouraging them to become more critically conscious of "how they know what they know."[55] In history classes, this might involve a content analysis of the images in a textbook. What kind of people are pictured and in what numbers? Who seems to be in control? Similar questions can be asked in geography. In social studies, current events are often used as a springboard for discussion. But do newspapers and television report the facts with complete objectivity? What parts of the story have been highlighted or ignored? In an English class dealing with required texts, a teacher might spend time talking about the limits of specific genres, the economics of publishing, and the separation of "high" culture from the everyday.[56]

In each of these instances media literacy begins to ask students to question the way their identities have been shaped as subjects in the school, the neighborhood, the nation, and the world. The point is that whether or not viewers realize it (in fact because they often *don't* realize it), they are always being interpellated by the media into quite specific roles. Every movie, every textbook, and every magazine addresses an ideal audience that is most often defined in terms of a national collectivity. This interpellation is so ubiquitous that it seems nonexistent. It is simply assumed.

This national interpellation is more than the brazen chauvinism of Bruce Willis and Ralph Lauren. It exists in an advertising industry that pictures the world as its playground, a commercial ethos of economic dominance rather than cooperation, and now, a military attitude of complete global control rather than negotiation. Images aside, the question these attitudes leave begging concerns the future role of the United States in the world community. Indeed, what is the relevance of any national identity in a world of transnational capital? The combined effects of the free flow of information and the breakdown of national boundaries have caused changes in the centers as well as the margins of international culture. U.S. media products now reach larger audiences abroad than at home. For this reason, production companies (many of which are owned by foreign companies) now tailor programs for international audiences. Increasingly the choices offered to U.S. viewers are determined by audiences located elsewhere. As the United States loses strength as an economic power, the influence of external culture will continue to grow.

Democracy Beyond the Classroom

The development of critical pedagogy, media literacy, and other philosophies of radical education owes a great deal to the writings of Antonio Gramsci. Concerned with finding practical applications for Marxist theories, Gramsci saw social change as a process of learning in which ordinary people come to formulate a new social order. Like Dewey, Gramsci stressed the importance of what he termed "creative" knowledge in which "learning takes place especially through a spontaneous and continuous effort of the pupil, with the teacher only exercising a function of a friendly guide."[57] Like Freire, he believed that principles of revolution would emerge from the oppressed themselves. For Gramsci, "every relationship of 'hegemony' is necessarily an educational relationship."[58] In this context he was referring not simply to the forms of teaching that one commonly associates with the classroom. Gramsci was describing the profoundly political process through which citizens are socialized to recognize and validate state power. This process infuses all components of the social apparatus: the office, the church, the museum, and particularly the school. If we think of these institutions as sites of potential ideological persuasion, then Gramsci's theory of education becomes significant. Obviously we are nearly always in a process of learning.

This form of radical pedagogy has great significance as a democratizing practice. In contrast to the conservative impulse to remove ever-larger regions of experience from public discussion, a Gramscian pedagogy recognizes the implications of everyday events. This means admitting that many areas that claim neutrality in our lives are in fact sites of profound ideological struggle. Television newscasts, school curricula, computer programs, scientific breakthroughs, "great" works of literature—these are not "objective" phenomena that somehow exist outside the realm of ideology. They are forms of representation invested with specific interests in every manifestation. Through these texts, dominance strives to replicate itself, often disguising its actions in the process. As Russell Ferguson characterizes it, "the place from which power is exercised in often a hidden place. When we try to pin it down, the center is always somewhere else."[59] This invisibility of the center is often accompanied by a quiet exclusion of otherness. People may be concerned about the violent suppression of certain dissenting voices, yet at the same time they may be unaware of those consigned to the "structured absences" of discourse. As Edward Said has suggested, the process of "representing (and hence reducing) others, almost always involves violence of some sort to the subject of the representation."[60] This process occurs with subtlety. It is a common experience among readers to forget what lies outside a text. Readers may be aware of the violent suppression of certain dissenting voices, yet they often don't consider those consigned to the "structured absences" of discourse. In this sense, every act of writing, of film production, of curriculum design, of institutional organization is an act of inclusion and exclusion. Therefore these and other social forms must be continually scrutinized for what they represent.

Recognition of educational potentials outside the classroom has led many teachers to rethink their roles. This same impulse has also helped cultural workers in such "non-educational" sites as arts organizations, neighborhood centers, recreational facilities, hospitals, theaters, and jails to reconfigure their programs along more pedagogical lines. This type of institutional "border crossing" has been encouraged by interdisciplinary academic areas like ethnic studies, media studies, and cultural studies.[61] Equally significant has been the broad-based recognition that conventional methods for reaching students, clients, or audiences are no longer adequate. New methods and structures are needed that can combine scarce resources and forms of expertise in ways that overcome rigid protocols and conventional institutional designs.

The emphasis of radical educators on participation and dialogue has encouraged many to focus on issues of critical literacy as an important democratizing tool. Not only can interpretive strategies assist viewers in understanding potentially manipulative media messages, these tools can also enhance the pleasure of consuming media. By affording audiences a role in the communicative transaction, one does not deny the overwhelming influences public media command. Instead, this view suggests that viewers and consumers of culture have a stake in the process that can be enhanced through education.

Reasonable as it seems, these premises of critical literacy run counter to the common-sense thinking of many parents, politicians, and educators. Arguments generally fall into two equally deficient categories: the first negatively asserts that popular culture deceives and degrades the thinking of viewers; the second claims that media innocently reflect the actual wants and needs of audiences. The difficult idea for some is that both assertions may be true simultaneously. Communications technologies are as much *descriptive* as they are *prescriptive*, existing in a dialectical relationship with lived experience. Each informs and is informed by the other.

Beyond this, the study of popular culture(s) holds importance as a means of validating the relevance of different vocabularies, canons, aesthetic registers, discursive forms, and sites of cultural articulation. A democratic society is enhanced by pedagogies that encourage the production of diverse identities and knowledge forms, rather than restricting such possibilities. The concerns of such education is well summarized by Henry Giroux and Roger Simon:

> Do such practices open up new notions of identities and possibilities? What identities and possibilities are disorganized and excluded? How are such practices articulated with forms of knowledge and pleasure legitimated by dominant groups? What interests and investments are served by a particular set of popular cultural practices and critiqued and challenged by the existence of such? What are the moral and political commitments of such practices, and how are these related to one's own commitments as a teacher (and if there is a divergence, what does this imply)?[62]

Answering these questions involves finding the means to interrogate and revise textual and material codes. It means revealing the ways received meanings are bound in specific histories and modes of address (or use) that act as limits to human possibility. Thus, the pedagogical task is to demystify these codes in the interest of new *productive* capacities.

In this sense production by students or audiences refers to the creative development of meanings and interpretations. It evolves from the understanding of the mediated character of all representation and consequent ability of human agents to invent new or alternate readings. Such activity might range from benign arguments following a film over what it really "meant" to the elaborate fantasy rituals, social events, and even conventions attached to such television programs as *Melrose Place* or *VR5*.

This more active posture of reception implies that viewers, users, or purchasers of texts and objects need not accept the subject positions they have been assigned by an author or manufacturer. Audiences possess the capacity to exceed their purportedly passive roles, to subvert given interpellations, or create new subject positions. Ultimately this can be a point of initiation for citizens to develop their own stories, or dream their own dreams. No better example of this exists than the practice in rap and hip-hop composition of "sampling"—a process enabled by relatively inexpensive recording technology. Sampling entails the often repeated use of a segment from one recording in another. In this act of appropriation the original piece is both used and changed by virtue of its new context. The individual sampling is at once a listener and a creator of the music.

These productive capacities entail a critical engagement with market forces. In this sense human agents need to recognize both the extent and limits of choice in the selection of narratives and consumer goods. Obviously, one is always constrained by the range of texts, ingredients, and commodities that are available and affordable. Yet at the same time, within these parameters options exist with tactical applications. As Mica Nava argues, it is time to move beyond the reproductionist "consumer-as-victim" mentalities that characterized much early writing on advertising.[63] Such negative discourses range from overdetermined suggestions of "false consciousness" to psychological claims of "subliminal seduction." What needs to be stressed instead is the degree to which audiences are not always fooled by the media. People *do* exercise agency in the acquisition and use of products; consumer advocacy groups and product boycotts *have* had an impact on what gets shown on television and what ends up on store shelves.[64] The corporate production of texts and objects does not exert a total authority over buyers, but functions in a relationship of exchange.

These critical understandings enhance democracy in expanding people's ability to choose, not merely from an array of preselected goods, but from among options to reject, alter, or creatively use what they view or buy. Since reception and use are active gestures, educators need to recognize that the potential for productive culture inheres in the very fabric of life. Like talking, it lives in the ways people communicate to each other, in the objects they make, and in the stories they tell. It permeates the rituals of meeting, listening, dancing, joke telling, playing sports, and making pictures. Most importantly, it inheres in the ways that people make choices, invent their lives, and adapt to difficult circumstances. In this latter sense, culture is, as Paul Willis has stated, the very stuff of survival.[65] Such a broadened definition of education constitutes a means of encouraging people to assert more control over their lives. This pedagogy suggests that choices exist where none were seen and creativity is possible where none was expected. In this renewed source of agency the promise of democracy can be rekindled.

Learning Democracy

If radical educators are to expand the parameters of democratic possibility, how do they proceed without replicating the essentialized political norms they seek to dismantle? The nagging epistemological question in this program of critical dialogue and expanded pedagogy is that of *whose* agenda of emancipation is being administered to *whom*. The answer may lie in deferring overarching prescriptions in favor of multiple approaches. Here again, the model of the "un-generation" is useful in paradoxically pointing to an object that refuses to identify itself.

On one level, this means accepting that no single solution exists for all problems. Such an understanding has been discussed by Chelda Sandoval in relation to the work of third world feminists. Sandoval offers the term "differential consciousness" to indicate a means of political action within mainstream paradigms, when appropriate, but also exceeding those constraints when necessary.[66] She identifies five categories of opposition to explain this principle. The first four entail arguments for equal rights, the respect of cultural difference, the privileging of particular experience (elsewhere termed "standpoint epistemology"), and separatism. To these she adds the differential consciousness category, which allows strategic movement among the other categories. This model permits a provisional closure upon which to base arguments and actions, but doesn't lock activists into a single program.

Beyond such tactical arrangements, a further reconceptualization is needed of the parties involved. Such an initiative must combine a politics and an ethics of a sort not typically drawn upon by radical activists. These entail types of practice that eschew both foundational closure and free-floating relativism. Such seemingly paradoxical practices respect differences, oppose oppressions, and permit the contingencies of provisional spaces of experiment with new social forms. Given such a challenge, it is incumbent upon radical cultural workers to reassert their roles in civic life. This calls for new understandings of identity and new forums for civic dialogue.[68] As described by Chantal Mouffe:

> If the task of radical democracy is indeed to deepen the democratic revolution and to link together diverse democratic struggles, such a task requires the creation of new subject positions that would allow the common articulation, for example, of antiracism, antisexism, and anticaptialism. These struggles do not spontaneously converge, and in order to establish democratic equivalences, a new "common sense" is necessary, which would transform the identity of different groups so that the demands of each group could be articulated with those of others according to the principle of democratic equivalence.[68]

As Mouffe suggests, this will involve promoting notions of shared responsibility for community life, along with the belief that change is indeed possible.[69] This is a profoundly pedagogical endeavor in that it is an act of political education. Such a pedagogy convinces people that individual acts of citizenship (like voting) can make a difference—that they themselves can command the authority to make community decisions.

At the heart of the struggle must stand a set of competencies through which cultural activists can dismantle structures that dictate societal norms and limit what issues can be considered political. At the same time, it is necessary to connect a pair of concepts that liberalism and conservatism seem unable to reconcile: *difference* and *egalitarianism*. To both of those political camps, differing needs or interests are to be overcome or suppressed because they frustrate the will to systemization, standardization, and normalization.[70] Implicit in this view is a hierarchy of subject positions supporting an idealized "national" identity that is impossible for most citizens to attain. The ethos of this new mandarin class is discursively constructed in the texts of culture, high and low, to be sure. But it is also learned through the myriad of institutionalized roles and naturalized rituals through which human actors are cast as either winners or losers. Moreover, it is profoundly inscribed in the production, exchange, and consumption of commodities in daily routines of work and play, where personal achievement and accumulation are held above any collective interest. Here conservatives have done the most damage, with attitudes such as those espoused by Margaret Thatcher: "There is no such thing as society, only individual men and women and their families."[71]

Challenging this on a representational level will mean that radicals must reclaim many icons and rituals that mainstream politicians have appropriated. If deconstruction has demonstrated anything, it is that the meanings of cultural signs are unstable. After all, it was through the false recontextualization of Robert Mapplethorpe and Andres Serrano as negative symbols that the right succeeded in limiting artistic expression.[72] Cultural activists can work to unmask such methods of image manipulation, while at the same time forging a positive iconography. Yet in approaching this endeavor, care must be taken to avoid replicating universalizing models.

An important metaphor of this new iconography is democracy itself. Not the idealized democracy of unproblematic civic verisimilitude so favored by the corporate order, but instead a radical democracy defined by continual struggle, change, and critical revision. This is not to suggest a return to nostalgic origins, but to propose a democratic imaginary yet unrealized in human history. The task has both political and ethical dimensions. In political terms, the common short-coming of all hegemonic regimes (including utopian ones) is their implication of totalizing ideology or subjectivity. As discussed at the beginning of this chapter, this problem becomes particularly evident within conventional liberalism. Although frequently presented as a pathway to emancipation, the neo-liberal ethos of the Clinton administration perpetuates distinctions between historical subjects and objects: those who act and those who are acted upon. It seeks to make surface corrections to a structurally flawed system without interrogating its underlying inequities.[73] Regrettably, this is the pitfall of much avant-garde artistic and intellectual practice, which makes the additional mistake of claiming vanguardist wisdom only for its own members. Such condescending logic has also been attributed to the prescriptive exhortations of "empowerment" associated with certain forms of emancipatory pedagogy. In contrast, a radical democracy defines itself on all levels in pluralistic terms. There is no single set of attitudes or social group to which all others must conform, because an acknowledgment is made of the impossibility of any one perspective's satisfying diverse needs. Instead, the unifying ethos is one of decentered authority. Owing to this latter principle, such a political program resists the vacuous amoralities of relativism and unexamined pluralism. For obvious reasons, such a scheme seems dangerously unstable to many neoconservatives, who warn of the "threat" of uncontained difference.

This is where the ethical dimension of radical democracy comes in. Beyond establishing a utilitarian program based simply on what works, and beyond an aesthetic attachment to transcendental ideals, lies a commitment among the members of the democracy to their mutual project. To put these theories into practice, activists need to develop the mutually supportive character of their struggles. This presents a challenge to the cooperative tolerances and communicative capacities of the interests involved. Groups defined by gender, sexuality, ethnicity, nationality, or occupation need to recognize their imbrication in the social totality. To encourage a degree of coalescence, boundaries (and the hierarchies often implied) must be softened that separate groups via such distinctions as amateur/professional or mass/elite.

Here it is necessary to work toward a world view that is horizontal rather than vertical. To many observers the stage is already set for a wide-scale reorganization of old forms of authority and knowledge. The tendencies exhibited thus far for the increasing corporate consolidation of emergent information and communication technologies need not advance unimpeded. A critically motivated citizenry committed to the democratization of such technologies only needs to

act to reverse these regressive patterns. Certainly, much has been made in contemporary computer literature of the theoretical decentering made possible by
hypertext and intermedia.[74] George Landow, a prominent proponent of this
view, contends that this democratic shift of authority from national to more local
sources has a long and continuous history:

> The history of information technology from writing to hypertext reveals an
> increasing democratization or dissemination of power. Writing begins this
> process, for by exteriorizing memory it converts knowledge from the posses-
> sion of one to the possession of more than one. . . . The democratic thrust of
> information technologies derives from their diffusing information and the
> power that such diffusion can produce.[75]

In international terms, recent history has demonstrated through the reforms
of Eastern Europe the willingness of large numbers of people with different interests to coalesce around the issue of their common estrangement from power. The
popular revolutions in Poland, Romania, Czechoslovakia, East Germany, and the
Soviet Union have proven the ability of ordinary people to topple massive
bureaucracies without resorting to violence.

At home, the radical potentials suggested by the multivalent, hip-hop, baby-
buster generation of young people seems to suggest that such a revolution may
not be so unthinkable. Rather than a cause of uncertainty and anxiety, recent
changes in the national and geopolitical landscape can be viewed as an indication of new democratic possibilities. In this context, radical activists have their
jobs cut out for them in working to educate populations about new definitions of
citizenship and civic responsibility, as discussed by Stuart Hall and David Held:

> It seems to be the case that citizenship belongs exclusively to neither Right or
> Left, nor indeed to the middle-ground. Like all the key contested political con-
> cepts of our time, it can be appropriated within different political positions—
> as its recuperation by the New Right clearly shows. The concept can only mean
> something decisive for the Left if we are prepared to do some theoretical and
> political work around it, actively integrating it within a whole set of related
> political ideas.[76]

Ultimately then, the approach to democratic citizenship returns to the motivation and belief that change is indeed possible. Such a democracy achieves its
moral dimension in its demand for participation from all quarters and, by necessity, its resistance to racism, homophobia, commodification, sexism, and all
other forms of objectifying, colonizing, and dehumanizing behavior.

seven

From Victim Aesthetics
to Postmodern Citizenship

Within the United States, the relationship of individual to community has evolved in a particularly schizophrenic manner, as notions of success, accumulation, and liberty are conflated with themes of patriotism, philanthropy, and social justice. In 1995, this glorification of the personal took an especially vicious turn in the assaults on civil rights and affirmative action led by California governor Pete Wilson. In a callous bid for the presidency, Wilson decried as unfair any policy favoring "group membership" over "individual merit." In Wilson's argument, efforts to compensate the disadvantaged do little more than perpetuate a "victim" mentality that infantilizes those it seeks to assist. Couching these arguments in a phraseology critical of "collective" impulses, the governor constructed a mutually exclusive opposition between personal agency and egalitarian concern.

The idea seems to be catching on. Increasingly, politicians and media personalities are capitalizing on public anxiety by suggesting that egalitarian impulses have gone too far. In fact, a recent public opinion poll indicated that seventy-two percent of respondents valued personal freedom more than human equality. Everywhere one is surrounded by institutions that encourage citizens to assume roles of selfish individualism—from television programs valorizing wealth and success to religious tracts promising personal salvation.[1] The collapse of economies in Eastern Europe is characterized as a triumph for the American system, a mechanism promising all citizens the opportunity to rise above their neighbors. These antagonisms are heightened by the growing list of xenophobic media demagogues promoting hatred of immigrants, the poor, and other "groups."

In his book *In Defense of Elitism*, William A. Henry suggests that the egalitarian drive threatens to overwhelm what he terms the other prime social force: the desire to excel. As Henry puts it, we need to accept:

> The simple fact that some people are better than others—smarter, harder working, more learned, more productive, harder to replace. Some ideas are

better than others, some values more enduring, some works of art more universal. Some cultures, though we dare not say it, are more accomplished and therefore more worthy of study. Every corner of the human race may have something to contribute. That does not mean that all contributions are equal.[2]

As discussed throughout this book, traditional liberal and conservative politics do little to ameliorate these difficulties, despite claims to the contrary. In their normative appeals to an assimilated mainstream, party politics reduce the particularities of human difference or group membership to vast fields of left-wing or right-wing verisimilitude. The gulf between individuals and parties frustrates the will of people to self-identify as citizens—as active agents seeking rights, bearing responsibilities, and holding membership in political communities.

Needed are definitions of citizenship and structures of political identification that can account for the specificities of group identity, facilitate their articulation, and mobilize them politically. These needs can be met by alternative definitions of how citizenship is defined and where it is exercised. Postmodern theory, with its emphasis on decentered subjectivity and the dispersion of power throughout society, offers great promise in this regard. It enables a view of citizenship like that articulated by Chantal Mouffe:

> A common political identity of persons who might be engaged in many different purposive enterprises and with differing conceptions of the good, but who accept submission to rules prescribed by the *res publica* in seeking their satisfactions and performing their actions. What binds them together is a common recognition of a set of ethico-political values. In this case citizenship is not just one identity among others—as in liberalism—or the dominant identity that overrides all others—as in civic republicanism. It is an articulating principle that affects the different subject positions of the social agent.[3]

This is not to minimize the importance of existing identity-based movements that have done so much to advance democracy in the name of civil rights, environmentalism, peace, and justice. Certainly the very success of groups ranging from the National Organization of Women and the ACLU to the Nation of Islam and ACT-UP is indicated by the extent that reactionary efforts are mounting against them. I want to suggest that a key strategy for continuing this egalitarian work lies in extending the democratic impulses of identity-based movements into yet-unpoliticized areas of social life. This is why it is so crucial to develop more decentered sites of cultural articulation.

In what follows, I will first discuss some of the reactionary movements that stand in the way of this emancipatory project. Focusing on the victim metaphors so popular in the current media, I will review ways that cultural difference is cast as a political threat to foundational, modernist views of citizenship and the nation. This will be followed by a discussion of resistant practices developing in music, community cultural work, and media activism. Specific emphasis will be placed on the importance of encouraging "group" articulation in a radical democracy. Crucial to the development of new political spaces for dialogue and debate are new institutional sites. Such emerging commercial enterprises, non-profit groups, and social clubs are increasingly appearing in the cultural void that larger institutions leave unfilled. Eminently interdisciplinary in character, these new postmodern hybrid organizations offer great promise for the development of democratic activism.

The Empire Strikes Back

Perhaps the most dramatic indication of the anti-egalitarian character of current popular discourse lies in portrayals of difference and dissent. Within this atmosphere any manifestation of disagreement with "mainstream" opinion is cast as disruptive or anti-patriotic. One doesn't have to look far these days to find a television program or news report decrying the ethos of "victimization" that is purportedly spreading across the nation. The response among numerous politicians, media personalities, and more recently, art critics has been a backlash against what *Time* magazine critic Robert Hughes called "the culture of complaint."[4] According to Hughes, the United States is increasingly becoming a nation of crybabies, in which assertions of injustice have exceeded legitimate grievance. Although affirmative action may once have served a purpose, such practices are seen as reverse discrimination in a society where workplace inequity no longer exists.

Similar arguments inspired the Contract with America's assaults on public assistance, food stamps, and environmental regulations, to cite but a few examples. Within this logic all claims for the redistribution of resources or authority are cast as manipulations. As Hughes puts it, "complaint gives you power—even when it's only the power of emotional bribery, of creating previously unnoticed levels of social guilt."[5]

What is motivating this apparently popular set of attitudes? What is behind the new politics of victimization? One easy answer, of course, is misinformation—the argument that the wealthy and powerful are successfully promoting a set of false beliefs. But a deeper dynamic gives these ideas credibility—having to do with public anxiety, and civic alienation, that is driving people back into private domains of fear and self-absorption. Rather than succumbing to the argument that selfish conservatives are tricking the public, more complex issues of ideological reception need to be considered. Only by addressing both the misinformation and the social anxieties supporting the misinformation can the situation be understood—and possibly changed.

Today's public is confronted with profound contradictions in the mass media, which help perpetuate the reactionary attitudes. As representation of diverse populations appears to be increasing on television, in movies, and in art galleries—government statistics and news reports continue to document the increasing gap between rich and poor citizens, the continued erosion of civil rights protections, and the rise of extremist bigotry and violence. Put another way, the recognition by marketing executives that people of all sorts do indeed watch TV, eat hamburgers, and buy beer has not afforded consumers the power to do much more than spend money. Yet the impression that social inequities have already been addressed is something one encounters almost daily. After all, it's not an audience of rabid extremists that is buying CDs of the Eagles' recent song "Get Over It," which argues that people should stop complaining and shut up. The song's audience includes people of all ages, searching for a way to explain why the quality of life in the United States is declining for all but a few .

One frequently offered explanation for this decline is that the people who always were to blame for social problems—the newcomers, the poor, and the otherwise "different"— have been rewarded rather than punished. Instead of asking immigrants to learn English or AFDC recipients to work, the nation has coddled these social others by encouraging the very terms of their otherness. By not insisting on their assimilation into the great all-American project, public policy has encouraged a disruptive cultural difference.

This difference has resulted in what Hughes calls the "fraying of America"— a loss of common purpose, a decline of mutual respect, a failure of the very principles that hold democracy together. Indeed, to critics like Hughes this pollution of American values by the culturally different is so detrimental that it is even infecting people like him. As Hughes explains, "Since our new-found sensitivity decrees that only the victim shall be hero, the white American male starts bawling for victim status too. Hence the rise of cult therapies which teach that we are all victims of our parents."[6]

Besides its obvious deployment to discredit genuine hardship, the backlash against the disadvantaged is being used to explain—and often rationalize—a growing reactionary movement among the status quo to strike back. Such is the logic behind the increasingly mean-spirited rhetoric of media personalities and politicians from Bob Grant to Pat Buchanan—an attitude that reached its ultimate expression in the unrestrained violence of the film *Falling Down*.[7] This is how abstract attitudes of distrust and suspicion turn into prescriptions for real gay bashing, clinic bombing, and racial attacks.

This backlash is nowhere more pronounced than in current congressional efforts to slash welfare. Not that efforts to reduce public assistance are particularly new. Historically, political attitudes toward welfare have been shaped by tendencies to categorize the poor in two ways: as either culturally marginal or morally deficient. With the transition to industrial capitalism in the early nineteenth century, scientific theories based on then-fashionable principles of eugenics provided a logic for blaming the economically oppressed for their own hardship. Popularized by thinkers like Charles Darwin, these arguments find contemporary expression in claims made by Richard Herrnstein and Charles Murray in *The Bell Curve: Intellectual and Class Structure in American Life*.[8]

In the 1960s liberals developed alternative theories to this brand of biological determinism. In books like Michael Harrington's *The Other America* the poor were cast as existing outside the realm of mainstream culture and bound within an inescapable "culture of poverty." Rather than the consequence of genetic disposition, poverty was seen as a behavioral propensity for failure passed from parent to child. Unfortunately, this assessment still attributed the source of poverty to the poor themselves rather than external factors.

More significantly, all notions of agency were absent. The urban poor were seen as incapable of resisting the powerful forces of cultural impoverishment. The goal of the liberal change agent was to rescue the failing individual, with salvation only possible through outside assistance.[10] Although developed by liberals like Harrington, these ideas were easily coopted by the conservative establishment. To Edwin Banfield, the poor were unable to recognize future needs and defer gratification.[11] To George Gilder, the threat was promiscuous sexuality and a deteriorating family.[12]

One of the most common manifestations of these views has been the depiction of poverty as an illness. Early in this century, writers drew on the emerging terminology of germ theory and epidemiology, to speak of "infections," contagions," and "plague spots" within impoverished communities.[13] To Herbert Spencer, such sickness was a necessary part of social evolution when he wrote that "we cannot repress and gradually diminish this body of relatively worthless people without inflicting much pain. Evil has been done and the penalty must be paid. Cure can only come through affliction."[14] Similar metaphors persist in today's humanitarian literature.

These issues were most profoundly brought home in the coverage of 1992 urban violence in Los Angeles, which a sensation-hungry media quickly framed in terms of social pathology. Reports in *Time* and *Newsweek* characterized the events as an "epidemic" of irrationality in which "violence became contagious" as it spread from block to block. In addition to metaphors of physical disease, the riots were also cast in terms of mental illness, with references to the insanity, craziness, and most of all "wilding."[15] The willingness to accept this misinformation in the anti-victim backlash stems in part from the sense of alienation that many people have from public life and civic institutions. We have become a more private society, less held together by that middle ground of churches, unions, and social clubs—what was once called the "civil society"—between individuals and the state.

This sense of distance and powerlessness in the face of public institutions has made it easy to criticize big government and big business, while encouraging people to focus on more personal issues like home and family. Add to this the insecurity of more than a decade of economic decline, and the need develops for people to blame for life's hardships. This is how public assistance recipients receiving two percent of the federal budget are blamed for the nation's deficit— and immigration is depicted as the cause of all problems in California.

The right has capitalized on this resentment by encouraging the anger of citizens who believe they haven't been getting what they've worked so hard to achieve. Here a major difference emerges between the political approaches of the left and right. In its appeal to primarily white elements within the middle and upper classes, Republicans have encouraged people to act in their own interests to demand tax breaks and local control of government resources. Meanwhile, as Democrats appeal to the same electoral demographic, they often speak on behalf of populations largely excluded from their ranks. This is because traditional attitudes of liberal benevolence fail to address structural issues that lie at the heart of social inequity. As Marc Cooper recently put it:

> Nary a populist can be found on the left (save Ralph Nader and Jesse Jackson), as the Rev. Martin Luther King Jr.'s yearning for the "beloved community" has been supplanted by liberals calling for boot camps and public executions, and the Democrats in general deteriorate into the Republicans' caricature of a party of lobbyists and lawyers in tasseled loafers, it is the Christian right that has

best taken up the challenge to fill the growing emptiness in American life, to soothe the fears and uncertainties provoked by the global market.[16]

By continuing to speak on behalf of others, liberals often perpetuate images of powerlessness. This creates an atmosphere in which people like Newt Gingrich can assert that many liberal groups actually require images of helpless people to justify their continued existence. Until relatively recently, a similarly condescending approach to human suffering has motivated much socially concerned media and artistic production.[17] Regrettably, this is part of what has opened these fields to charges that they promote a dogmatic political correctness. By speaking on behalf of the socially marginal in the interest of eliciting sympathy, many media producers in the 1970s and 1980s further rationalized the inevitability of failure.[18]

Although these practices are changing somewhat, the continued presence of such imagery in the art world has generated a parallel anti-realist, anti-political backlash—as audiences are increasingly irritated (or in some cases bored) by the display of human misfortune an aesthetic commodity. Documentaries of poverty like *American Refugees* by long-time homeless advocate Jim Hubbard are often targeted by this backlash, although similar assaults are made against works conveying political content, addressing sexual orientation, or practically any work produced by a person of color.[19] *American Refugees* argues that society permits people to become homeless because it fails to recognize their essential humanity. The collection depicts individuals and families in a variety of distressed circumstances: huddling over subway grates, standing in bread lines, being evicted from apartments. The selection of images is clearly intended to dramatize the exceptional character of these hardships. Hubbard suggests that "as you look at these photographs, I urge you to see similarities between you and the people shown here. These people are our neighbors. They are us."[20] But this plea is as far as Hubbard goes in making the connection. No real explanation is ever offered as to how these people arrived in their circumstances. There is no reason for a viewer to believe that "they are us."

Despite its intended purpose, documentary work that fetishizes difference in this way succeeds only in heightening the sense of distance between viewers and those viewed. As Martha Rosler put it, "documentary is a little like horror movies, putting a face on fear and transforming threat into fantasy, into imagery. One can handle imagery by leaving it behind. (It is them, not us.)"[21]

This is not at all to suggest, as certain critics have done, that social issues have no role in art or entertainment. It is only to say that important questions need to be asked about who is being represented, by whom, to what audience, in what context, and for what purpose. Certainly recent projects such as those organized by choreographer Bill T. Jones change these dynamics in important ways. For the last several years Jones has preceded his productions with workshops that enable audiences to join in the performances or to contribute narrative components. In addition to giving voice to local communities, such arrangements unseat traditional views of art works as events detached from those they speak about or speak to.

This is exactly what the prompted the assault by *New Yorker* Dance critic Arlene Croce against Jones's "Still Here," and the subsequent avalanche of letters and news coverage.[22] Because Jones's performance incorporated taped commentary and images of "real" people with HIV and AIDS, Croce argued that Jones had placed himself "beyond the reach of criticism."[23] She explained that "these are the prime exhibits of a director-choreographer who has crossed the line between theater and reality-who thinks that victimhood in and of itself is sufficient to the creation of an art spectacle . . . I can't review someone I feel sorry for or hopeless about."[24]

Although Croce's argument purportedly addresses an overly literal form of testimony, what it really boils down to is one of control—of deciding who does the speaking and what gets spoken about. In Croce's lexicon the term "victim art" is little more than a code word for the increasing presence of so-called "others" currently infiltrating the refuge of the dance studio. That the artist Croce chooses to assault is a gay person of color with HIV is hardly a coincidence in this case, for as Croce puts it "dissed blacks, abused women, and disenfranchised homosexuals" are reducing aesthetic quality to emotional blackmail.[25]

Attitudes like Croce's have two important consequences. On one hand they precludes disenfranchised communities from speaking for themselves. On the other they have mitigated against the engagement of audiences as active agents. This condescending view toward both publics has a historical legacy dating to the European avant-garde of early 1900s. This unfortunate tradition lives on in much of what is generated by cultural producers today. Of course, this recognition of liberal elitism is nothing new. Besides a favorite topic on talk radio programs, it's been a major issue in theoretical circles for several decades. The question is what to do about it. To a growing number of thinkers the answer lies in changing attitudes toward audiences to give them a little more credit as critical thinkers.

Certainly this lesson has not been lost on conservatives. Perhaps the most powerful weapon used in the recent congressional upset was the motivation of personal autonomy—the great social impulse to excel. The massive anti-incumbency, anti-government movement linked a sense of civic alienation to a powerful encouragement of self interest in such forms as tax relief and government decentralization. Cultural activists need to develop ways to encourage a sense of agency that do not succumb to the regressive side of this impulse. Fortunately, the appeal to self-interest is quite compatible with a radical democratic emphasis on decentralized politics.

Cultural Insurgency

In his book *The Revolt of the Elites and the Betrayal of Democracy,* Christopher Lasch discusses the decline of citizenship and the collective engagement so necessary to participatory politics. Lasch writes that "self-governing communities, not individuals, are the basic units of democratic society . . . It is the decline of those communities, more than anything else, that calls the future of democracy into question. Suburban shopping malls are no substitute for neighborhoods."[26] Lacking these intermediate structures of what some call the "civil society," a vast gulf develops between individuals and the large apparati that inform and govern their lives. As a consequence, people begin to feel powerless in the face of what is perceived to be an insurmountable edifice. Corporate maneuvers to remove matters of civic concern from public discourse further contribute to the perception that individual voices can do little to alter the course of current events. Add to this the devaluation of everyday experience, the delegitimization of human difference, and the message is complete: conformity is inevitable, dissent unthinkable, and resistance impossible.

At the same time, certain productive impulses emerge from this frustration with totalizing structures of authority. As corporate and government bureaucracies promote master narratives of submission and consent, the inadequacies of the these norms increasingly becomes apparent. For every scene of flag-waving jubilation, for every Pepsi-commercial vision of consumer ecstasy, there exists an opposite scene of lived discrimination and suffering. With each passing year, the distance between the dream and the reality widens. In the United States the number of children living in poverty grew by 2.2 million during the decade of the 1980s. Infant mortality rose to 9.8 per one thousand babies—a rate below that of sixteen other countries. Meanwhile, from 1965 to 1990, the income of African-American families fell by fifty percent, as black youth unemployment rose 400 percent.[27] To the objects of these economic conditions, being a victim is less a state of mind that a fact of daily life. As the number of people living out-side the dream grows, so does resistance to it. Is it any wonder that young people are dropping out of mainstream society and that urban poor seek solutions out-side the law? The task ahead is to organize that resistance and channel it into productive political energy.

The potential for such work is not hard to locate. On one level, the remark-able energy manifest in contemporary youth culture and music bespeaks a desire to explode the repressive myths of the monoculture on many fronts. This youthful expression is but one indication of the power of "voice" that historically has held great importance in the emancipation of oppressed groups of all ages. On another level, if one looks to the emerging cultural production of groups outside the so-called "mainstream" one finds a virtual explosion of activity in recent years. In part, this can be attributed to changing demographics. Some estimates suggest that by the year 2000 there will be no white majority in many parts of this coun-try. "We are the next chapter in the story of the Americas," declared Henry Cisneros, then-mayor of San Antonio.[28] Despite the economic ravages of the 1980s, artists and musicians from communities of color have made significant advances in cultural production. Similar steps forward are evident in the growing number of lesbian and gay writers, artists, performance groups, and film festivals. This is not to claim that oppositional thinking emerges unproblematically or consistently from oppressed groups. To assume so would be to attribute political attitudes exclusively to social location, thus promoting essentialized views of human agency. In this regard, it is also important to acknowledge that anti-egali-tarian relations harm the privileged also, and that groups with social advantage can similarly formulate radical correctives.

Arguably the most accessible medium for many people is popular music. Yet is it possible for popular music to help locate the ground for fresh articula-tions of citizenship? Although now competing with the televisual offerings of MTV and VH-1 (and to some extent telecommunication networks on the Internet), the recording and radio industries remain significant purveyors of an insurgent (albeit often unfocused) political consciousness. The history of rock and roll in the postwar period bespeaks a range of youth-oriented, technologically determined, and economically mediated styles and messages. Itself a synthesis of prior, primarily African-American, musical movements, rock embodies a mutable ensemble of resistant forms, which enabled its evolution from the 1950s through the 1980s. Ironically, despite its inherent iconoclasm rock often has functioned as a conservative medium: reinforcing market hierarchies and values of con-sumption, reproducing racial and sexual stereotypes, containing subversion in an ethos of escapism and self-destruction. This has led some critics to begin fore-casting "the death of rock."[29]

The argument is hardly that simple, of course. Like most cultural forms, music is capable of delivering an array of complex and often contradictory mes-sages. Rock is no exception. Just as it has served conservative interests, rock has also presented pointed critiques of economic exploitation, human oppression, and powerlessness. This is certainly most pronounced with its integration of tra-ditional folk styles to lend an aura of authenticity to the music's "message." Popularized by left-leaning entertainers in the 1960s and 1970s, this style of performing exploited the anti-technological and "natural" ethos of agrarian pop-ulism. The work of quintessential folk-auteurist Bob Dylan emphasized the importance of lyrical text over musical accompaniment or even the performer's vocal capacities. In its extreme forms, this cerebral emphasis on the spoken mes-sage mitigated against the more visceral experience of rock. Arguably, such an "anti-musical" approach was little more than a device used by groups prior and since to suggest a distancing from artifice and thereby imply homespun honesty or independent truth. Rhetorical strategies aside, this work proved enormously effective in communicating certain anthems of political concern. Still, its one-directional address replicated many of the alienating positions of passive audi-ence reception discussed in chapter 3.

This is not to suggest that spoken or written text is necessarily the preferred vehicle for democratic activism. In addition to matters of content lie the forms such messages take, for such forms mirror their enabling social relations. The development of the novel in the eighteenth century can be attributed to such fac-tors as the expansion of a literate middle class, new technologies of publishing, and a growing preoccupation with individualized narratives. Similar analyses have been written about phenomena ranging from the comic book to the video game. In this sense, cultural forms and messages constitute more than mere aes-thetic elaborations of social conditions. They are part of what enables and per-petuates those conditions.

Musicians and writers have frequently asked themselves whether these dynamics of cultural production can work in reverse. Might radical form provide the impetus for social revolution? Such radical formalist thinking achieved a remarkable sophistication between the first and second world wars in the work of the Eastern European avant-gardists. In this school of thought, art works were fashioned to intentionally draw attention to their means of production. Self-ref-erences to technical contrivances, optical systems, or artistic processes would be used to demystify the art object, undercutting its aura of fetishized value by "lay-ing bare the apparatus."

More to the point, in the works of performers and artists like Bertolt Brecht, Alexander Rodchenko, and Dziga Vertov lay a belief in the possibility of radical practice linked by necessity to the activation of a radicalized spectator.[30] Apprehension of the work required an alternative way of perceiving, a revolutionary paradigm brought about through the experience of the cultural work. The point of all of this was that content alone was insufficient in the conception of a radical vision. New containers, new structures, were required for the new messages of political reorganization. Much of this type of modernist thinking has been rejected in recent years as naive or romantically utopian. Yet one need only examine the reified formats of television soap operas, sit coms, indeed MTV, to confirm the determinative influence of form. Not only does the immediate instrumentality of form exert an influence (as in a thirty second spot), but it also creates a range of overdetermined viewer expectations. Raymond Williams dealt extensively with the importance of the social relations in which communication operates. The formats of television programs and music CDs both reflect and create a range of behaviors and attitudes that encourage audiences to act and think in particular ways. In his well-known analysis of television, Williams pointed out how the continuous sequence of entertainment programs, news, and commercials obliges viewers to concentrate on an entire "flow" of material rather than discrete shows. Implicit in this observation were the political potentials of making interventions at the level of cultural form. "These are the contemporary tools of the long revolution," Williams stated.[31]

This directly translates into the way contemporary cultural genres like hip hop, grunge, and even techno pop have been credited by many with more progressive capacities. As opposed to the political use of music for crude party cheerleading (as in Bill Clinton's use of Fleetwood Mac following his 1992 nomination address), music can also serve as a vehicle to amplify protest and consolidate community on deeper levels. In this sense, music can define alternative frames of reference for political thinking linked to new ways of articulating the body and means of experiencing the world. In offering listeners the opportunity to join in the performance by dancing, singing along, or participating in other ways, the distance between performer and audience is diminished—along with the passivity implied. In this respect, it might indeed be speculated that part of the excitement of live concerts lies the audience's perception of belonging to a group that actively creates meaning through collaboration with those on stage.

Beyond these types of audience participation and shareholding in meaning lie more direct forms of production that might be linked to forms of citizenship. The impulse of young people to organize street corner ensembles or garage bands has a very long history, which varies according to contexts of time, place, and social circumstance. As discussed by Tricia Rose, youth culture is hardly a homogeneous or static category, especially as it has been fragmented in the postmodern era of the 1990s. Rose's recent work has emphasized the importance of locating hip-hop culture within the broader framework of the postindustrial urban Afro-diaspora.[32] To Rose, the specific forms of hip-hop culture—graffiti, breakdancing, and rap music—constitute a direct response to constraints placed upon a particular community and the communicative strategies that arise as a consequence.

> Hip-hop replicates and reimagines the experiences of urban life and symbolically appropriates urban space through sampling, attitude, dance, style and sound effects. Talk of subway dress and posses, urban noise, economic stagnation, static and crossed signals leap out of hip-hop lyrics, sounds and themes. Graffiti artists spray-painted murals and name "tags" on trains, trucks and playgrounds. Early breakdancers' elaborate, technologically inspired, street-corner dances, involving head spins on concrete sidewalks, made the streets theater-friendly, and turned them into make-shift youth centers.[33]

The connection is frequently made between the way graffiti production and the act of sampling represent a disregard for conventional rules of property. One involves a physical reclamation of space; the other a flouting of copyright laws. In both instances producers use materials at hand to speak to their communities, often in quite powerful ways. It's not a coincidence that both of these expressive forms have been equated with criminality by law enforcement officials and civic authorities.

For often-unexamined reasons, conservatives and liberals alike take the issue of culture very seriously when it comes to hip hop. Increasingly, public concern has shifted from issue of flag burning and artistic obscenity to rap performers like 2-Live Crew, Da Lench Mob, KRS-1, and Snoop Doggy Dogg. Racially loaded arguments encourage the association of hip-hop nationalism with a plethora of ills, including crime, urban decay, drug and alcohol abuse, welfare dependency, and illiteracy. These abstract attitudes have very concrete consequences. The release of Ice-T's "Cop Killer" resulted in police seizures and record store closures in many states; the NWA (Niggaz With Attitude) album *Straight Out of Compton,* with its controversial single "Fuck the Police," became the subject of an FBI complaint to NWA's record company. Ignoring decades of televisual violence and musical misogyny by performers of all colors, attention focuses on the presumably inverted role modelling of "hard-core" and gansta rappers.[34]

Elsewhere, the mainstream press delegitimated hip-hop music and visual culture, identifying such forms as deviant or incompetent. When critics aren't calling for the containment of rap via censorship, labelling, or other regulatory means, the material is often assailed on aesthetic grounds as atonal "noise" or "anti-music." In the analysis of Houston Baker, this typifies the response of some citizens to what they perceive as a "sonic other." This argument partly can be rationalized as a generational distancing from youth culture. Yet to Baker such attitudes are more than generational; they are also "urbanely proprietorial. Who owns the public space? What constitutes information and what constitutes noise? Just what is visually and audibly pure and what precisely is noise pollution or graffiti?"[35]

These comments suggest that hip-hop culture is becoming increasingly politicized from outside itself in the way it motivates discussion about rights and responsibility in public discourse and physical space. Such issues get more pointed when the topic turns to graffiti—as the primarily white journalistic establishment degrades its expressive potential as mere vandalism. In one of corporate capitalism's ironic inconsistencies, rap music is insulated from its critics by the profit motive of the recording industry. The same cannot be said of graffiti artists. Aside from the brief cachet afforded to token artists like Jean Michael Basquait in the 1980s, such graffiti artists and "taggers" are more usually the subject of court dockets than art reviews.

In Philadelphia, where the incidence of tagging has been a continual source of distress for city officials, a novel program has been developed. The Anti-Graffiti Network, as it is called, takes a novel approach to the suppression of the voices of insurgent postmodern citizens. The effort is a collaboration of local business owners, city government, and the Philadelphia Police Department in which apprehended taggers receive an unusual form of punishment. Rather than going to jail or paying fines, the "misguided youngsters with paint" (as they are termed by the program) are sentenced to cover over graffiti spots with upbeat, socially palatable murals. In its initial stages the program limited such depiction to subjects like the Statue of Liberty, flags, or professional sports figures.[36] A more recent work featured a portrait of Malcolm X. The costs of each mural, which range from $5,000 to $10,000, are underwritten by local commercial groups and civic organizations. In addition to the mural program, the Anti-Graffiti Network also offers weekend workshops sponsored in collaboration with the Philadelphia Museum of Art, thus attaching itself to the cachet of the city's most respected cultural institution. So far, the program has received widespread praise and news coverage as a national model.

The Anti-Graffiti Network is clearly more than civic beautification program. It makes a symbolic statement about the appropriate subject matter and institutional sanctioning of public expression. Lois Nesbitt discusses the program as setting itself up as an:

> Arbiter of good and bad, legitimate and deviant, orderly (controlled, coercive) and spontaneous (anarchic, threatening) public art. Its choice of subjects for the murals reflects a desire to replace individual expression of such unmanageable emotions as pain and rage with cheerful symbols of "true" American values themselves problematic (liberty for whom?) of being questioned by the very subgroups the network hopes to help/rehabilitate.[37]

Unlike the anti-graffiti programs of cities like New York or Boston, which attempt to discourage tagging with increased police patrols or paint-resistant subway cars, the Philadelphia project replaces one form of expression with another. To Nesbitt, this constitutes a profound reversal of art's critical function to question the status quo. "Every scrawl or graffiti is a gesture of defiance against a social system in which people must fight for survival. . . . The Statue of Liberty has little to say to teenagers trapped from birth on the bottom of the social heap."[38] In this manner, the Anti-Graffiti Network reproduces the more socially palatable forms of censorship of the marketplace. Rather than directly silencing producers, it legitimizes one form of speech over another.

In many instances, nascent cultural producers are reaching for new technological tools to overcome expressive roadblocks. Both the style and volume of contemporary graffiti is enabled by advances in spray paint delivery systems that enable quick and inexpensive painting. But nowhere is the influence of technology more evident in hip-hop culture than in music. In hip-culture this process is enhanced by a unique confluence of changes in technology and market organization. Relatively recent advances in digital equipment have made sophisticated duplication and mixing techniques, once limited to recoding studios, available for consumer purchase. This has encouraged the development of new forms of collaged sound works incorporating fragments of music from other recordings. The ability to draw upon some of the newest electronic, digital, and computer technologies emerged within a population of young people consigned to impoverished vocational high schools. As budget cuts in public school music programs diminished the availability of conventional musical instruments, students found themselves increasingly obliged to turn to recordings for musical study and expression.

But this facility for high-tech wizardry indicates more than mere virtuosity with equipment. It is also a metaphoric component of a particular collective imaginary in which artifice and technology constitute ways of overcoming the oppressions of an order that presents itself as "natural." Mechanized styles of cyborg-like dance provide the means for people to exercise new identities through performance. In a society in which racism, sexism, and homophobia continue to limit and control the lives of so many, this technological mimicry offers a means of imaging new possibilities through the body itself. Judith Butler has discussed this use of the body as signifier, and is worth quoting at length:

> Acts, gestures, and desire produce the effect of an internal core or substance, but produce this *on the surface* of the body, through the play of signifying absences that suggest, but never reveal, the organizing principle of identity as a cause. Such acts, gestures, enactments, generally construed are *performative* in the sense that the essence or identity that they otherwise purport to express are *fabrications* manufactured and sustained through corporeal signs and other discursive means.[39]

Hence, dance routines develop in which participants assume robot-like "transformer" postures or "running man" syncopation. Young people with large car speakers and "boom boxes" accentuate the bass beats of music to transform and exert control over the environment they inhabit. The names of hip-hop DJs and musical personalities often reflect this fascination with technology and control: Sir Mix-A-Lot, Terminator X Assault Technician, DJ Cut Creator, Grand Master Flash.[40]

Postmodern Citizenship

Cultural production and civic identity do not emerge from a vacuum. These insurgent subjectivities are enabled by changing political spaces—of both metaphoric and material varieties. In a literal sense, such spaces have been made possible by the development of community organizations that provide a formal basis for expressions of citizenship. Yet the question remains—how political are these groups, really? Often lacking the kinds of government support available in the 1970s and 1980s, these entities devise ways to define themselves in the gaps left by larger structures. Bridging old divisions between social work, culture, education, and entertainment, these new postmodern community organizations both articulate and answer the needs of a citizenry unserved by prior models. These hybrids may yield the sort of political spaces that a radical democracy requires.

Enabling the growth of hip hop and other insurgent cultural forms have been hybrid institutional relationships brought about by a postmodern decentering and mixing in the commercial and non-profit sectors. In the profitmaking arena, new information technologies and delivery mechanisms have enabled the growth of "niche marketing," which enables manufacturers to target ever more narrow segments of the market. This has obvious benefits for groups excluded from the homogenized culture of mainstream media. As Nancy Hicks Maynard points out, "for American minority groups, the rising importance of niche markets is partly the result of mass media's failure to capture the essence of their lives and partly the result of technological possibilities. . . . As the ability to reach discrete communities skyrockets, the mass audiences scatter."[41] Maynard, a newspaper publisher in Oakland, California, cites the massive growth of specialized communications as evidence of this business trend. She documents the rise of African-American, Asian-American, and Latino-oriented newspapers in major cities, and the growing ownership of broadcast properties and cable franchises by people of color. Beyond this lie the opportunities for group-specific production in cyberspace, as evidenced in the emergence of such on-line services as the African American Information Network, Asian Pan American Resource Net, LatinoNet, and Net Noir.

Again the music industry is particularly revelatory in analyzing this phenomenon. In recent years, the dominance of the recording industry by a handful of specialized companies based in North America has given way to a new brand of multinational leisure and entertainment corporations like Warner, Sony, and Geffen. As in the motion picture business, this post-Fordist shift to transnational ownership and control has been paralleled by a decentralization of production and marketing into smaller, more "flexible" units. Former hostilities to "independent" recording companies (such as Harriet in Cambridge, Mass. and Kill Rock Stars in Olympia, Wash.) has diminished in favor of more narrowly segmented entrepreneurship. Although the industry continues to be controlled by a tiny oligarchy of corporate interests, the multinationals have come to recognize the business potential of using independent companies as a "farm league" to incubate and test potentially lucrative performers. This phenomenon was most widely evident in the meteoric eighteen-month rise (to many fans a sellout) of Seattle-based Nirvana from grunge obscurity to platinum stardom following its signing with Geffen.

Although this openness to obscure artists results from the desire to continually segment existing markets and define new product lines, it also creates new openings for cultural activism and democratic possibility. Contrary to the ideological proselytizing of both left and right, the entertainment industry is driven less by liberal or conservative ideology than it is by the hunger for continual profits. What gets produced is what will sell, regardless of the message. This attitudinal shift has hardly gone unnoticed among the more politically savvy producers of the hip-hop movement. For many, songwriting and-performing have become active efforts to exploit postmodern technologies and corporate structures to forge a new black nationalism. Rapper Chuck D has repeatedly asserted the strategic importance of exploiting corporate structures to promote solidarity within the black community. He explains that "rap is black America's TV station. It gives a whole perspective of what exists and what black life is about. And black life doesn't get the whole spectrum of information through anything else."[422]

Although the sincerity of such claims has been questioned both inside and outside the rap community, the issues D raises are significant. As suggested by Pharoahe Monch of Organized Konfusion in a recent editorial in *The Source*, "as it stands now, our industry does not reward intellect over ignorance, especially when the negative influences are a billion dollar commodity. The youth have to reach out for more and demand better from life and art. If we don't our culture will implode—growing smaller until we ultimately cease to exist."[43] The very mutability of cultural signifiers allows a CD or film to convey multiple and often contradictory meanings. The lyrics of a song can be both oppressive and emancipatory, depending on who is listening, at what moment, and in what setting. Just as new spaces of expression are opening up within the entertainment industry for formerly excluded groups, new understandings are developing about the indeterminacy of speech acts. Just as radical messages can be delivered directly, they can be appropriated, commodified, exaggerated, misunderstood, or forgotten.

Along with this decentering of production and destabilizing of meaning has been the emergence of new mixtures of institutional forms. Borders have softened between formerly separate communities and groups. Novel hybrid strains of organization have developed as commercial and non-commercial interests have formed partnerships and as single-purpose community institutions have diversified their programs. This has allowed people to assemble in new kinds of social, cultural, and political relationships—in effect forming new micro-communities and coalitions.

Many local communities in the United States are responding to the generalized depletion of social service monies by forging new collaborations across formerly rigid institutional boundaries. In many states, schools have joined forces with welfare, mental health, medical, legal, and day care facilities to provide comprehensive means of assisting students with difficulties in attending high school. These so-called "Classroom of the Future" projects developed from the recognition that the fragmented structure of social services is extremely difficult for young people to comprehend and engage. Beyond this practical rationale lies the fact, unacknowledged by many educational reformers, that performance in school is often linked to issues outside the classroom involving physical or emotional well-being and factors in a student's home and social environments.

Another novel instance of such institutional border crossing is the partnership forged between radio station KMEL and the San Francisco's Omega Boy's Club through the program "Street Soldiers." The impetus for the project came from rap performer Hammer, who convinced the station to develop a program where young people could discuss urban violence. Enlisting the participation of popular high school teachers Joseph Marshall and Margaret Norris, the station embarked on the unlikely mission of producing a call-in program for active gang members. But unlike similar shows in which callers simply provide conversational fodder, "Street Soldiers" made significant departures in both programming format and function. These innovations made the program a remarkable success.

Every Monday night from 10 p.m. till 2 a.m., the program is broadcast over KMEL, which is San Francisco's number one music station. Part of the novelty of "Street Soldiers" lies in the way it foregrounds the primacy of the caller's experience. On a typical Monday night, a fifteen-year-old named Eric phoned to say "Last Friday night I lost my brother. He was shot in a fight." Eric explains that he subsequently took his own gun to revenge his brother's death, but upon finding the killer he reconsidered. "I thought about what you said on the show and I put my gun away." The commentary from Marshall and Norris is probing and supportive—asking the young man how he felt—while reinforcing his decision to walk away from another killing. Eric is then told that he will receive a phone call later that night from "Little Monster," a former gang member who has become a frequent caller to the show. Marshall and Norris then invite Eric to attend a meeting that week at the Omega Boys Club to discuss the incident in more detail.

At the club, participants are able both to share their experiences and develop a sense of expertise in such issues. In this way, the young people like Eric are drawn into a network of peer co-counseling and community support, which can play an important role in restoring a lost sense of agency and control. As discussed by Ken Alutta, "the notion of family is at the core of the club," where young people are befriended and given academic or employment training.[44] Some even receive college scholarships from Omega. Marshall suggests that many of the young people who call or listen to the program "feel orphaned by all institutions—their families, their communities, the government, the media."[45] Rather than looking to gang membership for a sense of belonging, the youth find can support in the unique collaboration offered by the KMEL and the Omega Boys Club.

In these ways, "Street Soldiers" is providing a novel location for many of the impulses associated with citizenship. Moreover, the success of "Street Soldiers" has been nothing short of phenomenal. Since its first program in 1993, the program has garnered a local audience approaching 200,000 listeners. Media coverage of the program has appeared on every network news program, MTV, PBS, and numerous magazine and newspaper accounts. In recognition of the show's accomplishments, Marshall recently received an achievement award from *Ebony Magazine* and the Children's Defense Fund—as well as a "genius" grant from the MacArthur Foundation. Similar programs based on the "Street Soldiers" model are planned in New York, Los Angeles, and other cities.

This type of institutional border crossing is not exactly a new idea. Certainly within the United States the idea of multipurpose community cultural centers can be traced to the emergence of charitable organization societies and settlement houses at the end of the nineteenth century. Privately funded forerunners to the contemporary public welfare system, these entities experimented with ways to combine educational and social services for the urban poor. Settlement houses in particular had developed a reputation by the turn of the century for organizing groups the "were not quite classes and not quite clubs," as Jane Addams explained it.[46] To Addams, settlement houses could act as intermediate institutions that could provide a mix of education and social activity. Addams's well-known Hull House in Chicago, which opened its doors in 1889, was a model for what would become more than 100 such settlement houses nationwide within a decade. The activities offered included a kindergarten for young children, lectures and general education courses for adults, arts and crafts classes, a variety of clubs, and venues for neighborhood parties and social gatherings.

Certainly in historical terms, such hybrid entities were not necessarily incubators of radical democracy. Despite the progressive range of their activities, one should remember that these organizations were very much products of their times. They were largely financed and staffed by white, middle-and upper-class outsiders to the primarily immigrant neighborhoods they served. Although markedly less self-righteous than the quasi-fundamentalist charitable organization societies, settlement houses nevertheless judged urban working class life by its own elitist standards. As described in 1895 by Josephine Shaw Lowell, volunteer workers in these institutions saw themselves as missionaries in a primitive society, whose purpose was to "awaken nobler ambitions and create higher ideas" in the slums.[47] Even the more tolerant Addams viewed the neighborhood surrounding Hull House as a scene of deviance, which needed to be restored to the norms of middle class culture: "The lower-class environment of saloons, dance hall, and street life needed to be . . . made more like a middle-or upper-class neighborhood," she observed.[48]

This implies that one should be cautious about automatically attributing democratic impulses to such hybrids. Similarly, paternalistic overtones have characterized much community cultural work, and is manifest today in the moralizing prescriptions of liberals and conservatives alike.[49] Neither side has sustained a vision that integrates culture into everyday life. Instead, cultural matters have been considered "outside" social structure, or they have remained mired in condescending proselytizing.

Hybrid organizations that have been able to survive tend to be more local in character, serving a particular range of needs to a specific community. San Francisco's Galeria de la Raza is a good example. Founded in 1970, the Galeria is one of many *centros* to emerge from the Chicano reclamation movement of the 1960s and 1970s. Growing in cities with large Chicano/Latino populations, like San Antonio and San Diego, a key component of these organizations is an emphasis on everyday experience through a mixture of cultural and educational activities. San Francisco's Galeria de la Raza developed programs specifically geared to served the community of the city's Mission District through a wide range of exhibitions, poster brigades, mural projects, performances, street events, and parades. Cultural historian Amalia Mesa-Bains explains that such a connection to community requires an organization to be responsive to change— something than mainstream institutions often cannot:

> In the ongoing exchange with self and other, the artist finds new language. In an extended fashion the community institution must also find its language in the dialogue with its audience. Through the lived experience of their artists, the collaboration with neighborhood groups, their pursuit of critical scholarship, and experimentation with presentation strategies, the community cultural *centros* aim at an authentic service.[50]

Part of the success of the Galeria de la Raza lies in its dual commercial/non-profit organizational structure. Comprised of two adjacent spaces, the organization is half art gallery and half gift shop. The gallery side features a changing schedule of exhibitions of contemporary work by multicultural artists; the store offers

Mexican and Latin American crafts, books, and goods like jewelry and t-shirts. Hence, the organization is capable of supporting its community on a variety of levels, where "popular barrio syntax, ceremonial satire, personal family narrative, social activism . . . theater, and spirituality have blended and fused, in a profusion of forms and meanings."[51]

In the 1990s, innovations in hybrid profit/non-profit structure and decentralized production and marketing are gaining popularity among service organizations of all kinds. In some sense this can be interpreted as a convergence of the economic mandates of post-Fordism with cultural impulses of identity-based movements. Certainly, many groups within the arts community are beginning take an interest in such interdisciplinary models, especially at a time when such organizations are suffering budget cuts and are increasingly called upon to justify their existence. This has led some mainstream groups to seriously rethink the very definition of the cultural space. Hence, these emerging hybrids offer important opportunities for renewed articulations of citizenship. First and most obviously, they provide significant linkages among groups often separated by identity, interest, or bureaucratic design. Second, these organizations respond to needs unmet by conventional institutions or disciplines. Finally, by developing new definitions of service, such hybrid models create fresh experiential worlds— new spaces where previously hidden or unrecognized forms of political possibility can be imagined.

eight

Toward a Radical Cultural Democracy

In recent years, the United States has found itself bound in a set of political contradictions. On one hand, the nation has seen the gradual narrowing of democratic discourse due to a growing polarization of opinion and a decline in the quality of public debate. A sensation-hungry media provides superficial sound bites to audiences hungry for answers to complex social problems, while the inadequacy of conventional party politics drives people further from the electoral process. The result is that disagreements seem further and further from resolution, as citizens feel more and more frustrated by their estrangement from power.[1]

At the same time, this very crisis of democratic discourse is opening new social and political possibilities. What postmodernists would term the "failure of master narratives" is giving way to a dramatic decentering of authority, a new emphasis on the importance of the margins. These emerging political possibilities have appeared with the decline of state authority and the growth of new social movements. Factor in the potentials of new technologies and decentralized markets, the emergence of alternative organizational forms—and the picture is nearly complete. Conditions seem ripe for a radical political imaginary, if the United States can find the capacity to reorient its understanding of civic accords.

Central to this new understanding is the acceptance of difference as workable political principle in the United States. With its historic emphasis on such assimilationist metaphors as the "melting pot," the United States has developed an almost pathological drive toward cultural conformity. Indeed, to some theorists, such an obsession with an articulated "common culture" becomes synonymous with the integrity of national identity itself. In this context then, the form of democracy advocated in this book becomes "radical" in at least two senses of the term. Not only does it imply a fundamental rejection of monolithic party politics in favor of a decentralized model based on identity groupings. It also suggests the rejection of a set of national accords seen by many to constitute the very glue

179

that holds the nation together. These two factors make possible the type of new spaces for engagement and new definitions of citizenship that radical democracy implies.

In the preceding chapters, I have sought to delineate the problems produced by the binary epistemology of Enlightenment humanism across a range of disciplinary fields: photography, film, television, education, music, and new media. The roots of this Enlightenment model are perhaps nowhere more clearly articulated than in Hegel's phenomenology, which mapped out a basic theory of subject/object relations. Hegel postulated an abstract dyad of the self and other, constructed in the consciousness of individuals. Within this idealized rendering the subject envisions an external object that it comes to recognize as different from itself. This difference produces a dissatisfaction that prompts the subject to absorb the attributes of the external other. He termed this process "sublation."[2] According to Hegel, sublation was the motor force of human learning, as the subject is changed through the appropriation of new ideas and objects. What is important to remember is that this dialectic was a pure function of metaphysics. Although Hegel's fundamental subject/object dualism was replicated for many decades in Western philosophies and institutions, it was not a model of the world—as contemporary feminist, poststructuralist, and postcolonial theories have made clear. Indeed, it has become increasingly evident that it is less productive to view social relations in binary "either/or" terms than in multiple "ands."

Toward a Cultural Democracy

This renewed emphasis on culture and difference should not be mistaken for a retreat from issues of social structure. The deterioration of democratic agency certainly results in large part from structures of capitalist power. A workable radical democracy will require mechanisms to keep capitalist impulses in check. As Jim Hightower explains, this is the major disincentive to civic participation:

> The most important—and the most radical—political perspective in our country is not right to left . . . but top to bottom, and most Americans today realize they are no longer even in shouting distance of the economic and political powers at the top, whether those powers call themselves Republican or Democrat, Conservative or Liberal.[3]

In the top-to-bottom crisis that Hightower describes, citizens excluded from what has recently been termed the emerging "overclass" believe they have lost control of their democracy—and must resort to other means to secure basic rights and protections. Evidence of this popular resentment toward government and public officials found expression in massive anti-incumbency movements nationwide, the "voter rebellion" of the 1994 congressional elections, and in the seemingly inexplicable popularity of unelected fringe personas like Bob Grant and Rush Limbaugh. Fortunately, few citizens have chosen to join militias or bomb buildings. But many people find themselves attracted to a growing array of alternative avenues—from fan clubs to activist movements—through which they can experience and extend aspects of their identities.

Taken together, issues like environmentalism, civil rights, AIDS activism, peace and justice, the pro-choice efforts, lesbian and gay pride, religious fundamentalism, health care, immigration reform, tax resistance, sexual harassment, censorship, racial and ethnic discrimination, affirmative action, youth culture, veterans' rights, homeless advocacy, world hunger, neighborhood organization constitute the type of "new political spaces" in which a more immediate democracy becomes feasible. This horizon of a radical democracy is premised on a much more complex set of issues than conventional party politics can accommodate because it encompasses many issues typically viewed as "off limits" to politics.

As suggested earlier in the discussion of "victim" culture, radical democrats need to help clarify the issue of who is and who isn't entitled to voice dissent in the current political environment. Another way of looking at Robert Hughes's "culture of complaint" lies in recognizing that the portrait of normalcy he paints is so remarkably small.[4] After all, if you take the mythic model of the American mainstream and subtract those who have experienced racial or gender discrimination, sexual harassment, homophobia; if you take out people who have been troubled by physical or mental illness; if you remove people born into economic hardship or those who are old (or young) or who speak languages other than English—you are left with a tiny minority of the population.

Acknowledging then that most people have legitimate reasons for complaint, we might then address the role of complaint in public life. To argue that complainers or victims need to get over it so that we can stop the "fraying of America" suggests a romantic view of life in which disagreement and difference are erased. This is of course antithetical to the very concept of a democracy in which commonly held agreements are continually tested and reevaluated by divergent opinions. What the fraying of America really implies is that people can only consider themselves as citizens within the carefully drawn precincts of Enlightenment humanism and Western law.

Rather than asking those with different needs and discordant views to "get over it," we should recognize the inherent value of diverse opinion in the continual improvement of social accords. In more specific terms, educational and cultural institutions can help correct views of poverty as a personal or cultural illness, for example, by helping to explicate the complexity of its origins. The tendency to blame victims for their own misfortune is the direct result of attitudes that fragment society into categories with little impact on one another. Such a failure to see the world in interrelated terms promotes a vision of homelessness, for example, as the result of laziness rather than a function of the employment market, real estate values, educational opportunities, or the availability of mental health services. This permits the view of substance abuse as a moral weakness rather than a function of genetic disposition, physiological response, social practice, and psychology, among other factors. All of this suggests the need for approaches that stress the interconnectedness of human experience and social reality.

Is it possible for a new political consensus to cohere around a different set of principles than the simple left/right dichotomy? Certainly, a variety of economic and technological factors are pointing toward this possibility. Evolving practices of post-Fordist production and distribution are creating a vastly decentralized business climate. Rather than appealing to consumer "masses" with single product lines and nationally uniform advertising campaigns, corporations are maximizing the potentials of flexible manufacturing and computerized delivery techniques to both serve and build "niche markets." Although on one level this activity provides little more than a veneer of independence from powerful multinational corporations, it also affords a measure of opportunity for localized alternatives. Frankly speaking, corporate moguls have recognized the potential profit in serving people of color, lesbian and gay communities, iconoclastic youth, and other previously unexplored markets. Within this atmosphere of "corporate multiculturalism" exist occasional opportunities for subversion.

What would a radical cultural democracy look like? It would be considerably different from what exists today in the United States. Certainly the ideal of an area of civic "talk" like the public sphere would be an important component of such a formulation. However, the liberal notion of a single space of unmediated dialogue and exchange would be abandoned. As radical democratic theorists Ernesto Laclau and Chantal Mouffe have suggested, it is unrealistic to envision a participatory sphere free from antagonisms and power asymmetries. The environment for egalitarian dialogue should provide a stage for such antagonisms to play themselves out within a context that affords a measure of constitutional protection.

Such a model eschews both the unregulated competition created by the marketplace and the paternalistic control that systems of government patronage imply. Within the United States as well as other nations, opposing systems of private/public funding for cultural enterprises have proven inadequate for the sustenance of democratic exchange. Instead, they have contributed to the very polarization of opinion that has mitigated against the meaningful consideration of issues. Commercial television, movies, music, and the art market have demonstrated repeatedly their resistance to minority viewpoints or to ideas with little market potential. Although the recent diversification of commercial culture through the emphasis on "corporate multiculturalism" offers promising opportunities for diversity, these spaces will never represent a consistent venues of progressivism. They exist within a hierarchical capitalist structure fundamentally premised on resource consolidation and social stratification.

Similarly, public funding for media and the arts has shown itself to represent exclusionary constituencies of its own. Primarily owning to their reliance on liberal political support, entities like the Corporation for Public Broadcasting, The Public Broadcasting Service, The Institute for Museum Services, and the National Endowments for the Arts and Humanities must cater to a culture that is in large part both Eurocentric and bourgeois. Although for many recipients of such funding the direct role of the state has long ago been compromised by funding restrictions imposed by the legislature, the symbolic effect of a government imprimatur through even a small grant has the capacity to drive an institution's programming. Operating as a compensatory element of "balance" to the marketplace, public funding excludes the culture that many people value.

A radical cultural democracy would seem to imply a commitment to pluralism outside both the marketplace and the subsidized realm, without negating the possibility of either system. Clearly a structure would need to be put in place to effect this pluralist vision, possibly like the public/private "endowment" proposed by some to support the CPB. Although supplemented by tax dollars, this new pluralist model would not be operated by the state. Instead, it would provide a framework which would sustain a plurality of independent media institutions in different spheres.[5]

The overall purpose of the structure would be twofold: to effect a partial decentralization of existing commercial cultural and media industries; to insulate media institutions from the exercise of state power. In other words, such an endowment would sustain an independent institutional, governed by an independent body of administrators, between the unimpeded forces of the market and the regulatory control of the state. Such a structure could accommodate a variety of specific organizational forms, whether located within the public realm, the private realm, or in the type of hybrid organizations discussed earlier.

Resembling a type of international civil society, this model would have a legal charge not simply to admit diversity as a condition of its existence, but to actively seek it out. Disengaged from the mandates of grant requirements or Neilson ratings, this arena of cultural radical democracy could realize the utopian aspiration of the public sphere by offering a site of civic contestation and debate.

The future of radical cultural activism lies in the unified efforts of democratic cultural workers to work together, across the boundaries of individual struggles, to meet its challenges head on. These issues assume a heightened urgency in an era in which meaningful dialogue in the form of public gatherings and social rituals is increasingly undermined by the isolation of individualized culture and the binary oppositions of party politics. These issues take on even greater importance at a time when cultural difference advances to the front of the political agenda. It is clear that groups on the left can no longer afford to insist that issues of identity and representation have no place in material struggles. Overcoming these attitudinal problems will mean recognizing the reciprocal role of media as both reflective and constitutive of social formations.[6]

Indeed, within this moral environment culture has a dual function. It is both the means by which the oppressed come to know their oppression and the vehicle through which citizens struggle to find methods for change.

N O T E S

Chapter 1

1. The views of these authors on radical democracy have been recently anthologized in David Trend, ed., *Radical Democracy: Identity, Citizenship, and the State* (New York: Routledge, 1996). See also Hank Johnston and Bert Klandermans, *Social Movements and Cultures* (Minneapolis: University of Minnesota, 1995); and Douglas Lummis, *Radical Democracy* (Ithaca: Cornell University Press, 1996).

2. This latter impulse recently has been discussed in Amatai Etzioni, *Rights and the Common Good: The Communitarian Perspective* (New York: St Martins, 1995).

3. These issues are taken up in depth in Paul Piccone's comprehensive essay, "From the New Left to the New Populism," *Telos* 101 (Fall 1994): pp. 173–208. See also Jeffrey Alexander, "Modern, Anti, Post, Neo," *New Left Review* 210 (March/April 1995): pp. 63–104.

4. Molly Ivins, untitled address, National Public Radio, June 22, 1995.

5. Stanley Aronowitz, "The Situation of the Left in the United States," *Socialist Review* 93/3 (1994): p. 5. See also Matthew McAllister, *The Commercialization of American Culture: New Advertising, Control, and Democracy* (Thousand Oaks, Cal.; Sage, 1996).

6. Cornel West, *Race Matters,* (New York: Vintage Books, 1994), p. 19.

7. John Dewey, *Democracy and Education : An Introduction to the Philosophy of Education* (New York: Macmillan, 1944); John Rawls, *A Theory of Justice* (Cambridge: Harvard University Press, 1971).

8. John Locke, *The Second Treatise of Civil Government,* (Buffalo: Prometheus Books, 1986), p. 413.

9. Michael Walzer, "The Civil Society Argument," in Chantal Mouffe, ed., *Dimensions of Radical Democracy* (London and New York; Verso, 1991), pp. 89–107; Paul Hirst, "Associational Democracy," in David Held, ed. *Prospects for Democracy: North/South/East/West* (Stanford: Stanford University Press, 1993), pp. 112–135; Juan Linz and Alfred Stephan, "Toward Consolidated Democracies," *Journal of Democracy* 7, no. 2 (April 1996), pp. 14–33.

10. See for example, Robert Dahl, *A Preface to Economic Democracy* (Berkeley: University of California, 1984); David Held, *Models of Democracy* (Landen: Cambridge University Press, 1987); C. B. Macpherson, *The Life and Times of Liberal Democracy,* (New York: Oxford University Press, 1977).

11. John Dunn, ed., *The Economic Limits of Modern Politics* (Cambridge: Cambridge University Press, 1990); Samuel Bowles and Herbert Gintis, *Democracy and Capitalism: Property, Community, and the Contradictions of Modern Social Thought* (New York: Basic Books, 1986).

12. Norberto Bobbio, *Which Socialism? Marxism, Socialism, and Democracy,* trans. Roger Griffin (London: Polity Press, 1987), p. 24; See also Norberto Bobbio, *The Future of Democracy: A Defense of the Rules of the Game,* trans. Roger Griffin (London: Polity Press, 1987).

13. Chantal Mouffe, "Democratic Politics Today," in Chantal Mouffe, ed., *Dimensions of Radical Democracy* (London and New York: Verso, 1991).

14. Ernesto Laclau and Chantal Mouffe, *Hegemony and Socialist Strategy,* p. 122.

15. *Ibid.*

16. Despite their utopian aspirations (perhaps because of them), prescriptions for radical pluralism have been subject to strenuous critique. Many on the left assert that a focus on identity and on definitions of the subject tends to minimize the importance of economic issues and the particulars of social structure. Radical democracy may promise an egalitarian program but does little to spell out the details of how it will address redistributive issues. This lack of specificity is similarly critiqued from postcolonial quarters as one indication that this purportedly "postmodern" approach to politics simply may constitute another brand of modernism in disguise. In this critique, radical pluralism's failure to articulate where and how its program will be implemented is interpreted as a universalizing impulse that refuses to acknowledge social inequalities. The general "right" of citizens to vote is undermined by the absence of other privileges that such universalizing rhetoric obscures. Without acknowledging the ethnocentric and otherwise xenophobic character of these absences, radical democracy becomes simply "the latest" chapter in an enlightenment program of Western advancement. Evidence of this evolutionary view comes, for example, from radical democracy's preservation and adaptation of liberal principles Due to this allegiance to the liberal legacy, still other critics claim that radical democracy represents little more than a new name devised by disaffected socialists, who are drifting toward liberal democracy but who can't bring themselves to embrace it.

17. Lani Guinier, *The Tyranny of the Majority: Fundamental Fairness in Representative Democracy* (New York: Free Press, 1994).

18. Hilton Kramer, "A Note on the New Criterion," *New Criterion* 1, no. 1 (September 1982): p. 7.

19. Chandra Talpade Mohanty, "On Race and Voice: Challenges for Liberal Education in the 1990s," *Cultural Critique* (Winter 1988/89), pp. 179–208.

20. Christopher Lasch, *The Revolt of the Elites and the Betrayal of Democracy*

(New York: W.W. Norton, 1995); Jerry Adler, "The Rise of the Overclass, "*Newsweek* 126, No. 5 (July 31, 1995): pp. 32–48; and Lani Guinier, *The Tyranny of the Majority*. See also, Paul Gorman, *Left Intellectuals and Popular Culture in Twentieth Century America* (Chapel Hill: University of North Carolina, 1996).

21. U.S. Department of Education, *America 2000: An Education Strategy* (Washington, D.C.: U.S. Government Printing Office, 1991). For an updated analysis of Goals 2000, see, "Education in the Clinton Administration," a special section of *Teacher's College Record* 96, no. 3 (Spring 1995), with contributions by Peter Cookson, Eugene Garcia, René Gonzalez, Richard Elmore, Susan Fuhrman, and William Reilly, among others.

22. Samuel Lipman, "Redefining Culture and Democracy," *The New Criterion* 8 (December 1989): p. 11.

23. See Theodor Adorno and Max Horkeimer, *The Dialectic of Enlightenment*, trans. John Cumming (New York: Herder and Herder, 1972); Hans Magnus Enzenberger, "Constituents of a Theory of Media," in *The Consciousness Industry*, trans. Stuart Hood (New York: Seabury Press, 1974). A significant discussion of the cultural populism/elitism debate is found in Jim Cullen, The *Art of Democracy: A Concise History of Popular Culture in America* (New York: Monthly Review Press, 1996).

24. James Madison, "Letter to Edmund Randolph (31 May 1789)," in *The Writings of James Madison*, Gaillard Hunt, ed. vol. 5 (New York: 1904), p. 377.

25. Jürgen Habermas, *The Structural Transformation of the Public Sphere*, trans. Thomas Berger with Frederick Lawrence (Cambridge, Mass.: MIT Press, 1989). Originally published 1962. See also Robert C. Holub, *Jürgen Habermas: Critic in the Public Sphere* (London and New York: Routledge, 1991); Oskar Negt, *Public Sphere and Experience: Toward an Analysis of the Bourgeois and Proletarian Public Sphere* (Minneapolis: University of Minnesota, 1993); Bruce Robbins , ed. *The Phantom Public Sphere* (Minneapolis: University of Minnesota, 1993); Roberto Alejandro, *Hermeneutics, Citizenship, and the Public Sphere* (Albany: SUNY Press, 1993); Daniel Hallin, *We Keep America on Top of the World: Television Journalism and the Public Sphere* (London and New York: Routledge, 1994); Farid Syed Alatas, *The Post-Colonial State: Dual Functions in the Public Sphere* (Singapore: National University of Singapore, 1994); Patrick McHugh, "Democracy, Cultural Politics and *The Phantom Public Sphere*," *Review of Education, Pedagogy, and Cultural Studies* 17, no. 2 (April 1995): pp. 235–248; Maurizio Passerin d'Entrèves and S. Seyla Benhabib, eds. *Habermas and the Unfinished Project of Modernity* (Cambridge: MIT Press, 1996).

26. Habermas, p. 282.

27. For a summary of these views, see Douglas Kellner, *Television and the Crisis of Democracy* (Boulder and San Francisco: Westview, 1990); James Fishkin, *The Voice of the People: Public Opinion and Democracy* (New Haven: Yale University Press, 1996); James Fallows, *Breaking the News; How the Media Undermine Democracy* (New York: Pantheon, 1996).

28. John Thompson, *Ideology and Modern Culture: Critical Social Theory in the*

Era of Mass Communication (Stanford: Stanford University Press, 1990); Erwin Hargrove, "Self-Rule: A Cultural History of American Democracy," *American Political Science Review*, 90 no. 2 (June 1996), pp. 443-444.

29. James Jefferson Hunter, *Before the Shooting Starts: Searching for Democracy in America's Culture War* (New York: The Free Press, 1994), p. 98.

30. Patricia Aufderheide, "The Big Grab," *In These Times* 19, no 15 (June 12, 1995): pp. 8–9.

31. Ben Bagdikian, *The Media Monopoly*, 4th edition (Boston: Beacon Press, 1992).

32. John Keane, *The Media and Democracy* (London: Polity Press, 1991), p. 68.

33. David Harvey, "The Condition of Postmodernity"; see also, David Harvey, "Flexibility: Threat or Opportunity," Socialist Review 21, no 1. (Jan.-Mar. 1991): pp. 64–77.

34. Marshall McLuhan, *Understanding Media: Extensions of Man* (New York: McGraw-Hill, 1964).

35. Robert Wright, "Hyper Democracy," *Time*, 145, no. 3 (Jan. 23, 1995): pp. 15–25.

36. An excellent collection of essays addressing this question is Peter Dahlgren and Colin Sparks, eds, *Communication and Citizenship: Journalism and the Public Sphere in the New Media Age* (London and New York: Routledge, 1991).See also Stephen Ansolabert and Shante Ivengar, *Going Negative: How Political Advertisements Shrink and Polarize the Electorate* (New York: Free Press, 1996).

37. Nancy Fraser, "Rethinking the Public Sphere: A Contribution to the Critique of Actually Existing Democracy," in *Unruly Practices: Power, Discourse and, Gender in Contemporary Social Theory* (Minneapolis: University of Minnesota, 1989), pp. 93–112; See also Michael Schudson, " Was There Ever a Public Sphere? If So, When? Reflections on the American Case." Manuscript, Department of Communication, University of California, San Diego, Dec. 1989.

38. Sara Evans and Harry Boyte, *Free Spaces: The Sources of Democratic Change in America* (New York: Harper and Row, 1986).

39. Lani Guinier, "Democracy's Conversation," *The Nation* (Jan 1995).

Chapter 2

1. Patrick Buchanan, "In the War for America's Culture the 'Right' Side is Losing," *Richmond News Leader*, June 24, 1989. Republished in Richard Bolton, *Culture Wars: Documents from the Recent Controversies in the Arts* (New York: The New Press, 1992), pp. 31–33.

2. See Bolton, *Culture Wars;* Ira Schor, *Culture Wars: School and Society in the Conservative Restoration, 1969–1985* (London and New York: Routledge, 1986); Geoffrey Hartman, *Minor Prophesies: The Literacy Essay in the Culture Wars* (Cambridge: Harvard University Press, 1991); James Davison Hunter, *Culture Wars: The*

Struggle to Define America (New York: Basic Books, 1992); Henry Louis Gates, *Loose Canons: Notes on the Culture Wars* (New York Oxford University Press, 1992); Gerald Graff, *Beyond the Culture Wars: How Teaching the Conflicts Can Revitalize American Education* (New York: WW Norton, 1992); Margaret Heins, *Sex, Sin, and Blasphemy* (New York: The New Press, 1993); Fred Whitehead, *Culture Wars: Opposing Viewpoints* (San Diego: Greenhaven Press, 1994); Russell Jacoby, *Dogmatic Wisdom: How the Culture Wars Divert Education and Distract America* (New York: Doubleday, 1994); Elaine Rapping, *Media-tions: forays into the culture and gender wars* (Boston: South End Press, 1994).

3. Buchanan, in Bolton, *Culture Wars*, p. 32.

4. In a recent development that has mortified free speech advocates, in March 1993 the Clinton administration appealed the federal court decision that struck down the National Endowment for the Arts' "decency clause" the previous summer. Like George Bush, Clinton is arguing that content restrictions of federally funded art are legal. It's worth noting that during his election campaign, Clinton staunchly insisted that he would lift all such restrictions. See C. Carr, "Artful Dodging: The NEA Funds the Defended Four," *Village Voice* (June 15, 1993): pp. 30–31.

5. As one commentator responded to Bill Clinton's nomination of Sheldon Hackney to head the National Endowment for the Humanities, "Once you have convinced people, as the right wing has, that multiculturalism and deconstruction are barbaric forms of nihilism, how can you expect an NEH nominee to speak favorably of them in public." See Stephen Burd, " Hackney Attacked and Praised for Criticizing Literary Theory," *Chronicle of Higher Education* (July 14, 1993): p. A21.

6. James Davison Hunter, *Before the Shooting Starts: Searching for Democracy in America's Culture War* (New York: The Free Press, 1994). See also, Stephen Ansolabert and Shante Ivengar, *Going Negative: How Political Advertisements Shrink and Polarize the Electorate* (New York: Free Press, 1996).

7. James Fallows, *Breaking the News: How Media Undermine American Democracy* (New York: Pantheon, 1996).

8. David Rieff, "Multiculturalism's Silent Partner," *Harpers Magazine* 287, no. 1717 (Aug. 1993) p. 64. See also Lawrence Soley, *Leasing the Ivory Tower: The Corporate Takeover of Academia* (Boston: South End Press, 1995).

9. As cited in Rieff, p. 65. See also, Richard Ohman, "On 'PC' and Related Matters," in Jeffrey Williams, ed, *PC Wars: Politics and Theory in the Academy* (New York: Routledge, 1995), pp. 11–21.

10. "Hot Type," *Chronicle of Higher Education* XL, no. 46 (July 20, 1994): p. A10.. The statistics were drawn from Steven Brint, *In an Age of Experts: The Changing Role of Professionals in Politics and Political Life* (Princeton: Princeton University Press, 1994).

11. Joel Bleifuss, "Building Plans, " *In These Times* 19, no. 17 (July 10, 1995): pp. 12–15. See also, Randy Shaw, *The Activist's Handbook: A Primer for the 1990s and Beyond* (Berkeley: University of California, 1996).

12. William J. Bennett, *To Reclaim a Legacy: A Report on the Humanities in*

Higher Education (Washington, D.C.: U.S. Government Printing Office, 1984); T. E. Bell, *A Nation at Risk: The Imperative for Educational Reform* (Washington, D.C.: U.S. Government Printing Office, 1983).

13. E.D Hirsch, Jr., *Cultural Literacy: What Every American Needs to Know,* (New York: Vintage, 1987), p. 20.

14. Paul Lauter, "'Political Correctness' and the Attack on American Colleges," *Radical Teacher* 44, (Winter 1993): pp. 34–40.

15. Issued in the final year of his presidency, Bush's "America 2000: A Plan for the Nations Schools" proposed vouchers and a school choice option, which would allow parents to move their children into private schools at government expense.

16. Svi Shapiro, "Clinton and Education: Policies without Meaning," *Tikkun* 9, no. 3 (May-June 1994): pp. 17–20, 90. An incisive review of Clinton administration education policy appears in a special "Goals 2000" issue of *Teachers College Record* 96, no. 3 (Spring 1995).

17. L .Fraser, "Tyranny of the Media Correct: The Assault on the New McCarthyism," *Extra!* 4, no 4 (1991): p. 6.

18. Adler, p. 54.

19. Roger Kimball, *Tenured Radicals : How Politics Has Corrupted Our Higher Education* (New York: Harper and Row, 1990); Dinesh D'Sousa, *Illiberal Education: The Politics of Race and Sex on Campus.* (New York: The Free Press, 1991); Lawrence Soley, *Leasing the Ivory Tower: The Corporate Takeover of Academia* (Boston: South End Press, 1995).

20. Kimball, p. 166.

21. D'Sousa, p. 257.

22. See Jerry Adler, "Taking Offense," *Newsweek* (Dec. 24, 1990): p. 54.

23. Rosa Ehrenreich, "What Campus Radicals? The P.C. Undergrad Is a Useful Spectre," in F. Beckwith and M. Bauman, eds., *Are You Politically Correct?: Debating America's Cultural Standards* (New York: Prometheus Books, 1993), pp. 33–39.

24. Gregory S. Jay, "Knowledge, Power, and The Struggle for Representation, *College English* 56, no. 1 (Jan. 1994): p. 20.

25. Page Smith, *Killing the Spirit: Higher Education in America* (New York: Viking, 1990).

26. Charles J. Sykes, *Profscam: Professors and the Demise of Higher Education* (New York: St Martins Press, 1988).

27. Jay. p. 20.

28. Leon Wieseltier, "All or Nothing at All: The Unreal World of Cornel West," *The New Republic* 212, no. 10 (Mar. 6, 1995): p. 31.

29. Salim Mukakkil, "The Public Mind," *In These Times* 19, no. 13 (May 15, 1995): p. 25.

30. Victor Burgin, "Questions of Feminism: 25 Responses," *October* 71 (Winter 1995): pp. 20–21.

31. This error of technological determinism is most eloquently made in the much-

celebrated essay by Walter Benjamin, "The Work of Art in the Age of Mechanical Reproduction," in *Illuminations*, trans. Harry Zohn (New York: Schocken Books, 1969).

32 Ben J. Bagdikian, *The Media Monopoly*, 4th ed. (Boston: Beacon Press, 1992). See also, Philo Washburn, "Democracy and Media Ownership," *Media, Culture, and Society*, 17, no. 4 (October 1995), pp. 647–676.

33. Bagdikian, p. 3.

34. Bagdikian, p. 18.

35. Bagdikian, p. 4.

36. Michael W. Apple, *Teachers & Texts: A Political Economy of Class & Gender Relations in Education* (New York: Routledge, 1989).

37. Apple, p. 98.

38. Bagdikian, p. xii.

39. Elayne Rapping, "Who Needs the Hollywood Left?" *The Progressive* 57, no. 9 (Sept. 1993): p. 34.

40. William Hoynes, *Public Television for Sale: Media, the Market, and the Public Sphere* (Boulder and San Francisco: Westview, 1994).

41. Marshall McLuhan, *Understanding Media: Extensions of Man* (New York: McGraw-Hill, 1964), p. 23.

42. Pat Aufderheide, "The Media Monopoly Muscles In," *The Nation* (Jan. 3/10, 1994): pp. 1, 18–21.

43. See Dick Netzer, *The Subsidized Muse: Public Support for the Arts in the United States* (New York: Cambridge University Press, 1978), p. 6.

44. Michael S. Joyce, "The National Endowments for the Humanities and the Arts," *Mandate for Leadership*, Charles L. Heatherly, ed. (Washington, D.C.: The Heritage Foundation, 1981), pp. 1040–1041.

45. Joyce, p. 1041.

46. Martha Rosler, "Theses on Defunding," *Afterimage* 11, nos. 1–2 (Summer 1982): pp. 6–7.

47. Rosler, p 7.

48. Arian, pp. 42–44.

49. NEA Annual Report 1988, p. 239.

50. David Trend, "NEA Watch, " *Artpaper* (Oct. 1992).

51. Admittedly, during the initial decades following the patenting of the daguerreotype in 1839, photographic equipment was expensive , the chemical processes were complex, and its practitioners tended to be wealthy. But by the turn of the century, photography had become a commonly available technology, which was quickly adapted to mass production and amateur use by George Eastman.

52. Karl Marx, *Grundisse: Foundations of the Critique of Political Economy*, trans. Martin Nicolaus (Harmondsworth: Penguin, 1973); Karl Marx, *Capital* 3 vols., Frederick Engels, ed, Samuel Moore and Edward Aveling, trans. (London: Lawrence and Wishart, 1974).

53. In fact, the perceived boom in cultural studies is an illusion. Although a hand-

ful of cultural studies practitioners have attracted some publicity, cultural studies (and media studies) has failed to gain a substantial foothold in the academy as a whole. While cultural studies courses are taught in some schools, less than half a dozen universities have elevated the endeavor to the status of a department. A recent discussion of this situation appears in Liz McMillen, "New York U. Becomes a Magnet for Scholars in Cultural Studies," *Chronicle of Higher Education* 39, no. 41 (July 28, 1993): p. A10.

54. Lawrence Grossberg, Cary Nelson, Paula Treichler, eds. *Cultural Studies* (London and New York: Routledge, 1992).

55. See Stuart Hall, "The Emergence of Cultural Studies and the Crisis of the Humanities," *October* 53 (Summer 1990): pp. 11–24.

56. *Ibid.*, p. 15.

57. Pat Aufderheide, "Charting Cultural Change: The Role of the Critic," in *Reimaging America: The Arts of Social Change,* eds. Mark O'Brien and Craig Little, (Santa Cruz, Cal.: New Society Publishers, 1990), p. 359.

58. Stanley Fish, "Being Interdisciplinary Is So Very Hard to Do," *Profession 89* (New York: Modern Language Association, 1989): pp. 15–22.

59. Judith Williamson, "Woman is an Island: Femininity and Colonization," in *Studies in Entertainment: Critical Approaches to Mass Culture,* Tania Modleski, ed. (Indianapolis: Indiana University Press, 1986), pp. 100–101.

60. Meaghan Morris, "Banality in Cultural Studies," *Block* 14 (1988): pp. 15–26.

61. See Teresa Ebert, "Ludic Feminism, the Body, Performance, and Labor: Bringing Materialism Back into Feminist Cultural Studies," *Cultural Critique* 23 (Winter 1992–93): p. 17. In this remarkably reductive essay, Ebert collapses the work of such diverse thinkers as Judith Butler, Nancy Fraser, Donna Haraway, Kobena Mercer, Ernesto Laclau, Diana Fuss, Andrew Ross, and Frederic Jameson into a category she identifies as "ludic" postmodernism. See also, Antonio Callari and David Ruccio, eds., *Postmodern Marxism and the Future of Marxist Theory* (Middletown, Conn.: Wesleyan, 1996).

62. In the early writing of Jean Baudrillard the dual logics of materialist and textualist positions fuse in the figure of the "commodity sign." Like Marx, Baudrillard blames the representation of commodities for generating an "abstract" exchange value from a "concrete" use value. In this manner, Baudrillard identifies signification as the central logic of late capitalism. As seen in much of consumer society, the rendering of the commodity as text becomes the driving force of objectification, surplus valuation, and, ultimately, alienation. See Mark Poster, "Translator's Introduction," from Jean Baudrillard, *The Mirror of Production* (St Louis: Telos Press, 1975), p. 5.

63. As Christopher Newfield , "What Was Political Correctness?" *Critical Inquiry* 19 (Winter 1993): pp. 308–336.

64. Linda Chavez, "Demystifying Multiculturalism, *National Review* 156, no. 3 (Feb. 21, 1994): p. 30.

65. Michael Omi and Howard Winant, *Racial Formation in the United States: From the 1960s to the 1980s,* second ed. (New York: Routledge, 1994).

66. D'Sousa, p. 250.

67 Todd Gitlin, "The Rise of 'Identity Politics,'" *Dissent* (Spring 1993): p. 172.

68. Jeffrey Escoffier, "The Limits of Multiculturalism," *Socialist Review* 21, nos. 3–4 (July-Dec. 1991): pp. 61–74.

69. Barbara Epstein, "Political Correctness and Collective Powerlessness," *Socialist Review* 21, nos. 3–4 (July-Dec. 1991): pp. 14–15.

70. The literature in this area is voluminous. Selected examples include: Benjamin Barber, *Strong Democracy: Participatory Politics for a New Age* (Berkeley: University of California Press, 1984); Paul Hirst, *Associative Democracy* (1994); Chantal Mouffe, *The Return of the Political* (London and New York: Verso, 1993); Ernesto Laclau and Chantal Mouffe, *Hegemony and Socialist Strategy: Notes Toward a Radical Democratic Politics* (London: Verso, 1985); Stuart Hall and Martin Jacques, eds., *New Times: The Changing Face of Politics in the 1990s* (London and New York: Verso, 1990); and Sara Evans and Harry Boyt, *Free Spaces: The Sources of Democratic Change in America* (New York: Harper and Row, 1986).

71. Cornel West, *The Ethical Dimensions of Marxist Thought* (New York: Monthly Review Press, 1991), p. 1.

72 Amarpal Dhaliwal, "Response to Stanley Aronowitz," *Socialist Review* 93, no. 3 (1994): p. 97.

73. Selected examples of the culture-as-substitute argument resurface in Ebert; Heins; Epstein, and Thomas Crow, "I'll Take the High Road, You Take the Low Road," *Artforum* 19 (Jan. 1991): pp. 104–107.

74. Mable Haddock and Chiquita Mullins, "Whose Multiculturalism?: PBS, the Public, and Privilege," *Afterimage* 21, no. 1 (Summer 1993): pp. 14–19.

75. Michael Bérubé, "Exigencies of Value," *Minnesota Review* 36 (Fall/Winter 1992/93): pp. 63–87.

76. This has been made apparent in Hillary Rodham Clinton's concern, following that of *Tikkun* editor Michael Lerner, over what has been termed the "politics of meaning."

77. Quotations from Rush Limbaugh radio broadcasts, November 1994. For a detailed discussion of the Limbaugh phenomenon, see Kurt Anderson, "Big Mouths" *Time* 142, no. 18 (Nov. 1, 1993): pp. 60–66.

78. Barber; John Dewey, *Democracy and Education*. See also, Amy Gutman, *Democratic Education* (Princeton: Princeton University Press, 1987).

79. Mark Achbar, ed., *Manufacturing Consent: Noam Chomsky and the Media* (Montreal and London: Black Rose Books, 1994).

Chapter 3

1. Donald Wildmon, as quoted in Richard Bolton, "The Cultural Contradictions of Conservatism, " in the *New Art Examiner* 17, no. 10 (June 1990): p. 26.

2. *The American Public's Perspective on Federal Support for the Arts and the Controversy over Funding for the National Endowment for the Arts* (Washington, D.C.: People for the American Way, 1990).

3. Robert Samuelson, "Highbrow Pork Barrel, Washington Post, August 16, 1989," in Bolton, ed. *Culture Wars,* p. 95.

4. Christopher Lasch, *The Revolt of the Elites and the Betrayal of Democracy* (New York: WW Norton, 1995). See also, George Scialabba, "'A Whole World of Heroes'": Christopher Lasch on Democracy," *Dissent* 42, no. 3 (Summer 1995): pp. 407–413; Jim Cullen, *The Art of Democracy: A Concise History of Popular Culture in America* (New York: Monthly Review Press, 1996).

5. Michael Denning, "The Academic Left and the Rise of Cultural Studies," *Radical History Review* 54 (1992): pp. 21–47.

6. Eric Barnouw, *Documentary: A History of the Non-Fiction Film* (New York: Oxford University Press, 1983), p. 5.

7. Herbert Marcuse, *An Essay on Liberation* (Boston: Beacon Press, 1969), p. 21. See also, Paul Gorman, *Left Intellectuals and Popular Culture in Twentieth Century America* (Chapel Hill: University of North Carolina, 1996).

8. As cited in Mark Acbar, ed., *Manufacturing Consent: Noam Chomsky and the Media* (Montreal and New York: Black Rose Books, 1994), p. 52.

9. Grant Kester, "Rhetorical Questions: The Alternative Arts Sector and the Imaginary Public," *Afterimage* 20, no. 6 (Jan. 1993): p. 12.

10. Grant Kester, "Aesthetic Evangelists: Conversion and Empowerment in Contemporary Community Art," *Afterimage* 22, no. 6 (Jan. 1995): p. 6.

11. Christian Metz, *The Imaginary Signifier: Psychoanalysis and the Cinema* (Bloomington: Indiana University Press, 1982), p. 51.

12. John Belton, *American Cinema/American Culture* (New York: McGraw-Hill, 1994), p. 17.

13. Ella Shohat and Robert Stam, *Unthinking Eurocentrism: Multiculturalism and the Media* (New York: Routledge, 1994): p. 103.

14. Jan Pieterse, *White on Black: Images of Africa and Blacks in Western Popular Culture* (New Haven: Yale Univ. Press, 1992), p. 77.

15. Barsam, pp. 42–44.

16. Shohat and Stam, p. 107.

17. Rosalind Krauss, Art Journal, and Jan Zita Grover, "Landscapes Ordinary and Extraordinary," *Afterimage* 11, no. 5 (December 1983): pp. 4–5.

18. Ross, p. 69.

19. "Report on the Proceedings of the 30th Annual Convention of the American Federation of Labor," *New York Call,* May 15, 1911, as cited in Ross, p. 77.

20. Hugo Munsterberg, *Psychology and Industrial Efficiency* (Boston: Houghton Mifflin, 1913), p. 24.

21. Steven J. Ross, "Cinema and Class Conflict: Labor, Capital, the State, and the

American Silent Film," in *Resisting Images: Essays on Cinema and History*, Robert Sklar and Charles Musser, eds. (Philadelphia: Temple University Press, 1990), p. 172.

22. Herbert Marcuse, "Some Social Implications of Modern Technology," *The Essential Frankfort School Reader*, ed., Andrew Arato and Eike Gebhardt (New York: Continuum, 1985), p. 138.

23. Arthur, p. 116.

24. Among these programs were the Resettlement Administration and the Farm Security Administration.

25. Don Adams and Arlene Goldbard, "Learning to Read the World, " *exposure* 28, nos. 1/2 (1991): p. 15.

26. Jonathan Buchsbaum, "Left Political Filmmaking in the West; The Interwar Years," in Musser and Sklar, p. 136.

27. For a detailed discussion of this revisionism, see Robert Sklar, "Oh! Althusser!: Historiography and the Rise of Cinema Studies," in Musser and Sklar, pp. 12–35. In this essay Sklar presents an overview of significant texts in this reevaluation of the role of working-class audiences. These works include: Miriam Hansen, "Early Cinema: Whose Public Sphere?" *New German Critique* 29 (Winter 1983): pp. 147–184; Roy Rosensweig, *Eight Hours for What We Will: Workers and Leisure in an Industrial City, 1870–1920* (Cambridge: Cambridge University Press, 1980); Lary May, *Screening Out of the Past: The Birth of Mass Culture and the Motion Picture Industry* (New York: Oxford University Press, 1980); Daniel J. Czitrom, *Media and the American Mind: From Morse to McLuhan* (Chapel Hill: University of North Carolina, 1982).

28. Rosenzweig, p. 223. See also Bill Nichols, *Blurring Boundaries: Questions of Meaning in Contemporary Cinema* (Bloomington and Indianapolis: Indiana University Press, 1994).

29. As cited in Barsam, p. 80.

30. Brian Neve, *Film and Politics in America: A Social Tradition* (New York and London: Routledge, 1992), p. 15.

31. Neve, p. 28.

32. *Ibid.*

33. Neve, p. 31.

34. James Combs, *American Political Movies: An Annotated Filmography of Feature Films* (New York and London: Garland, Press, 1990).

35. Combs, p. 24.

36. Belton, p. 121.

37. David Grimsted, "Melodrama as Echo of the Historically Voiceless, " in Tamara Hareven, ed. *Anonymous Explorations in Nineteenth Century Social History* (Englewood Cliffs, N.J.: Prentice-Hall, 1971), p. 178.

38. Terry Christiansen, *Reel Politics: American Political Movies from Birth of a Nation to Platoon*, (New York: Basil Blackwell, 1987), p. 93.

39. Belton, p. 258.

40. Warren Miller, as cited in Richard M. Barsam, *Nonfiction Film: A Critical History* (Bloomington and Indianapolis: Indiana University Press, 1990), p. 292.

41. Marita Sturken, " An Interview with George Stoney," *Afterimage* 11, no 6. (December 1983): pp. 7–11.

42. These two films are discussed at length in Christiansen, pp. 137–140.

43. It is important to mention that both *Philadelphia* and *Longtime Companion* were widely criticized for limiting their portrayal of HIV and AIDS to the white, middle-class gay community.

44. J. Hoberman, "Back to the Garden," *Village Voice* 39, no. 29 (July 12, 1994): p. 41.

45. Kirsty McClure, "On the Subject of Rights: Pluralism, Plurality, and Political Identity," in Chantal Mouffe, ed. *Dimensions of Radical Democracy* (New York and London: Verso, 1992), p. 108.

46. Trinh. T. Minh-Ha, *Framer Framed* (New York and London: Routledge, 1992), p. 252.

47. Fred Herman, "Clinton and the Left, Encore," *The Nation* 259, no. 4 (July 25/Aug. 1, 1994): p. 110.

48. Paulo Freire has discussed this issue at length. He stresses the responsibility of oppressed peoples to engage oppressors in a process of education about social inequity. See, Paulo Freire, *Pedagogy of the Oppressed,* (New York: Continuum, 1971).

49. Sharon D. Welch, *A Feminist Ethic of Risk* (Minneapolis:, Fortress Press, 1990), p. 38.

50. See John Hess, "Notes on US Radical Film, 1967–80" in *Jumpcut: Hollywood, Politics, CounterCinema,* (New York: Praeger, 1985), pp. 134–151.

51. See Alice Echols, "We Gotta Get Out of this Place: Notes Toward a Remapping of the Sixties," *Socialist Review* 92, no 2 (1992): pp. 9–36.

52. J. Ronald Green, "Media Arts Center: A Report to the National Endowment for the Arts Media Arts Program," unpublished report, 1980.

53. Colin Young, "An American Film Institute: A Proposal," *Film Quarterly* (Summer 1961): pp. 37–50.

54. Annie Goldson, "The Difference is Academic: Theory and Production in Media Education," *exposure* 28, nos. 1/2 (1991): p. 68.

55. *Ibid.*

56. Letter dated Sept. 7, 1983 from Lawrence Sapadin, executive director of the Association for Independent Video and Filmmakers, to Sharon Rockefeller, chair, Corporation for Public Broadcasting.

57. National Endowment for the Arts, Application Guidelines, Media Arts: Film/Radio/Television (Washington, D.C.: NEA, 1991).

58. Self-censorship at PBS has been well documented in recent years. See, Barbara Osborn, "Coalition Blasts Self-Censorship at PBS" *The Independent* 16, no 3 (April 1993): pp. 9–10.

59. Andrew Kopkind, "The Rising of the Wretched," *The Nation* 252, no. 7 (May

6, 1991): p. 588. The cultural implications of this issue are taken up exhaustively in Brian Wallis, ed., *Democracy: A Project by Group Material* (Seattle: Bay Press, 1990); and more recently bell hooks, *Art on My Mind: Visual Politics* (New York: The New Press, 1995).

Chapter 4

1. Walter Lippmann, *Public Opinion* (New York: Free Press, 1965, first published 1922), p. 158.

2. Noam Chomsky, *Necessary Illusions: Thought Control in Democratic Societies* (Boston: South End Press, 1989); Noam Chomsky, *Deterring Democracy* (Scarborough: Harper Collins Canada, 1992); Noam Chomsky, *Keeping the Rabble in Line* (Monroe, Me.: Common Courage Press, 1994); Michael Parenti, *Make Believe Media: The Politics of Entertainment* (New York: St Martin's Press, 1992); Michael Parenti, *Inventing Reality: The Politics of the News Media* (New York: St Martin's Press, 1993); Herbert I. Schiller, *Mass Communications and American Empire* (New York: Beacon Press, 1969); Herbert I. Schiller, *Communication and Cultural Domination* (White Plains: International Arts and Sciences Press, 1970); Douglas Kellner, *Television and the Crisis of Democracy* (Boulder and San Francisco: Westview, 1990); Douglas Kellner, *The Persian Gulf TV War* (Boulder: Westview Press, 1992); Jeff Cohen and Norman Solomon, *Through the Media Looking Glass: Decoding Bias and Blather in the News* (Monroe, Me.: Common Courage Press, 1995). With the exception of Kellner, who attempts to survey a broad range of approaches to media politics, all of these authors tend to stress the role of cultural institutions and political economy in media at the expense of audience agency or reader response.

3. Mark Achbar, ed., *Manufacturing Consent: Noam Chomsky and the Media* (Montreal and New York: Black Rose Books, 1994).

4. Tom Leykis, as quoted in Micah L. Sifry, "Anti-Ditto," *The Nation* 260, no. 20 (May 22, 1995): p. 708. See also, Paul D. Colford, *The Rush Limbaugh Story: Talent on Loan from God: An Unauthorized Biography* (New York:St Martins Press, 1993); Christopher Kelly, *The Great Limbaugh Con: And other Right Wing Assaults on Common Sense* (Santa Barbara: Fithian Press, 1994).

5. David Lusted, Introduction," in *The Media Studies Book*, ed. David Lusted (London and New York: Routledge, 1991), p. 5.

6. Benedict Anderson, *Imagined Communities: Reflections on the Origin and Spread of Nationalism* (London: Verso, 1983).

7. Anderson, p. 22.

8. David Morley and Kevin Robins, "Spaces of Identity: Communications Technologies and the Refiguration of Europe," *Screen* 30. no. 4 (Autumn 1989): p. 12.

9. David Buckingham, "Teaching About the Media," from *The Media Studies Book*, p. 12.

10. Raymond Williams, *Television: Technology and Cultural Form* (Hanover, N.H.: Wesleyan University Press, 1974).

11. Williams, p. 19.

12. Kellner, p. 29.

13. RCA was forced by the FCC to divest itself of ABC in 1946.

14. Brian Winston, *Misunderstanding Media*.

15. Joe S. Foote, *Television Access and Political Power: The Networks, the Presidency, and the "Loyal Opposition,"* (New York: Praeger, 1990), p. 1. See also, Leo Bogart, "Media and Democracy: Hand in Hand?" *Current,* 380 (Feb. 1996), pp. 3–9.

16. Kellner, p. 42.

17. As cited in Kellner, p. 43.

18. The relationship of audiences to producers is taken up from varying perspectives in Tania Modleski, ed., *Studies in Entertainment: Critical Approaches to Mass Culture* (Bloomington and Indianapolis: University of Indiana, 1986). Contributors include Steven Heath, Margaret Morse, Judith Williamson, Dana Polan, Andrea Huyssen, Patricia Mellencamp, and Gillian Skirrow, among others.

19. Achbar, p. 18.

20. M.P. Crozier, S. J. Huntington, and J. Watanuki, *The Crisis of Democracy: Report on the Governability of Democracies to the Trilateral Commission* (New York: New York University, 1975), pp. 2–3.

21. Daniel C. Hallin, We Keep America on Top of the World," in Todd Gitlin, ed., *Watching Television* (New York: Pantheon Books, 1986), p. 19.

22. Kellner, p. 64.

23. Kellner, p. 134.

24. *Ibid.*

25. Foote, p. xv.

26. Henry Luce, as quoted in Schiller, *Mass Communications and American Empire,* p. 1.

27. Schiller, *Communication and Cultural Domination,* pp. 25–26.

28. Schiller, *Communication and Cultural Domination,* p. 44.

29. Anderson, pp. 14–15.

30. Schiller, *Communication and Cultural Domination,* p. 40.

31. UNESCO, International Commission for the Study of Communication Problems, Many Voices One World (London: Kogan Page, 1980).

32. John Tomlinson, *Cultural Imperialism: A Critical Introduction* (Baltimore: Johns Hopkins University Press, 1991), p. 71.

33. Jody Bertrand, "Angels Dancing: Cultural Technologies and the Production of Space," in *Cultural Studies,* eds. Lawrence Grossberg, Cary Nelson, and Paula Treichler (London and New York: Routledge, 1992), pp. 38–51.

34. Morley and Robins, p. 20.

35. Morely and Robins, p. 22.

36. See, Anderson, "Patriotism and Racism," in *Imagined Communities*, pp. 129–141.

37. The racist underpinnings of nationalistic impulses is explored in depth in Etienne Balibar and Immanuel Wallerstein, *Race, Nation, Class* (London and New York: Verso, 1991). In separate essays, both authors link racism in the capitalist nation state to antagonisms among people over monetary competition and national origin.

38. Tomlinson, pp. 68–99.

39. See Paul Mattick, Jr., "Art and the State: The NEA Debate in Perspective," *The Nation* 251, no. 10 (Oct. 1, 1990): p. 354.

40. Homi K. Bhabha, "DissemiNation: Time, Narrative, and the Margins of the Modern Nation," in *Nation and Narration*, p 310.

41. Achbar, p. 58.

42. This impulse toward technological determinism is most eloquently made in the much-celebrated essay by Walter Benjamin, "The Work of Art in the Age of Mechanical Reproduction," in *Illuminations*, trans. Harry Zohn (New York: Schocken Books, 1969).

43. Justin Lewis, *The Ideological Octopus: An Exploration of Televison and Its Audiences* (New York and London: Routledge, 1991), p. 6.

44. These four points of national and international communication are summarized in Noel King and Thomas Rowse, "'Typical Aussies': Television and Populism in Australia," in Manual Alvarado and John. O Thompson, eds., *The Media Reader* (London: British Film Institute, 1990), pp. 36–49. In elaborating this typology, the authors borrow the concept of "flow" introduced by Raymond Williams in *Television: Technology and Cultural Form* (New York: Schocken Books, 1975).

45. William Hoynes, *Public Broadcasting for Sale: Media, The Market, and the Public* (Boulder and San Francisco: Westview Press, 1994, p. 39.

46 Hoynes, p. 17. See also, Frank Reuven, "Showtime for Democracy," *Media Studies Journal*, 10, no. 1 (Winter 1996), pp. 81-90.

47 These and subsequent public broadcasting statistics are drawn from CPB and PBS surveys cited in Hoynes, pp. 17–18.

48. Hoynes, p. 17.

49. In 1994, a group calling itself Coalition vs. PBS Censorship initiated a series of protests across the nation. See, Holly Metz, "PBS Censors Called Off," *The Progressive* 58, no. 8 (August 1994): p. 12.

50. Ralph Lee Smith, *The Wired Nation: Cable TV: The Electronic Communications Highway* (New York: Harper Colophon: 1972), p. 38. The original version of this book appeared as a special issue of *The Nation*, May 19, 1970.

51. Hoynes, p. 9.

52. The implications of Marx's thinking in this regard are explored in Stuart Hall, "Ethnicity: Identity and Difference," in *Radical America* 23, no. 4 (June 1991): pp. 9–20.

53. Marshall McLuhan, *Understanding Media: Extensions of Man* (New York: McGraw-Hill, 1964), p. 23.

54. See, Michael Shamberg and the Raindance Corporation, *Guerrilla Televison* (New York: Holt, Reinhart, and Winston, 1971).

55. David Armstrong, *A Trumpet to Arms: Alternative Media in America* (Boston: South End Press, 1981), p. 71.

56. Martha Gever, "Video Politics: Early Feminist Projects," in Diane Neumaier and Douglas Kahn, eds., *Cultures in Contention* (Seattle: Real Comet Press, 1985), pp. 92–101. The overwhelming dominance of white men in the New Left is taken up in Alice Echols, "We Gotta Get Out of this Place: Notes Toward Remapping the Sixties," *Socialist Review* 22, no. 2 (April-June 1992): pp. 9–33.

57. Dorothy Todd Hénaut, "Asking the Right Questions: Video in the Hands of Citizens," unpublished manuscript, National Film Board of Canada, 1975.

58. bell hooks, *talking back: thinking feminist, thinking black* (Boston: South End Press, 1989).

59. Deedee Halleck, "Paper Tiger Television," in *Cultures in Contention*, p. 35.

60. Jim Naureckas, "We Want the Airwaves," *In These Times* 9, no,. 11 (April 17–30, 1995): pp. 19–20.

61. Paper Tiger organizer Jesse Drew, telephone interview with author, July 27, 1993.

62. Lawrence Daressa, "The Politics of Distribution," *Afterimage* 15, no 2 (Sept, 1987): pp. 8–9.

63. Michele Shapiro, "ITVS Trial by Fire," *Independent* 16. no. 2 (March 1993): pp. 10–12.

64. Jeffrey Chester and Kathryn Montgomery, "Technology in Transition: From Video Dialtone to DBS—Where Do Independents Fit In?" *Independent* 16, no. 3, (April 1993): p. 29.

Chapter 5

1. Douglas Kellner, *Television and the Crisis of Democracy* (Boulder and San Francisco: Westview, 1990), p. 1. See also, Douglas Kellner, *Media Culture: Cultural Studies, Identity and Politics between the Modern and the Postmodern* (New York and London: Routledge, 1995).

2. These distinctions are adapted from a variety of recent writings on technology, including Andrew Feenberg, *Critical Theory of Technology* (New York and Oxford: Oxford University Press, 1991) and Verena Andermatt Conly, ed., *Rethinking Technologies* (Minneapolis: University of Minnesota Press, 1993).

3. Marshall McLuhan, *Understanding Media: Extensions of Man* (New York: McGraw/Hill, 1964).

4. Christopher Scheer, "The Pursuit of Techno-Happiness," *The Nation* 260, no. 18 (May 8, 1995): p. 632.

5. Martin Heidegger, "The Question Concerning Technology," in *Basic Writings,* ed., David Farrell Krell (New York: Harper and Row, 1977), pp. 284–317.

6. Avatal Ronell.

7. Andrew Feenberg, *Critical Theory of Technology* (New York and Oxford: Oxford University Press, 1991), p. 9.

8. Teresa de Lauretis, *Technologies of Gender: Essays of Theory, Film, and Fiction* (Bloomington and Indianapolis: Indiana University Press, 1987).

9. George Landow, *Hypertext: The Convergence of Contemporary Critical Theory and Technology* (Baltimore: Johns Hopkins University Press, 1992), p. 169.

10. Kirkpatrick Sale, "Setting Limits on Technology," *The Nation* 260, no. 22 (June 5, 1995): p. 785.

11. Michel Foucault, *The Order of Things: An Archeology of the Human Sciences* (New York: Vintage Press, 1973) and Paulo Freire, *Pedagogy of the Oppressed,* trans. Myra Ramos (New York: Continuum, 1970).

12. Anderson, p. 22.

13. Anne Friedberg, *Window Shopping Cinema and the Postmodern* (Berkeley and Los Angeles: University of California, 1993).

14. Walter Benjamin, "The Work of Art in the Age of Mechanical Reproduction," trans. Harry Zohn, in *Illuminations,* (New York: Schocken Books, 1969).

15. Friedberg, p. 184.

16. Friedberg, p. 141.

17. William Gibson, *Neuromancer* (New York: Ace Books, 1986).

18. Gibson, p. 43.

19. Douglas Crimp, "Pictures," catalogue essay (New York: Committee for the Visual Arts, 1977), p. 3.

20. Donna Haraway, *Simians, Cyborgs, and Women: The Reinvention of Nature* (New York: Routledge, 1991), p. 154. See also, Anne Balsamo, *Reading Cyborg Women: Technology and the Gendered Body* (Durham: Duke University, 1996).

21. Gary Chapman, "Tired Wired," *San Francisco Examiner* (Jan 4, 1994): p D-4. See also, Paul Keegan, "The Digerati," *New York Times Magazine* (May 21, 1995): pp. 38–46.

22. Chapman.

23. Rheingold, p. 3.

24. Rheingold, p. 10.

25. As quoted in Rheingold, p. 24. For a further discussion of new public spaces see, Ray Oldenburg, *The Great Good Place: Cafes, Coffee Shops, Community Centers, Beauty Parlors, General Stores, Hangouts and How They Get You Through the Day* (New York: Paragon, 1991).

26. Robert Wright, "Hyper-Democracy," *Time* 145, #3 (Jan. 23, 1995): p. 15.

27. Jonathan Gill, quoted in Craig McLaughlin, "Virtual Democracy," *San Francisco Bay Guardian* (June 14, 1995) p. 30.

28. McLuhan, p. 23.

29. Rheingold, p. 81. See also, Dan Trighoff, "Reinventing Democracy via the Net," *Broadcasting & Calde,* 126, no. 30 (July 15, 1996), pp. 53–55.

30. Andrew Shapiro, "Street Corners in Cyberspace," *The Nation* 261, no. 1 (July 1, 1995): pp. 10–13.

31. Rheingold, p. 260.

32. Landow. See also, Richard Coyne, *Designing Information Technolgy in the Postmodern Age: From Method to Metaphor* (Cambridge: MIT Press, 1996).

33. Landow, p. 4.

34. Mikhail Bakhtin, *The Dialogic Imagination,* ed. Michael, trans. Caryl Merason and Michael Holquist (Austin: University of Texas Press, 1981), p. 426.

35. Michel Foucault, *The Archaeology of Knowledge,* trans. A. M. Sheridan Smith (New York: Harper Colophon, 1976), p. 23.

36. Foucault, as cited in Landow, p. 91.

37. Constance Penley and Andrew Ross, eds., *Technoculture* (Minneapolis: University of Minnesota, 1991); Henry Jenkins, *Textual Poachers: Television Fans and Participatory Culture* (New York and London: Routledge, 1992); Allucquére Rosanne Stone, *The War of Desire and Technology at the Close of the Mechanical Age* (Cambridge: MIT Press, 1996).

38. Jenkins, p. 34.

39. Marsha Kidner, *Playing with Power in Movies, Television, and Video Games* (Berkeley: University of California, 1991).

40. Jean Piaget, as cited in Kidner, p. 4.

41. Kidner, p. 95.

42. Kidner, p. 103.

43. Kidner, p. 104.

44. Julian Bleecker, "Urban Crisis: Past, Present, and Virtual," *Socialist Review* 24, nos. 1/2 (1995). It's worth noting that some users of *SimCity* subvert these normative parameters of play by rewriting the rules of the game.

45. Bleecker.

46. Paula A. Treichler and Lisa Cartwright , "Introduction," to "Imaging Technologies, Inscribing Science 2," a special issue of *Camera Obscura* 29 (1992): p. 6.

47. Ann Barry Flood, "Empowering Patients: Using Interactive Video Programs to Help Patients Make Difficult Decisions," *Camera Obscura* 29 (May 1992): pp. 225–232.

48. Flood, p. 230.

49. Chantal Mouffe, "Democratic Politics Today," in Chantal Mouffe, ed., *Dimensions of Radical Democracy: Pluralism, Citizenship, Community* (London: Verso, 1992), p. 4. See also, Jeremy Rifkin, "Civil Society in the Information Age," *The Nation* 262, no. 8 (Feb. 26, 1996): pp. 11–16. A thorough discussion of the need for activists in

different spheres to consider new sites for their political work appears in Henry A. Giroux, *Border Crossings: Cultural Workers and the Politics of Education* (New York: Routledge, 1992). Specific discussions of these concerns as they relate to media and arts activism appear in David Trend, *The Crisis of Meaning in Education and Culture* (Minneapolis: University of Minnesota, 1995). The important issue of dialogue was prominently introduced to the left community in Paulo Freire, *Pedagogy of the Oppressed*, trans. Myra Bergman Ramos (New York: Continuum, 1970). These ideas have recently been examined at length in Peter McLaren and Peter Leonard, eds., *Paulo Freire: A Critical Encounter* (New York: Routledge, 1993); Peter McLaren, *Critical Pedagogy and Predatory Culture: Oppositional Politics in a Postmodern Era* (London and New York: Routledge, 1995); and Henry A. Giroux, *Fugitve Cultures: Race, Violence, and Youth* (New York: Routledge, 1996).

Chapter 6

1. Jeff Giles, "Generalizations X," *Newsweek* 123, no. 23 (June 6, 1994): p. 62.

2. *Ibid.*

3. Michael Kinsley, "Back from the Future," *The New Republic* 4, no. 131 (March 21, 1994): p. 6.

4. Andrew Ross, "Introduction," in Andrew Ross and Tricia Rose, eds., *Microphone Fiends: Youth Music & Youth Culture* (New York: Routledge, 1994), p. 4.

5. Giles, p. 65. A decidedly more pessimistic outlook on youth culture appears in Mike Males and Faye Docuyanan, "Crackdown on Kids: Giving Up on the Young," *Progressive* 60, no. 20 (Feb. 26, 1996): pp. 24–26.

6. Giles, p. 62.

7. Eric Weisbard, "I Never Promised You a Rose Garden," *Socialist Review* 22, no. 3 (July-Sept., 1992): p. 25.

8. *Ibid.*

9. ("Crisis of Values") *Newsweek* (June 12, 1994).

10. Henry A Giroux, "Slacking Off: Border Youth and Postmodern Education," in *Fugitive Culture* (New York: Routledge, 1996).

11. George Lipsitz, "We Know What Time It Is," in Ross and Rose, p. 27. See also, Liza Featherstone, "Young, Hip, and Loud," *Nation* 262, no. 8 (Feb. 26, 1996): pp. 17–20.

12. Cheney, p. 5.

13. Lipman, p. 16.

14. Samuel P. Huntington, *The Crisis of Democracy: A Report on the Governability of Democracies to the Trilateral Commission* (New York: New York University Press, 1975).

15. Jeffrey Escoffier, "The Limits of Multiculturalism," *Socialist Review* (Spring 1992): pp. 61–73.

16. Chandra Talpade Mohanty, "On Race and Voice: Challenges for Liberal Education in the 1990s," *Cultural Critique* (Winter 1988/89): pp. 179–208.

17. John Dewey, *The Quest for Certainty* (New York: Capricorn, 1960), pp. 6–7.

18. A thorough interpretation of these issues is discussed in Stanley Aronowitz and Henry A. Giroux, Education Still Under Siege, 2nd ed. (New York: Bergin and Garvey, 1993) pp. 6-10.

19. John Dewey, *Education and Democracy* (New York: Macmillan, 1915).

20. Samuel Bowles and Herbert Gintis, *Schooling In Capitalist America: Educational Reform and the Contradictions of Economic Life* (New York: Basic Books, 1976).

21. Michael Apple, *Education and Power* (New York: Routledge and Kegan Paul, 1982).

22. Louis Althusser, "Ideology and Ideological State Apparatuses (Notes Toward an Investigation)," in *Lenin and Philosophy and Other Essays,* trans. Benjamin Brewster (London: New Left Books, 1971), pp. 121–173.

23. Herbert Marcuse, *An Essay on Liberation* (Boston: Beacon Press, 1969), p. 21.

24. Paul Willis, *Learning to Labour: How Working Class Kids Get Working Class Jobs* (Hampshire, England: Gower, 1981). For a discussion of the connections between critical pedagogy and cultural studies, see Henry A. Giroux, "Is there a Place for Cultural Studies in College of Education?" *Review of Education, Pedagogy,and Cultural Studies* 17, no. 2 (1995): pp. 127–142.

25. Among numerous reader response theorists, see especially works by Jonathan Culler, Stanley Fish, Wolfgang Iser, and Jane Tompkins.

26. Dick Hebdige, *Subculture: The Meaning of Style* (New York: Methuen, Inc.,1979). See also, Sarah Thornton, *Club Cultures: Music, Media, and Subcultural Capital* (Middletown, CT: Wesleyan, 1996).

27. Paulo Freire, *Pedagogy of the Oppressed* (New York: Continuum, 1970); Paulo Freire, *Cultural Action for Freedom* (New York: Penguin Press, 1972); Paulo Freire, *The Politics of Education* (South Hadley, Mass.: Bergin and Garvey, 1985). Freire's significance is discussed in Peter McLaren and Peter Leonard, eds. *Paulo Freire: A Critical Encounter* (New York and London: Routledge, 1993) and Henry A. Giroux and Donaldo Macedo, *Paulo Freire: History, Pedagogy, and Struggle* (Minneapolis: University of Minnesota Press, 1994).

28. Paulo Freire, *Pedagogy of the Oppressed* (New York: Continuum, 1970), p. 123. A range of recent books address Freire's work in a contemporary context. Of note is Peter McLaren and Peter Leonard, eds., *Paulo Freire: A Critical Encounter* (New York: Routledge, 1993).

29. Michael Apple, *Ideology and Curriculum* (New York: Routledge, 1979); Michael Apple, *Teachers and Texts* (New York: Routledge, 1987); Henry A. Giroux, *Ideology, Culture, and the Process of Schooling* (Philadelphia: Temple University Press, 1981): Henry A. Giroux, *Theory and Resistance in Education* (South Hadley, Mass.:

Bergin and Garvey, 1983); Henry A. Giroux, *Schooling and The Struggle for Public Life* (Minneapolis: University of Minnesota Press, 1988); Peter McLaren, *Life in Schools: An Introduction to Critical Pedagogy in the Social Foundations of Education* (New York: Longman, 1988); Peter McLaren, *Schooling as a Ritual Performance: Towards a Political Economy of Educational Symbols and Gestures* (London: Routledge, 1986); Ira Schor, *Culture Wars: School and Society in the Conservative Restoration, 1969–1985* (London and New York: Routledge, 1986).

30. See, Deborah Britzman, *Practice Makes Practice: A Critical Study of Learning to Teach* (Albany: SUNY Press, 1991); Linda Garber, ed., *Tilting the Tower: Lesbians, Teaching, Queer Subjects* (New York: Routledge, 1994); Patti Lather, *Getting Smart: feminist research and pedagogy with/in the postmodern* (New York and London: Routledge, 1991); Carmen Luke and Jennifer Gore, eds., *Feminisms and Critical Pedagogy* (New York and London: Routledge, 1993); Jennifer Gore, *The Struggle for Pedagogies: Critical and Feminist Discourses as Regimes of Truth* (New York: Routledge, 1993); Cameron McCarthy and Warren Critchlow, eds., *Race, Identity, and Representation in Education* (New York: Routledge, 1993); Christine Sleeter, ed., *Empowerment through Multicultural Education* (Albany: SUNY Press, 1991).

31. See, Elizabeth Ellsworth, "Why Doesn't This Feel Empowering: Working through the Repressive Myths of Critical Pedagogy," *Harvard Education Review* 59, no, 3 (1989): pp. 297–324.

32. William J. Bennett, *The Book of Virtues: A Treasury of Great Moral Tales.* (1993). For a critical discussion of Bennett's career, see Michael Kelly, "The Man of the Minute," *New Yorker* 71, no. 20 (July 17, 1995): pp. 25–29.

33. As cited in Nancy Warehime, *To Be One of Us: Cultural Conflict, Creative Democracy, and Education* (SUNY Press, 1993), p. 12.

34. Branda Miller, *Talkin Bout Droppin Out* (Boston: Boston School District, 1990).

35. Robert M. Diamond, "Single Room Television," in *A Guide to Instructional Media,* Robert M. Diamond, ed., (New York: McGraw-Hill, 1964), p. 3.

36. John M. Hofstrand, "Television and Classroom Observation," in *A Guide to Instructional Media,* p. 149.

37. The terms "visual literacy" and "media literacy" have been employed in a variety of differing contexts during the past two decades. The formalist media literacy of the 1970s should not be confused with the critical media literacy movement of the 1980s and 1990s.

38. Linda R. Burnett and Frederick Goldman, *Need Johnny Read? Practical Methods to Enrich Humanities Courses Using Films and Film Studies* (Dayton: Pflaum, 1971), p. xv.

39. These issues are taken up in depth in Elizabeth Ellsworth and Miriamne H. Whatley, eds., *The Ideology of Images in Educational Media: Hidden Curriculums in the Classroom* (New York: Teachers College Press, 1990); and David Sholle and Stan Denski,

Media Education and the (Re) Production of Culture (Westport, CT: Bergin and Garvey, 1994)

40. Anderson, pp. 14–16.

41. This expression was coined by Juan Bautista Alberti in his *Bases* (1952) for the Argentine constitution.

42. Andrew Parker, Mary Russo, Doris Sommer, and Patricia Yeager, "Introduction," in Andrew Parker, et al., eds., *Nationalisms and Sexualities* (New York and London: Routledge, 1992), p. 5.

43. Lorraine Kenny, "The Birds and the Bees: Teen Pregnancy and the Media," *Afterimage* 16, no. 1 (Summer 1988): p. 6–8. For a further discussion of media bias against adolescent female sexuality, see Lorraine Kenny, "Amy Fisher, My Story: Learning to Love the Unlovable," *Socialist Review* 24, no. 3 (1995): pp. 81–128.

44. Kenny, p. 6.

45. *Ibid.*

46. This banality of culture is taken up at length in the often-quoted Raymond Williams essay, "Culture is Ordinary," *Resources of Hope* (London: Verso, 1989).

47. A representative sampling of recent texts on critical pedagogy: Michael Apple, *Teachers and Texts* (New York: Routledge, 1989); Stanley Aronowitz and Henry A. Giroux, *Postmodern Education: Politics, Culture, and Social Criticism* (Minneapolis: Univ. of Minnesota Press, 1990); Henry A. Giroux, *Border Crossings: Cultural Workers and the Politics of Education* (New York: Routledge, 1992); Peter McLaren, *Critical Pedagogy and Predatory Culture* (London and New York: Routledge, 1995); Peter McLaren, ed., *Postmodernism, Post-colonialism, and Pedagogy* (Albert Park, Australia: James Nicholas Publishers, 1992); Chandra Talpade Mohanty, "On Race and Voice," *Cultural Critique* 14 (Winter 1989); Roger I. Simon, *Teaching Against the Grain* (New York: Bergin and Garvey, 1992).

48. Cary Bazalgette, as quoted in Ben Moore, "Media Education," in Lusted, *The Media Studies Book*, p. 172.

49. Stanley Fish, *Is There a Text in this Class? The Authority of Interpretive Communities* (Cambridge, Harvard University Press, 1980).

50. Donna Lloyd-Kolkin and Kathleen Tyner, *Media and You: An Elementary Media Literacy Curriculum* (San Francisco: Strategies of Media Literacy, 1991).

51. John Fiske, "Cultural Studies and the Culture of Everyday Life," in Grossberg, et al., p. 156.

52. Len Masterman, "British View: Achieving and Impossible Task," *Mediacy* 11, no. 3 (Fall 1989): p. 3.

53. Ella Shohat and Robert Stam, *Unthinking Eurocentrism: Multiculturalism and the Media* (London and New York: Routledge, 1995).

54.] Shohat and Stam, p. 180–181.

55. Moore, p. 173.

56. Moore, p 181.

57. Antonio Gramsci, *Selections from the Prison Notebooks*, Quinten Hoare, ed. (New York: International Publishers, 1972), p. 33.

58. Particularly in recent years the all-encompassing aspects of Gramscian principles have been overstated in pedagogical theory. Clearly, the institutional matrix in which schools reside exerts an influence upon the individual that is partial, at best. However, as one of the last great totalizers, Gramsci provides an important means of bridging gaps among disparate fields.

59. Russell Ferguson, "The Invisible Center," from Russell Ferguson, Martha Gever, Trinh T. Minh-ha, and Cornel West, eds., *Out There: Marginalization and Contemporary Cultures* (Cambridge: MIT Press, 1991), p. 9.

60. Edward Said, in Phil Mariani and Jonathan Crary, "In the Shadow of the West: An Interview with Edward Said," in Russell Ferguson, William Olander, Marcia Tucker, and Karen Fiss, eds., *Discourses: Conversations in Postmodern Art and Culture* (Cambridge: MIT Press, 1990), p. 94.

61. This notion of "border crossing" has been developed in detail in Henry A. Giroux, *Border Crossings: Cultural Workers and the Politics of Education* (New York: Routledge, 1992); and Henry A. Giroux and Peter McLaren, eds., *Beyond Borders: Pedagogy and the Politics of Cultural Studies* (New York: Routledge, 1994).

62. Giroux and Simon, p. 202.

63. Mica Nava, "Consumerism Reconsidered: Buying and Power," *Cultural Studies* (1991): pp. 157–173.

64. Susan Willis, *A Primer for Daily Life* (London and New York: Routledge, 1991).

65. Paul Willis, *Common Culture: Symbolic Work at Play in the Everyday Cultures of the Young* (Boulder and San Francisco: Westview, 1990).

66. Chelda Sandoval, "US Third World Feminism: The Theory and Model of Oppositional Consciousness," *Genders* 10 (1991): pp. 2–23.

67. See, Jurgen Habermas, *The Theory of Communicative Action*, trans. Thomas McCarthy (Boston: 1984).

68. Chantal Mouffe, "Radical Democracy: Modern or Postmodern," in Andrew Ross, ed., *Universal Abandon* (Minneapolis: University of Minnesota Press, 1988), pp. 31–45. (1988) p. 42. See also, David Trend, ed., *Radical Democracy: Identity, Citizenship, and the State* (New York: Routledge, 1995).

69. See, John Dewey, *Democracy and Education* (New York: Macmillan, 1910), pp. 321–360.

70. See, Philip. R. D. Corrigan, "Towards a Celebration of Difference(s): Notes for a Sociology of a Possible Everyday Future (1981)," in Philip. R. D. Corrigan, *Social Forms/Human Capacities* (New York: Routledge, 1990), pp. 130–153. Of course, on another level the right is very much committed to supporting the differences that install people at varying points in the meritocratic social hierarchy.

71. Hall and Held, p. 173.

72. See, David Johnson, "Stormy Days and Sleepless Nights for 'Lightening Rod' at Arts Agency," *The New York Times* (May 3, 1991): p. A 14; Brian Wallis, "Slow Burn at the NEA," *Art in America* 79, no. 2 (February 1991): p. 37; Richard Bolton, "The Cultural Contradictions of Conservativism," *New Art Examiner* 17, no. 10 (Summer 1990): pp. 24–29; Carole S. Vance, "The War on Culture," *Art in America* 77, no. 8 (Sept. 1989): pp. 39–45.

73. Samuel Bowles and Herbert Gintis, *Schooling in Capitalist America: Educational Reform and the Contradictions of Economic Life* (New York: Basic Books, 1976), pp. 20–26.

74. George P.Landow, *Hypertext: The Convergence of Contemporary Critical Theory and Technology* (Baltimore: Johns Hopkins, 1992) ; Bob Cotton sand Richard Oliver, *Understanding Hypermedia: From Multimedia to Virtual Reality* (London: Phaidon, 1993) ; Verena Andermatt Conley, ed., *Rethinking Technologies* (Minneapolis: University of Minnesota, 1993); Peter Ludlow, ed., *High Noon on the Electronic Frontier: Conceptual Issues in Cyberspace* (Cambridge: MIT Press, 1996).

75. Landow, p. 174.

76. Stuart Hall and David Held, "Citizens and Citizenship," *New Times: The Changing Face of Politics in the 1990s* (London: Verso, 1990), pp. 173–174.

Chapter 7

1. Jesse Goodman, "Education for Critical Democracy," *Journal of Education* 171, no. 2 (1989): pp. 88–116.

2. William. A Henry, *In Defense of Elitism* (New York: Doubleday, 1992), as cited in Roger Kimball, "What's Wrong with Equality?" *New Criterion* 13, no. 2 (Oct. 1994): p. 5.

3. Chantal Mouffe, "Citizenship and Political Community, " in Miami Theory Collective, ed., *Community at Loose Ends* (Minneapolis: University of Minnesota, 1991), p. 79.

4. Robert Hughes, *Culture of Complaint: The Fraying of America* (NY: Oxford University Press, 1993). See, David Trend, "The New Politics of Victimization," *Art Papers* 4, no. 19 (July/August 1995): pp. 32–35.

5. Hughes, p. 9.

6. Hughes, p. 7.

7. See, Richard Goldstein, "Save the Males: The Making of the Butch Backlash," *Village Voice* (March 7, 1995): pp. 25–27.

8. Richard Herrnstein and Charles Murray, *The Bell Curve: Intellectual and Class Structure in American Life* (New York: Free Press, 1994). See also, Russell Jacoby and Naomi Glauberman, eds., *The Bell Curve Debates: History, Documents, Opinions* (New

York: Times Books, 1995); and Steven Fraser, ed., *The Bell Curve Wars: Race, Intelligence, and the Future of America* (New York: Basic Books, 1995).

9. Michael Harrington, *The Other America* (New York: MacMillan, 1962).

10. For a detailed analysis of this phenomenon, see William Ryan, "The Art of Savage Discovery," in Ira Colby, ed., *Social Welfare Policy* (Chicago: Dorsey Press, 1989), pp. 16–33.

11. Edwin Banfield, *The Unheavenly City* (Boston: Little Brown, 1970).

12. George Gilder, *Wealth and Poverty* (New York: Basic Books, 1981).

13. Paul Boyer, "Building Character Among the Urban Poor," in Colby, pp. 113–134.

14. Herbert Spencer, *The Principles of Ethics, vol. 1* (New York: Appleton & Co., 1904).

15. See, Frank Washington, " A Night of Hell at Ground Zero," *Newsweek*, (May 11, 1992): p. 35; Lance Morrow, "Video Warriors in Los Angeles," *Time* (May 11, 1992): p. 68; Tom Matthews, "The Siege of LA," *Newsweek* (May 11, 1992): p. 11.

16. Marc Cooper, "God and Man in Colorado Springs," *The Nation* 260, no. 1 (Jan 2, 1995): pp. 9–10.

17. For a recent discussion of these issues, see, Vicki Goldberg, "Looking at the Poor in a Gilded Frame," *New York Times* (April 9, 1995): Sec. 2, pp. 1, 36.

18. John Szarkowski, as quoted in Martha Rosler, "in, around, and afterthoughts (on documentary photography)," *Martha Rosler: 3 Works* (Halifax: Nova Scotia College of Art and Design, 1981), p. 78. This essay by Rosler remains one of the most thorough-going critiques of documentary photographic practice written to date.

19. Jim Hubbard, *American Refugees* (Minneapolis: University of Minnesota Press, 1991).

20. Hubbard, p. xiv.

21. Rosler, p. 73.

22. Arlene Croce, "Discussing the Undiscussable," *The New Yorker* (Dec, 16, 1994/Jan. 2, 1995): pp. 54–60; John Leo, "The Backlash Against Victim Art," *US News & World Report* (Jan, 16, 1995): p. 22; Laura Shapiro, "The Art of Victimization," *Newsweek* (Feb. 6, 1995): p. 63; Martha Duffy, "Push Comes to Shove," *Time* (Feb. 6, 1995) : pp. 68–70.

23. Croce, p. 56.

24. Croce, p. 57.

25. *Ibid.*

26. Christopher Lasch, *The Revolt of the Elites and the Betrayal of Democracy* (New York: WW Norton, 1995), p. 8. See also, George Scialabba, "'A Whole World of Heroes': Christopher Lasch on Democracy," *Dissent* 42, no. 3 (Summer 1995): pp. 407–413.

27. George Lipsitz, "We know What Time It Is," from Andrew Ross and Tricia

Rose, *Microphone Fiends: Youth Music, Youth Culture* (New York: Routledge, 1994), pp. 18–19.

28. As cited in Lucy Lippard, *Mixed Blessings: New Art in a Multicultural America* (New York: Pantheon, 1990), p. 152.

29. These arguments are taken up at length in Lawrence Grossberg, *We Gotta Get Out of this Place* (New York: Routledge, 1992). Grossberg counters the pessimism of these arguments in a subsequent essay entitled "Is Anybody Listening? Does Anybody Care?" in Ross and Rose, pp. 41–58.

30. See, Abigail Solomon Goddeau, *Photography at the Dock* (Minneapolis: University of Minnesota, 1992).

31. Raymond Williams, *Television:Technology and Cultural Form* (Hanover and London: Wesleyan Press, 1974), p. 145.

32. Tricia Rose, "A Style Nobody Can Deal With," in Rose and Ross, pp. 71–88. See also, Tricia Rose, *Black Noise: Rap Music and Black Culture in Contemporary America* (New York and London: Routledge, 1994); Paul Gilroy, "'After the Love Has Gone,' Biopolitics and Ethno Poetics in the Black Public Sphere," *Third Text* 28/29 (Summer 1994): pp. 25–46.

33. Rose, p. 71.

34. Houston Baker, *Black Studies, Rap, and the Academy* (Chicago: University of Chicago, 1993), p. 33.

35. Baker, p. 43.

36. Lois E. Nesbitt, "Graffiti/ Anti-Graffiti/Anti-Anti-Graffiti," *ACME Journal* 1, no. 1 (1992): p. 57.

37. *Ibid.*

38. Nesbitt, p. 58.

39. Judith Butler, *Gender Trouble* (New York: Routledge, 1990), p. 136. See also, Jan Nederveen Pieterse, "Aesthetics of Power: Time and Body Politics," *Third Text* 22 (Spring 1993): pp. 33–43.

40. Rose, p. 80.

41. Nancy Hicks Maynard, "Diversity, Democracy, and Niche markets, " *Media Studies Journal* 9, no. 3 (Summer 1995): p. 142.

42. Chuck D, as cited in Jeffrey Louis Decker, "The State of Rap," in Ross and Rose, p. 102.

43. Pharoahe Monch, "Evolve," in *The Source*, 70 (July 1995): p. 10.

44. Ken Auletta, "The Electronic Parent," *The New Yorker* (Nov. 8, 1993): p. 69.

45. Auletta, p. 20. See also, Joseph Marshall and Lonnie Wheeler, *Street Soldier: One Man's Struggle To Save a Generation—One Life at a Time* (New York: Delacorte Press, 1996).

46. Jane Addams, "First Days at Hull House," in Ira Colby, ed., *Social Welfare Policy: Perspectives, Patterns, Insights* (New York: The Dorsey Press, 1989), p. 162.

47. Paul Boyer, "Building Character among the Urban Poor: The Charity Organization Movement," in Colby, p. 125.

48. *Ibid.*

49. Grant Kester, "Aesthetic Evangelists: Conversion and Empowerment in Contemporary Community Art," *Afterimage* 22, no. 6 (Jan. 1995): pp. 5–10.

50. Amalia Mesa-Bains, "Galeria de la Raza: A Study in Cultural Transformation," in Mark O'Brien and Craig Little, eds., *Reimaging America: The Arts of Social Change* (Philadelphia and Santa Cruz: New Society Publishers, 1990), p. 146.

51. Mesa-Bains, p. 147. See also, Randy Shaw, *The Activist's Handbook: A Primer for the 1990s and Beyond* (Berkeley: University of California, 1996).

Chapter 8

1. See, Raymond Williams, *Resources of Hope: Culture, Democracy, Socialism* (New York and London: Verso, 1989); Wim Weetens, *Writing and Democracy: Literature and Culture in Transition* (New York: Harvester Wheatsheaf, 1991); Andrew Buchwalder, ed., *Culture and Democracy: Social and Ethical Issues in Public Support for the Arts and Humanities* (Boulder, Col.: Westview, 1992); Larry Diamond, *Political Culture and Democracy in Developing Countries* (Boulder: Rienner, 1993); Renato Rosaldo, "Cultural Citizenship and Educational Democracy," *Cultural Anthropology* 9, no. 3 (August 1994): pp. 402–412; Aaron Wildavsky, "Democracy as a Coalition of Cultures: Democracy and Balance," *Current* 360 (Feb. 1994): pp. 13–17; Yehudah Mirsky, "Democratic Politics, Democratic Culture: Democratization and Civil Society," *Current* 359 (Jan. 1994): pp. 29–36; Jodi Cohen, "Critical Viewing and Participatory Democracy," *Journal of Communication* 44, no. 4 (Autumn 1994); pp. 98–114; Graham Murdock, "Across the Great Divide: Cultural Analysis and the Condition of Democracy," *Critical Studies in Mass Communication* 12, no. 1 (March 1995): pp. 89–96; Harold DeRienzo, "Beyond the Melting Pot: Preserving Culture, Building Community," *National Civic Review* 84, no. 1 (Winter 1995): 5–16.

2. Georg Wilhelm Frederich Hegel, *Phenomenology of the Spirit,* trans. A. V. Miller (Oxford: Clarendon Press, 1977).

3. Jim Hightower, "Foreword," in Jeff Cohen and Norman Solomon, *Through the Looking Glass: Decoding Bias and Blather in the News* (Monroe, Me.: Common Courage Press, 1995), p. x. See also, Harvey Kaye, *Why Do Ruling Classes Fear History?* (New York: St Martins Press, 1996).

4. Robert Hughes, *Culture of Complaint: The Fraying of America* (New York: Oxford, 1993).

5. John Thompson, *Ideology and Modern Culture: Critical Social Theory in the Era of Mass Communication* (Stanford: Stanford University Press, 1990), p. 19.

6. A thorough discussion of the need for activists in different spheres to consider new sites for their political work appears in Henry A. Giroux, *Fugitive Cultures: Race, Violence, and Youth* (New York: Routledge, 1996). Specific discussions of these concerns as they relate to media and arts activism appear in David Trend, *The Crisis of Meaning in Education and Culture* (Minneapolis: University of Minnesota, 1995). The important issue of dialogue was prominently introduced to the left community in Paulo Freire, *Pedagogy of the Oppressed,* trans., Myra Bergman Ramos (New York: Continuum, 1970). These ideas have recently been examined at length in Peter McLaren, *Critical Pedagogy and Predatory* Culture (New York Routledge, 1995).

Index